Unseen Places
Gregor Sailer

Unseen Places

Gregor Sailer

KEHRER

KUNST HAUS WIEN
MUSEUM HUNDERTWASSER

Inhaltsverzeichnis   Content

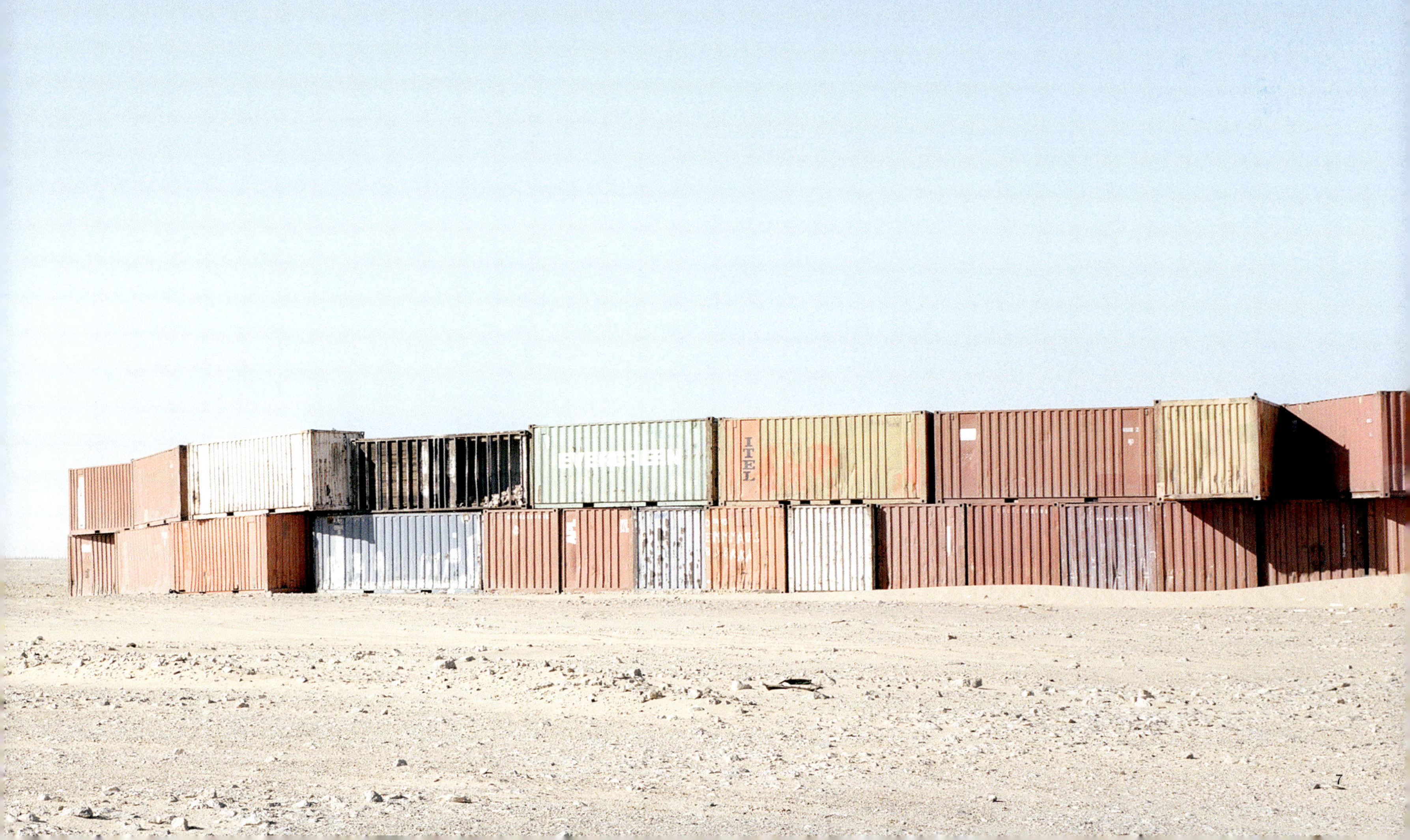

Ungesehene Orte

Verena Kaspar-Eisert

Ausrangierte, verblichene und verrostete Seecontainer pflügen sich von rechts kommend in einen tief liegenden, flachen Horizont. Zwischen dem trockenen, steinigen Wüstenboden und dem gleißend blauen Himmel sind ausrangierte Frachtbehälter in Doppelreihe gestrandet. Auf einem der Container in verblasstem Grün ist in weißer Schrift „Evergreen" zu lesen. „Immergrün" ist in dieser unwirtlichen Gegend allerdings nichts.

Diese unheimliche Situation hat Gregor Sailer 2010 im Westen Algeriens nahe der Stadt Tindūf festgehalten. Dort, in der Sahara, wurde die Containermauer zum Schutz des dahinterliegenden Flüchtlingslagers vor Sandstürmen und anderen Widrigkeiten errichtet. Weitgehend vergessen von der Weltöffentlichkeit leben hier maurische Sahrauis schon seit über 40 Jahren im Exil.

Es sind solch verborgene, vergessene und ungesehene Orte, die Gregor Sailers fotografisches Interesse wecken. Er will sie finden, sehen, fotografieren. Seit über 20 Jahren hält Sailer unserer komplexen Gegenwart seine präzisen, überlegt komponierten und zeitlos wirkenden Fotografien entgegen.

Gregor Sailer geht konzeptuell und strategisch an seine Projekte heran. Er schafft umfangreiche, inhaltlich und formal konzise Werkgruppen, die als Ganzes betrachtet einen Überblick über ein von ihm abgestecktes Themenfeld geben. Jedes Elnzelbild behauptet sich jedoch auch allein, changierend zwischen visuellem Beweis einer realiter vorgefundenen Gegend und ästhetisch aufgeladener, künstlerischer Komposition als Bestandteil des fotografischen Dispositivs.

Unseen Places

Verena Kaspar-Eisert

Scrapped, faded, and rusted sea containers plough their way from the right into a low-lying, flat horizon. Between the dry, stony desert soil and the blazing blue sky, decommissioned freight containers are beached in a double row. "Evergreen" can be read in white lettering on one of the pale-green containers. Nothing is "deciduous," however, in this inhospitable region.

Gregor Sailer captured this unearthly situation near the town of Tindouf in Western Algeria in 2010. There, in the Sahara, the container wall was built to protect the refugee camp behind it against sandstorms and other adversities. Largely forgotten by the global public, the Sahrawi people have been living here in exile for more than 40 years.

It is hidden, forgotten, and unseen places like these that awaken Gregor Sailer's photographic interest. He wants to find, see, photograph them. For more than 20 years, Sailer has been holding up his precise, judiciously composed and timeless-looking photographs to our complex present day.

Gregor Sailer takes a conceptual and strategic approach to his projects. He creates comprehensive, substantially and formally concise groups of works, which, contemplated as a whole, provide an overview of the topic area he is staking out. Each individual image, however, stands its ground alone, changing between visual proof and an aesthetically charged, artistic composition as a component of the photographic dispositif.

Zu Beginn von Sailers Karriere sind Themenspektrum und geografischer Radius der Werke noch enger gefasst. So erforscht er fotografisch eine Kokerei in Dortmund und folgt dabei in fast sinnlichen und doch strengen Schwarz-Weiß-Bildern dem Produktionsweg der Kohle zum Koks (*Kokerei Hansa,* 2003/2005); er fotografiert unterirdische Infrastruktur im Ruhrgebiet (*Subraum,* 2004–2005) wie auch die von Tourismusarchitektur verunstaltete alpine Hochgebirgslandschaft (*LADIZ_alpen™,* 2006/2008) oder lichtet in beunruhigender Art und Weise eine unzugängliche militärische Produktionsstätte aus dem Zweiten Weltkrieg in einem ehemaligen Bergwerk ab (*The Box,* 2014–2015).

Seine fotografischen Ambitionen haben den gebürtigen Tiroler, der in einem kleinen Ort in den Alpen wohnt, im Laufe der Jahre aber immer weiter in die Welt hinausgezogen und in sehr entlegene, spärlich besiedelte Weltgegenden geführt. Für die Serie *The Potemkin Village* (2015–2017) machte sich Gregor Sailer etwa nach Vårgårda (Schweden) oder Baschkortostan (Russland) auf, für *Closed Cities* (2009–2012) reiste er von Mirny (Jakutien, Russland) bis nach Chuquicamata (Chile); seine jüngste Serie *The Polar Silk Road* (2017–2022) führte ihn in die nördlichste Weltgegend, etwa nach Kangerlussuaq (Grönland) oder Tuktoyaktuk (Kanada).

Gregor Sailer hält weltweit nach sonderbaren, bisweilen dystopischen Szenerien Ausschau. Er hat ein ausgeprägtes Interesse an Architekturen, die auf politische, militärische oder wirtschaftliche Aspekte der Gegenwart verweisen. Anlagen, Infrastrukturen, Gebäude, Produktionsstätten, Forschungseinrichtungen – sie alle reflektieren in konzentrierter Form Themen unserer Zeit. Seine Bilder sind konsequent menschenleer, die gebauten Strukturen oder industrialisierten Landschaften bilden den zentralen Bildinhalt. Dabei blickt Sailer nie romantisierend auf das gewählte Sujet, sondern strebt nach einer nüchternen Wiedergabe des Gesehenen. Keinesfalls aber erliegt er dem Trug, eine Fotografie könnte objektiv sein; vielmehr unterstreicht er mit seinen klassischen Bildkompositionen den konstruktiven Charakter der Fotografie. Er verwendet eine Fachkamera und arbeitet mit analogem Mittel- und Großformat. Eine aufwendige Technik, die Sailer aber nicht nur zu dem gewünschten visuellen und ästhetischen Ergebnis verhilft, sondern auch den Vorteil hat, bei extremen Temperaturen – von 65 Grad Celsius in Katar bis minus 55 Grad in den Nordwest-Territorien in Kanada – nicht auf Akkubatterien angewiesen zu sein.

Sailers Werk lässt sich der Neuen Sachlichkeit in der Fotografie zuordnen, zugleich handelt es sich um Autorenfotografie im Sinne des Fototheoretikers Klaus Honnef, da „bestimmte Muster erkennbar und identifizierbar [sind], die darauf hinweisen, dass da ein Mensch tätig war, der seine ganz eigene Einstellung zur Realität – oder zum Sichtbaren, um es neutral zu sagen – gehabt hat".[1] Mit „beunruhigender Ausgewogenheit" lassen sich Gregor Sailers charakteristische Ästhetik und Bildinhalte zusammenfassend beschreiben.

At the start of Sailer's career, the works' topical spectrum and geographic radius are still more narrowly encompassed. For example, he undertakes a photographic exploration of a cokery in Dortmund and, as he does so, follows, in almost sensual and yet stringent black-and-white images, the production route from coal to coke (*Kokerei Hansa,* 2003/2005); he photographs subterranean infrastructure in the Ruhr region (*Subraum,* 2004–2005) and also the high alpine landscape blemished by tourism architecture (*LADIZ_alpen™,* 2006/2008). Alternatively, he captures, in a disquieting manner, an off-bounds World War II military production shop in a former mine (*The Box,* 2014–2015).

Over the years, though, his photographic ambitions have drawn the native Tyrolean, who resides in a small place in the alps, ever further into the world and into very remote, sparsely populated global regions. For the series *The Potemkin Village* (2015–2017), for instance, Gregor Sailer set off to Vårgårda (Sweden) or Bashkortostan (Russia); for *Closed Cities* (2009–2012), he travelled from Mirny (Yakutia, Russia) to Chuquicamata (Chile); while his latest series, *The Polar Silk Road* (2017–2022), took him to the northernmost global region, to Kangerlussuaq (Greenland), for instance, or Tuktoyaktuk (Canada).

Gregor Sailer keeps a lookout for singular, sometimes dystopian scenarios around the world. He has a pronounced interest in architectures that point to political, military, or economic aspects of the present day. Facilities, infrastructures, buildings, production shops, research institutions — all of them reflect, in concentrated form, the major themes of our times. His images are consistently devoid of people; the built structures or industrialised landscapes form the focal visual content. At the same time, Sailer never casts a romanticising eye on the chosen subject, but rather aspires to a sober rendering of what has been seen. Under no circumstances, though, does he succumb to the deception that a photograph could be objective; rather, with his classical image compositions, he underlines the constructional character of photography. He uses a professional camera and works in analogue medium and large format. This is an elaborate technique, which, however, not only helps Sailer attain his desired visual and aesthetic outcome, but also has the benefit, at extreme temperatures — from 65 degrees Celsius in Qatar to minus 55 degrees in the Northwest Territories in Canada — of not being reliant on rechargeable batteries.

Sailer's oeuvre can be classified under New Objectivity in photography; simultaneously, his is author photography as defined by photography theorist Klaus Honnef, since "certain patterns are discernible and identifiable which indicate that a person has been active there, who has had his own particular attitude towards reality — or towards the visible, to put it neutrally."[1] "Disquieting equilibrium" is the description by which Gregor Sailer's characteristic aesthetic and visual content can be summarised.

1
Klaus Honnef, „So gesehen", Interview von Damian Zimmermann, in: *Photo Presse* 12/2019, S. 24.

Klaus Honnef, "So gesehen," interview by Damian Zimmermann, in *Photo Presse* 12 (2019), 24.

Seine fotografischen Expeditionen führen ihn an entlegene, meist unzugängliche Orte. Die Vorbereitungszeit nimmt jeweils sehr viel Zeit in Anspruch. Sind die Ziele nach intensiver Recherche erst einmal festgelegt, muss sich Sailer nicht nur um Visa, sondern vielfach auch um Sondergenehmigungen und Zugangsberechtigungen kümmern, etwa wenn die Orte, die er aufsuchen will, in militärischen Sperrgebieten liegen oder geheime Forschungseinrichtungen sind. Ausgerüstet mit den notwendigen Dokumenten und mindestens 25 Kilogramm Fotoequipment begibt Gregor Sailer sich wiederholt auf mehrtägige Expeditionen. Von diesen bringt er seine außergewöhnlichen Bilder ungesehener Orte mit, die wir in Ausstellungen oder in Buchform betrachten können.

Sailers gesamtes Werk zeichnet sich durch seine ruhige, unprätentiöse und ernsthafte künstlerische Herangehensweise aus, die sich auch formal in seinen Fotografien manifestiert: Er versucht, einer unübersichtlichen Welt mit seinen Bildern Struktur zu geben. Wenngleich diese keine Menschen zeigen, ist der Mensch immer indirekt in ihnen präsent, verweisen die Architekturen, Landschaften und Infrastrukturen auf ihn zurück. So berichten Sailers Bilder von Migration und Krieg, von Ressourcenverschwendung und Klimakrise; sie erzählen von Arbeit, Haltung und Glauben, von Isolation, Täuschung und Schmerz, von Sicherheit und Bedrohung – es geht um Menschen und um den Zustand der Menschheit und der Welt.

Das KUNST HAUS WIEN widmet diesem herausragenden Protagonisten zeitgenössischer Fotografie eine erste große Mid-Career-Retrospektive in Österreich und präsentiert in einer über 160 Bilder umfassenden Zusammenstellung zentrale Werkgruppen aus 20 Schaffensjahren. Der vorliegende Katalog begleitet die Ausstellung und will wie diese einen Überblick über das einzigartige Schaffen Sailers geben, dem mit seinen außergewöhnlichen Bildern kritische, verdichtete Darstellungen unserer industrialisierten, kapitalisierten, globalisierten Gegenwart gelingen, der er an den absurdesten, entlegensten Orten habhaft wird.

Ich möchte mich im Namen des gesamten Teams des KUNST HAUS WIEN bei Gregor Sailer für sein Vertrauen, seine Offenheit und seine Professionalität in der Zusammenarbeit bedanken. Seine neugierige, analysierende, mutige und aufrichtige Haltung gegenüber der Welt spiegelt sich auch in seiner Haltung gegenüber Menschen wider und macht die Arbeit mit ihm besonders inspirierend. Mein großer Dank gilt meinen Kolleg:innen im KUNST HAUS WIEN, den Leihgeber:innen (Land Tirol, Sammlung Raiffeisen-Landesbank Tirol, LUMEN. Museum of Mountain Photography) und den vielen weiteren Menschen, die mit ihrem Fachwissen und Engagement zur Realisierung dieser Ausstellung und dieses Katalogs beigetragen haben.

Gregor Sailers Bilderwelten ermutigen zum Hinschauen, schulen das Sehen, laden ein, sich auf Ungesehenes und Ungedachtes einzulassen. Ich hoffe, Sie nehmen die Einladung an.

His photographic expeditions lead him to remote, usually inaccessible places. The preparation time takes an extensive period on each occasion. Once the goals have been established following intense research, Sailer needs to take care not only of visas but, in multiple cases, of special approvals and access permits as well; for instance, if the places he wishes to visit are located in exclusion zones or are secret research institutions. Armed with the necessary documents and at least 25 kilograms of photographic equipment, Gregor Sailer repeatedly embarks upon expeditions lasting several days. From these, he brings back his extraordinary images of unseen places, which we are able to contemplate in exhibitions or in book form.

Sailer's oeuvre as a whole is characterised by his quiet, unpretentious and serious artistic approach, which also manifests formally in his photographs: he attempts, with his pictures, to lend structure to a confusing world. Even though these images show no people, humanity is always indirectly present in them, back-referenced by architectures, landscapes, and infrastructures. Thus, his images report migration and war, the wasting of resources and climate crisis; they tell of work, attitude, and faith; of isolation, deception, and pain; of security and threat — they are about people and about the state of humanity and the world.

To this outstanding protagonist of contemporary photography, KUNST HAUS WIEN debuts a major mid-career retrospective in Austria, and presents, in a roundup comprising more than 160 images, focal groups of works from 20 creative years. The present catalogue accompanies the exhibition and, like the latter, aims to provide an overview of Sailer's unique artistry. With his extraordinary images, Sailer achieves critical, condensed portrayals of our industrialised, capitalised, globalised present day, which he captures in the most absurd, remote places.

On behalf of the whole team at KUNST HAUS WIEN, I would like to thank Gregor Sailer for his trust, openness, and professionalism during our collaboration. His curious, analytical, courageous, and candid attitude towards the world is also reflected in his attitude towards people and makes working with him especially inspiring. My great thanks go to my colleagues at KUNST HAUS WIEN as well as to the lenders (Land Tirol, Sammlung Raiffeisen-Landesbank Tirol, LUMEN. Museum of Mountain Photography) and the many other people who have contributed to producing this exhibition and catalogue with their expert knowledge and dedication.

Gregor Sailer's visual worlds train the eye and encourage us to look, while inviting us to engage with all things unseen and unthought. Please accept the cordial invitation.

The Box *The Box I*, Messerschmitthalle, Schwaz, Österreich | Austria, 2017

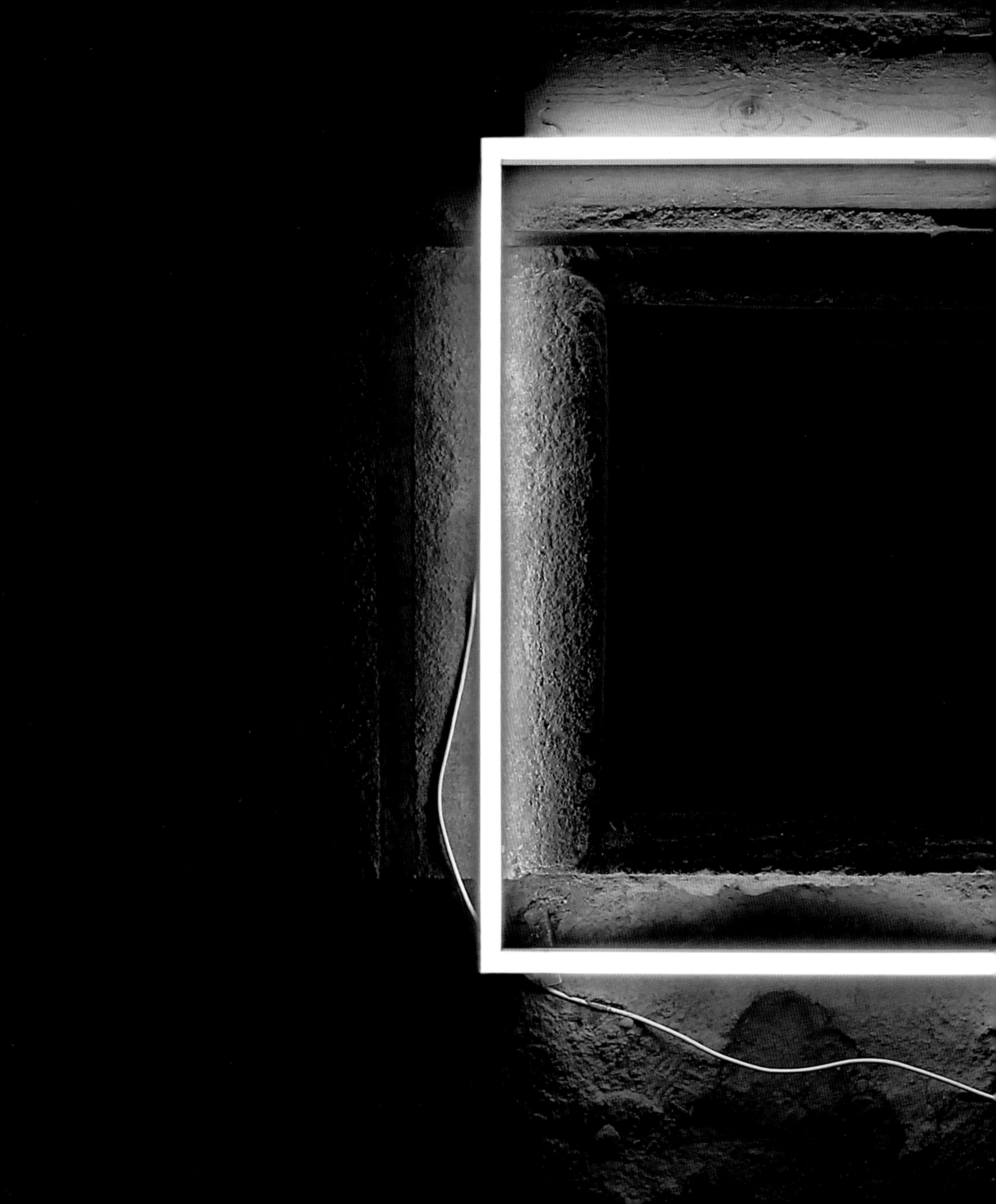

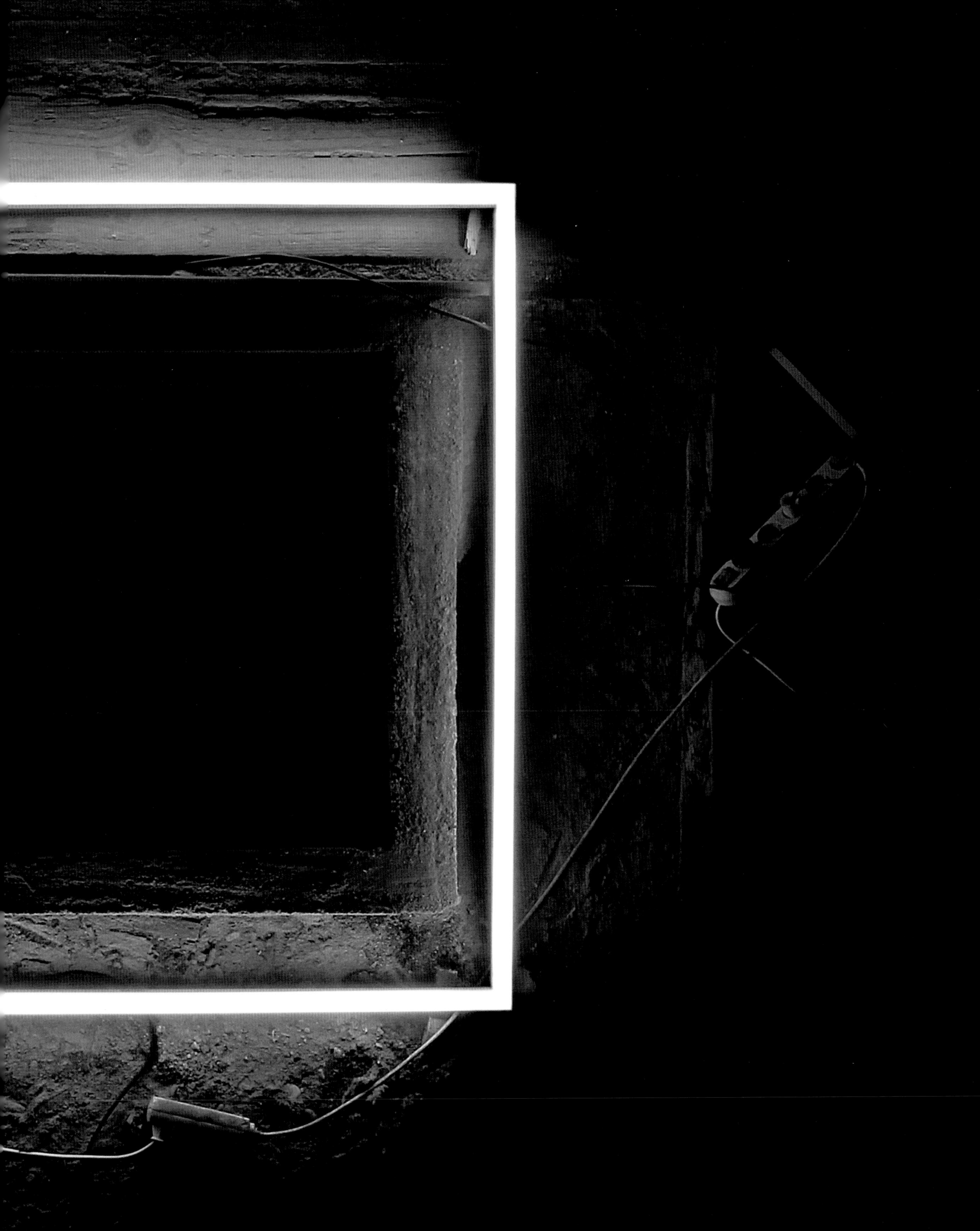

„Nichts ist so offensichtlich,
dass es offensichtlich ist.“

Errol Morris

„Manches von dem,
was die Kamera kann,
macht sprachlos.“

Maria Stepanova

"Nothing is so obvious,
that it's obvious."

Errol Morris

"Some of what the
camera can do makes
you speechless."

Maria Stepanova

Doppelte Wendung

Eine vorläufige Werkbetrachtung zu Gregor Sailer

Christoph Schaden

Wie wäre es, wenn sich die Apparatur der Fotografie als eine Architektur begreifen ließe? Als eine Art Gehäuse, das unsere Welt kategorisch in ein Innen und ein Außen unterteilt. In seinem Inneren würde das Gehäuse bekanntermaßen einen abgedunkelten Raum beherbergen, um auf eine seiner Wandeinheiten über Silbersalze ein Bild zu zeitigen. Was in diesem Lichtbild dann sichtbar werden würde, käme einem Vexierspiel gleich: Denn wiederum würde ein Raum erscheinen, der diesmal jedoch in ein Außen gekehrt und in seinen sichtbaren Verweisen zugleich paradoxerweise auf jene Außenwelt gerichtet wäre, die auf physische Weise jene Apparatur – man könnte auch von einer Architektur der Fotografie sprechen – umfängt. In dem Sinne ließe sich das Fotografische als eine höchst eigentümliche Denkfigur verstehen. Wie über eine Membran würde sie in gleich zwei entgegengesetzte Richtungen tendieren, eben ein Innen und ein Außen. Und stets wäre da noch ein weiterer Gedanke, der mitschwingt. Denn allein – ohne das Licht – ginge es nicht.

Nordstadt (Camera obscura)

Architektur, Raum, Bild, vice versa und mitunter ein Licht, das all diese Zonen auf magische Weise zu durchdringen vermag … Wäre das eine Wahrheit der Fotografie? Es liegt nahe, die faszinierende Bildarbeit von Gregor Sailer über solch diametrale Bewegungslinien nachzuvollziehen. Wie das Fotografische in seiner Wendung nach innen zu denken sein könnte, zeigt sich beispielhaft in einer der frühesten Werkserien des 1980 in Tirol

Essay

Inside-Out, Outside-In

A Current Overview of Gregor Sailer's Work

Christoph Schaden

Imagine that the apparatus of photography could be grasped as an architectural structure. As a type of housing, which categorically subdivided our world into an Inside and an Out. In its interior, the housing would, as is familiar, accommodate a darkened space, onto the wall of which was brought forth an image, through the use of silver salts. The apparition then to be seen in the picture would equate to a game of deception: for, in turn, a space would manifest that this time, however, would be turned into an Outside and, in its visible references, simultaneously — paradoxically — would focus on that exterior world which, physically, encompasses that apparatus — or that architecture of photography, one could also say. In that sense, the photographic would have itself to be understood as a highly idiosyncratic figure of thought. As via a membrane, this figure would drift into two opposing directions, precisely into an Inside and an Out. And another thought would constantly resonate too. For, alone — without light — it would not work.

Nordstadt (Camera obscura)

Architecture, space, image, vice versa, and, from time to time, a light, able to penetrate all these zones by magical means … Might that be a truth of photography? It is self-evident to comprehend the fascinating visual work of Gregor Sailer via such diametral lines of movement. A potential conception of the photographic on its inward turn is offered

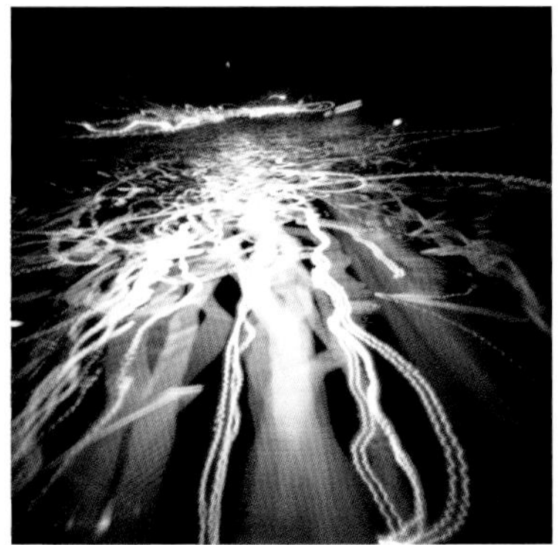

Nordstadt (Camera obscura)

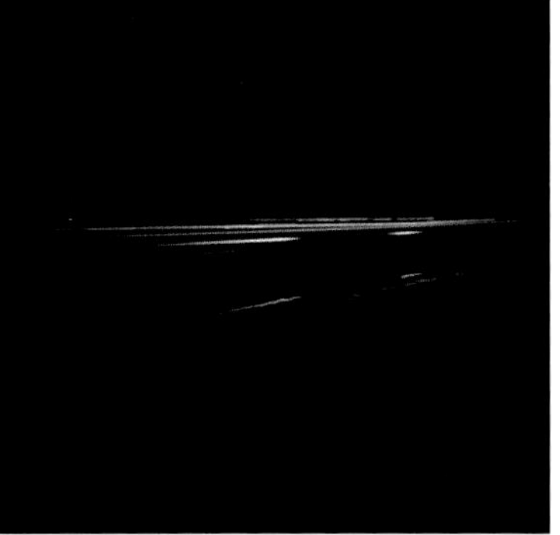

Nordstadt (Camera obscura)

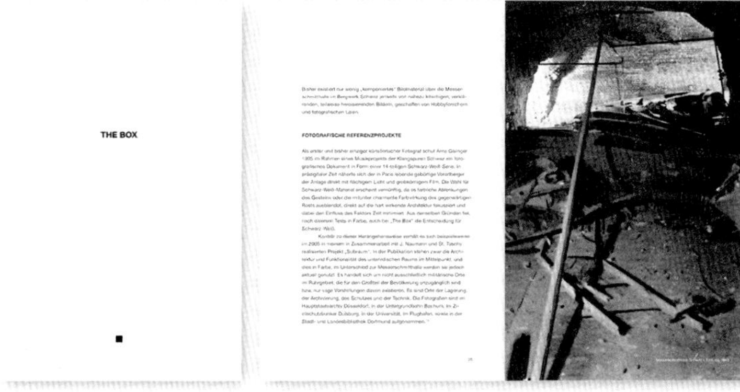

The Box, Cover   *The Box*

geborenen Bildermachers, die einem spezifischen Impuls nach Vergewisserung folgt. Im Jahr 2005, noch während seines ersten Studiums, baut sich Sailer eine Camera obscura, also jenes archaische Urgehäuse der Fotografie, um in einem Stadtteil von Dortmund experimentelle Nachtaufnahmen zu machen. Einmal befestigt er die Kamera an verschiedenen Körperteilen, ein andermal nimmt er von einem fixen Standpunkt aus Aufnahmen seiner Umgebung auf. Was dann über das belichtete Silbersalz der Schwarz-Weiß-Abzüge in die Anschauung transponiert wird, scheint sich in einem Grad ebenso zu entziehen wie zu offenbaren. Es sind Lichtspuren, allesamt spärlich und motivisch kaum zuordenbar, bezeugend und dennoch abstrakt. Wohin soll sich der Blick richten, scheinen die Aufnahmen der Serie nicht ohne Zweifel zu fragen. Auf ein Innen oder ein Außen? Seinen Zugriff kommentiert Sailer wie ein Leitmotiv zu seinen späteren Arbeiten. Es gelte, so bekennt er, den „urbanen Raum im Kontext der Zeit so weit zu reduzieren, dass er seine dem Betrachter bekannte Oberfläche weitgehend verliert".[1] Ästhetische Wirkungsstrategien von Konzentration und Desorientierung, die gerade in der Kombination den Blick auf subtile Weise zu irritieren wissen, zeichnen seine fotografische Arbeitsweise von Beginn an aus. Konsequent bleibt der menschliche Körper darin außen vor, die Physis der bildgebenden Technologie hingegen bewahrt. Bis heute operiert der Fotograf ausschließlich mit einer analogen Fachkamera im Groß- und Mittelformat.

The Box

Jahre später, im Frühjahr 2015, überschreibt Gregor Sailer eine Werkserie mit dem schlichten Titel *The Box.* Wer spekuliert, dass es sich hierbei um den Verweis auf ein Kameragehäuse handelt, könnte sich auf den ersten Blick getäuscht sehen, zumal in diesem Projekt stillgelegte Stollenareale dokumentiert worden sind. Sie finden sich inmitten eines Bergwerks, das in unmittelbarer Nähe zu Sailers österreichischer Heimatregion Schwaz in Tirol gelegen ist. Einst diente das unterirdische Labyrinth den Nationalsozialisten zur Herstellung und Deponierung

by one of the earliest series of works by this picture-maker, who was born in Tyrol in 1980, as it pursues a specific impulse for reassurance. In 2005, during his first course of study, Sailer builds himself a camera obscura — photography's archaic primal housing — in order to take experimental night-time pictures in a district of Dortmund. One time, he secures the camera on various parts of his body; another, he takes shots of his environs from a fixed standpoint. What is then conveyed to the eyes via the exposed silver salt of the black-and-white prints seemingly withdraws to a degree equal to its revelation. These are light traces, all of them sparse and thematically well-nigh unclassifiable, testifying and nevertheless abstract. What is the gaze meant to turn on, the shots in the series seem to ask, not without doubts. On an Inside or an Outside? Sailer's commentary on his approach resembles a keynote for his later works. The task, he avows, is to reduce the "urban space in the context of time so extensively that it largely loses its surface known to the viewer."[1] From the start, his photographic working method is characterised by concentrating and disorientating aesthetic effect strategies, which understatedly know how to puzzle us, precisely in combination with the gaze. Therein, consistently, the human body is left out in the cold; the physique of the image-giving technology, by contrast, persists. The photographer operates exclusively with an analogue professional camera to this day, in large and medium format.

The Box

Years later, in spring 2015, Gregor Sailer captions a series of works with the simple title, *The Box.* A first glance would quash any speculation that this refers to a camera housing, particularly as decommissioned tunnels are documented in this project. They are located in the middle of a mine that is in direct proximity to Sailer's Austrian birthplace region, Schwaz, in Tyrol. The underground labyrinth was once used by the National Socialists for the manufacture and disposal

1
Gregor Sailer, *Nacht,* Ausst.-Kat. Wien 2012, o. S.

Gregor Sailer, *Nacht,* exh. cat. (Vienna 2012), n. p.

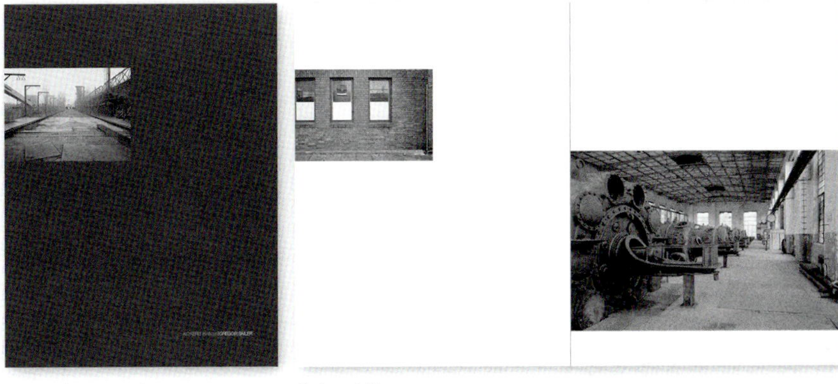

Kokerei Hansa, Cover   *Kokerei Hansa*

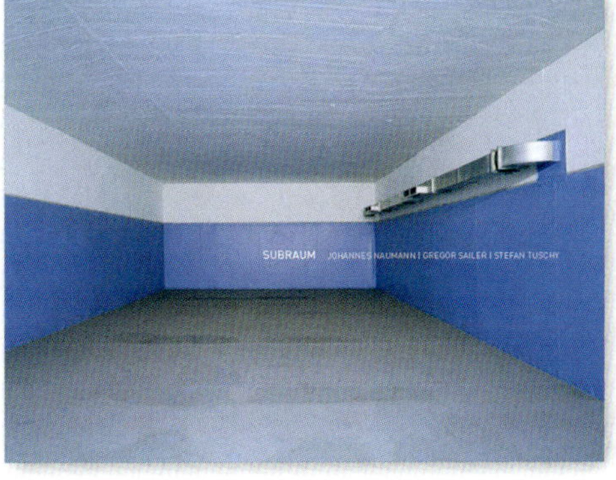

Subraum, Cover

von Waffenkontingenten. „Gegen Ende des Weltkriegs wurden hier von Zwangsarbeitern unter widrigsten Umständen Leitwerke für den Kampf-Düsenjet ME 262 hergestellt", heißt es in einem Katalogkommentar. „Diese Produktionsstätte wurde von den Alliierten nach Ende des Krieges 1947 gesprengt und liegt heute abgekapselt in absoluter Dunkelheit unter Tag. Erst das durchdachte Ausleuchten holt die riesigen Kavernen aus der Tiefe von Raum und Zeit."[2]

Über ein schlaglichtartiges Anleuchten der Kriegsrelikte und Restarchitekturen, die in den Stollen überdauert haben, löst die Bilderfolge tatsächlich den Anspruch an eine fotodokumentarische Arbeit ein. Verborgenes gerät in den Blick, Vergessenes tritt zutage. Was die Bilder freilich auf rezeptive Weise freilegen, ist etwas anderes, nämlich ein Unbehagen. Der Schwarz-Weiß-Abzug *The Box I,* als Prototyp der Serie noch in einer nahe gelegenen Kistenmacherfabrik entstanden, zeigt aus der Dunkelheit eines undefinierten Raums heraus auf ein Rechteck, dessen Kontur erst durch umgebende Neonröhren hervortritt. Es wird kaum kenntlich, dass es sich um einen Schacht handelt, der von oben fotografisch erfasst worden ist. Stattdessen charakterisiert sich das karge Setting als fast reines Abstraktum, ein Bild im Bild, dessen Künstlichkeit in der Anschauung umso stärker hervortritt. Paradox genug, wähnt sich das erkundende Auge urplötzlich wieder in einem verstörenden Innen. Wohin verortet sich Sailers Territorium der Fotografie? Wohin weisen seine Kulissen des Realen?

Kokerei Hansa

Äußere Zuschreibungen haben reflexartig nach Vereinfachungen gesucht. Ein Presseartikel ist jüngst wieder zu der Einschätzung gekommen, bei Gregor Sailer handele es sich um einen „Tiroler Extremfotografen" mit einem „Faible für surreale Architekturen".[3] Solcherlei Etikette verkennen, wie ausdifferenziert der Reflexionsgrad ist, mit dem der Bildermacher von Beginn an sein Medium einzusetzen versteht. Auch mit dem

of arms contingents. "Towards the end of the world war, tailplanes for the ME 262 combat jet were produced here by forced labourers under the most repugnant circumstances," one catalogue comment notes. "This production shop was detonated by the Allies after the war's end, in 1947, and today it lies encapsulated in total darkness underground. Only well thought-out illumination retrieves the giant caverns from the depths of space and time."[2]

In point of fact, via the spotlight-like lighting of the war relicts and residual architectures that have survived in the galleries, the succession of images does honour the claim to be photodocumentary work. The concealed comes into view, the forgotten comes to light. What the images reveal, albeit receptively, is something else: namely, a discomfiture. The black-and-white print *The Box I,* created as a series prototype in a box-making factory nearby, points out of the obscurity of an undefined space to a rectangle, whose contour only emerges courtesy of circumferential neon tubes. It is barely recognisable that this, here, is a shaft, photographed from above. Instead, the barren setting is characterised as almost pure abstraction, an image within an image, whose artificiality comes to the fore all the more strongly when it is looked at. Paradoxically enough, suddenly the exploring eye finds itself once more in an unsettling Inside. What will be the location of Sailer's territory of photography? Which way are his reality backdrops pointing?

Kokerei Hansa

Outside attributions have reflexively sought simplifications. One press article recently revisited the appraisal that, with Gregor Sailer, we have a "Tyrolean extreme photographer" with a "foible for surreal architectures."[3] Labels of this kind fail to recognise how fully differentiated the degree of reflection is with which the photographer has always deployed his medium. Probably even using the trendy buzzwords

2
Carl Kraus, „Von den Kitzbüheler Alpen bis zum Gardasee. Eine künstlerische Bestandsaufnahme", in: *Kunst Landschaft Tirol. Eine Entdeckungsreise von der Romantik bis zur Gegenwart,* Ausst.-Kat. Kitzbühel, 30.6.– 30.9.2018, Innsbruck 2018, S. 72.

Carl Kraus, "Von den Kitzbüheler Alpen bis zum Gardasee. Eine künstlerische Bestandsaufnahme," in *Kunst Landschaft Tirol. Eine Entdeckungsreise von der Romantik bis zur Gegenwart,* exh. cat. (Innsbruck 2018), 72.

3
Ivona Jelčić, „Seide, tiefgefroren", in: *Der Standard,* 9. September 2021, S. 25.

Ivona Jelčić, "Scide, tiefgefroren," in *Der Standard,* September 9, 2021, 25.

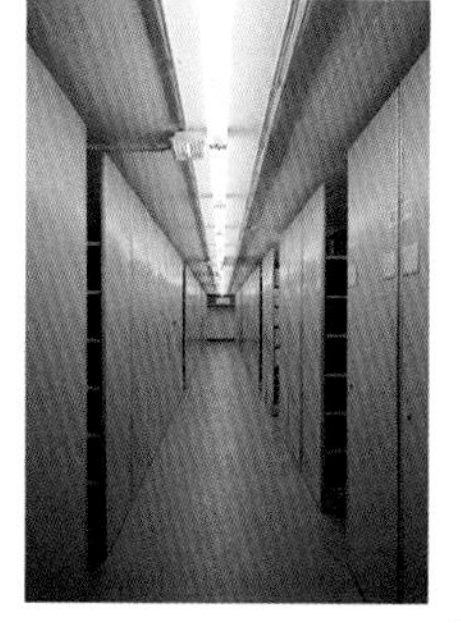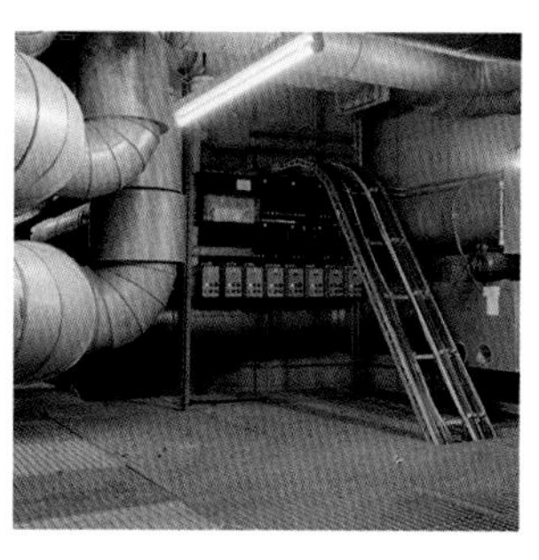

Subraum

trendigen Schlagwort eines konzeptuell geprägten Dokumentarismus wird man Sailers Bildarbeit wohl nur in Teilen gerecht. Kategorisierungsversuche, die ihn mal bildjournalistischen, mal fotokünstlerischen Milieus zuordnen, greifen ebenfalls nicht. Eher bietet es sich an, Sailers solitäres Schaffen, das sich in zahlreichen Publikationen und Ausstellungen widerspiegelt, aus den beiden schon genannten ortsgebundenen Koordinaten herzuleiten, die die Eckpunkte seiner Biografie markieren. Sie könnten kaum gegensätzlicher sein: Tirol und das Ruhrgebiet, konkreter der Wohnort Vomp und der Studienort Dortmund. Erst wenn man es wagt, die beiden topografischen Bezugspunkte zusammenzudenken, lässt sich rückblickend wohl jenes Spannungsfeld benennen, das Sailers unverwechselbare Position in der Gegenwartsfotografie auszeichnet.

Werkimmanent markiert die Folie der Dortmunder Studienzeit den Auftakt. Dass sich Sailers dokumentarischer Impuls schon früh in eine Motivtradition einreiht, die eng mit dem fotografischen Erbe zur Schwerindustrie in Westdeutschland verbunden ist, belegt ein frühes, ambitioniertes Buchprojekt. Es erscheint 2005 in Kooperation mit der Stiftung Industriedenkmalpflege und Geschichtskultur unter dem Titel *Kokerei Hansa*. Dahinter verbirgt sich eine von siebzehn Großkokereien, die in den 1920er-Jahren im Zuge umfassender Rationalisierungsmaßnahmen in der Schwerindustrie im Ruhrgebiet errichtet wurden. In Anlehnung an das kanonische Werk des einflussreichen Düsseldorfer Dokumentaristenpaars Bernd und Hilla Becher entscheidet sich Sailer dafür, in den laubfreien Wintermonaten eine Serie von Schwarz-Weiß-Aufnahmen über das gewaltige Kokereigelände in Dortmund zu erstellen. Jedoch befreien sich seine Motive bereits in einigen ästhetischen Aspekten vom streng neusachlichen Stil der genannten Vorbilder. „Aufgenommen in einem diffusen, kontrastlosen Licht, erscheinen die Bauwerke ruhig, würdevoll und zeitlos. Die Wege, die Gregor Sailer wählt, führen über Ofendecken, Meistergänge, Bandbrücken oder Bahngleise und weisen ins Unendliche", heißt es weitsichtig in dem Fotoband.[4]

"conceptually characterised documentarism," one will do only partial justice to Sailer's visual work. Attempts at categorisation, assigning him now to press photography, now to art photography milieus, likewise fail to stick. Rather, it is useful to deduce Sailer's solitary creativity, which is reflected in numerous publications and exhibitions, by the two place-bound coordinates already named, which mark the key points of his life story. They could hardly be more contrasting: Tyrol and the Ruhr region. Or more specifically: place of residence, Vomp; and place of study, Dortmund. Retrospectively, it seems that there can only be a name for the field of tension that distinguishes Sailer's unmistakable position in contemporary photography if one ventures to think of the two topographic reference points together.

An intrinsic part of the oeuvre marks its opener: the Dortmund study period. An early, ambitious book project is proof that Sailer's documentary impulse joins a motif tradition closely associated with the photographic heritage of heavy industry in West Germany. It appears in 2005 in partnership with the Stiftung Industriedenkmalpflege und Geschichtskultur under the title, *Kokerei Hansa*. Behind this title is one of seven large cokeries that were built in the 1920s, in the course of comprehensive rationalisation measures in Ruhr region heavy industry. Basing himself on the canonical work of the influential Düsseldorf documentary makers, Bernd and Hilla Becher, Sailer opts to create a series of black-and-white shots of the vast cokery compound in Dortmund in the leafless winter months. However, his motifs liberate themselves from the stringently New Objectivity style of his Becher predecessors in a number of aesthetic aspects. "Shot in a diffuse light devoid of contrast, the structures appear serene, dignified, and timeless. The paths chosen by Gregor Sailer lead across furnace roofs, galleries, conveyor bridges, and rail tracks and point to infinity," runs a far-sighted comment in the photobook.[4]

4
Ursula Mehrfeld, „Kokerei Hansa", in: *Kokerei Hansa. Gregor Sailer*, hrsg. von der Stiftung Industriedenkmalpflege und Geschichtskultur, Dortmund 2005, o. S.

Ursula Mehrfeld, "Kokerei Hansa," in *Kokerei Hansa. Fotografien von Gregor Sailer*, ed. Stiftung Industriedenkmalpflege und Geschichtskultur (Dortmund 2005), n. p.

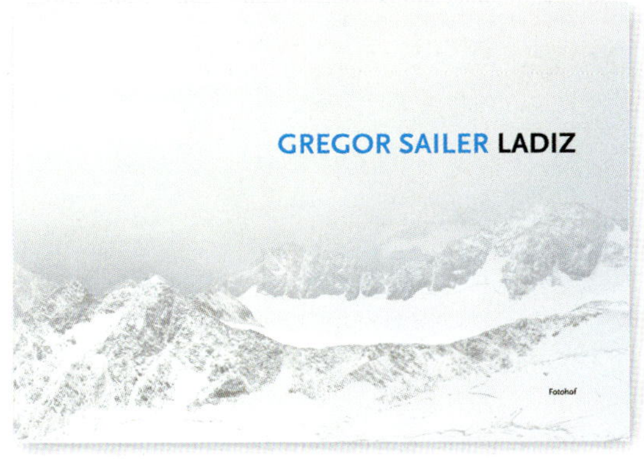

Ladiz, Cover

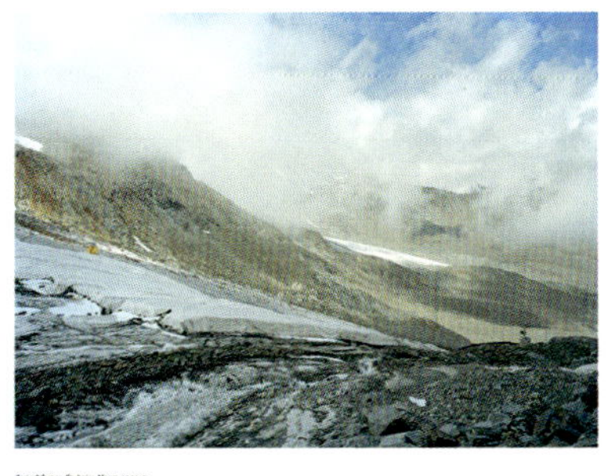

Ladiz

Subraum

Auch das Folgeprojekt *Subraum,* 2005 in Zusammenarbeit mit Johannes Naumann und Stefan Tuschy entstanden und fünf Jahr später unter Herausgeberschaft der Kunsthalle Wien in Buchform veröffentlicht, bleibt dem Ruhrgebiet verbunden. Das Fotografenkollektiv, das sich auf eine nahezu einheitliche Stilistik einigt, erfasst in nüchterner Präzision zahlreiche unterirdische Areale und Architekturen der Industrieregion, deren Funktionen ein breites Spektrum aufzeigen. Es reicht von Staatsarchiven, Versorgungsanlagen von Universitäten und Flughäfen über Untergrundbahnen und Depoträume für Bibliotheken bis hin zu Zivilschutzbunkern. Man mag das Fotoprojekt als Korrektiv am tradierten Bildklischee jener Industrieregion interpretieren, die ihr Image zuweilen immer noch aus einer überholten Ikonografie der Zechenkultur unter Tage schöpft. Allerdings greift auch dieser Gedanke zu kurz. Mal werden Blicke auf endlos anmutende Regalkorridore gelenkt, mal auf Gleisspuren, die über Tunnelröhren in die Dunkelheit führen. Hypnotisch drängen die Fluchten in die Tiefe des Bildraums, um sich dann im Erdinnern zu verlieren. Alles Situative ist ausgemerzt, alles elementhaft Erfasste seltsam erstarrt. Es scheint, als verharre jene streng funktionale Parallelwelt unter Tage in beckettscher Manier, als warte sie auf eine Zeit ohne Licht.

Ladiz

Das nachfolgende Projekt *LADIZ_alpen™,* das Gregor Sailer 2006 realisiert und zwei Jahre später in Buchform bei der Edition Fotohof in Salzburg veröffentlicht, stülpt sich in radikaler Wendung erstmals in ein Außen. Der Titel verweist auf den Namen einer alten Alm im Karwendelgebirge, „die im Familienbesitz der Sailers gewesen war, bis sie vor etwa 150 Jahren beim Kartenspiel verzockt wurde".[5] Was im Ton salopp daherkommt, lenkt im Gehalt augenblicklich auf ein biografisches Moment, das zu gleichen Teilen von Verwurzelung und Verlust erzählt. Bis heute ist Sailer mit seiner Familie in der Tiroler Ortschaft Vomp

Subraum

The subsequent project *Subraum,* created in 2005 in collaboration with Johannes Naumann and Stefan Tuschy, and published in book form five years later by Kunsthalle Wien, also retains ties to the Ruhr region. The photographers' collective, which agrees on an almost uniform style, captures, with sober precision, numerous subterranean areas and architectures of the industrial region, whose functions exhibit a broad spectrum. This ranges from state archives, university and airport supply facilities, through underground railways and library storerooms, to civilian bunkers. One may interpret the photographic project as a corrective of the handed-down visual cliché of an industrial region which still, occasionally, draws its image from an outdated iconography of mine culture below ground. Even that thought is inadequate, though. The gaze is steered one moment onto endless-looking corridors of shelving, the next onto tracks that lead into the darkness across tunnel tubes. Hypnotically, the vanishing points penetrate the depth of the pictorial space, in order, then, to lose themselves in the Earth's interior. All that is situated is eradicated, all that is elementarily captured is oddly rigid. It is as though this strictly functional parallel world below ground were poised in a Beckettian manner, as if waiting for a time without light.

Ladiz

The next project, *LADIZ_alpen™,* which Gregor Sailer produces in 2006 and publishes as a book at Edition Fotohof in Salzburg two years later, represents a first radical turning inside out. The title refers to the name of an old alpine farmhouse in the Karwendel mountains, "which had been owned by the Sailer family, until it got gambled away in a card game 150 years ago."[5] What comes across as lackadaisical in tone immediately draws one's attention to a biographical instance that tells of uprooting and loss in equal parts. To

5
N. N., „o. T.", in: *Triennale Linz 1.0. Gegenwartskunst in Österreich,* Ausst.-Kat. Linz 2010, S. 192.

Anonymous, "Untitled," in: *Triennale Linz 1.0. Gegenwartskunst in Österreich,* exh. cat. (Linz 2010), 192.

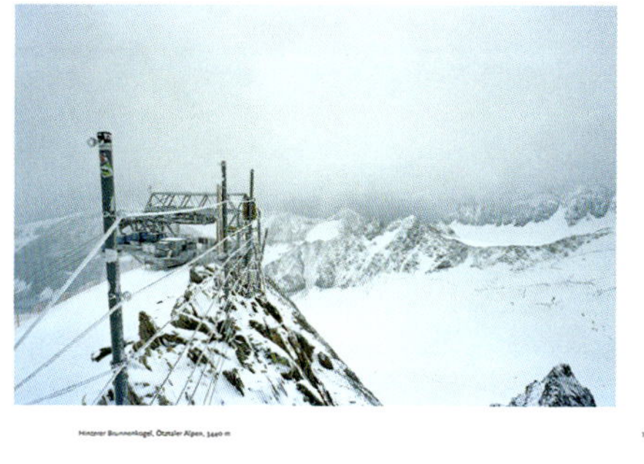

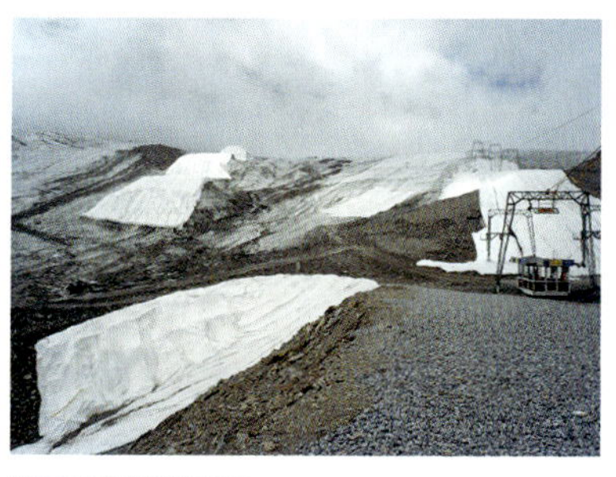

Ladiz

beheimatet, in dieser Peripherie tankt er nach eigenem Bekunden Kraft für seine Unternehmungen, hier findet sich sein Rückzugs- und privater Lebensbereich. Der Vater betreibt in der Region ein Architekturbüro, sein jüngster Bruder, der ihm auf Reisen zuweilen assistiert, verdingt sich in der Informationstechnik bei einem Optikkonzern. Existenzen wie diese lassen sich nur schwerlich mit jenen romantischen Vorstellungen in Verbindung bringen, die bis heute die kollektiven Sehnsuchtsklischees des Alpenbilds prägen – im Gegenteil. Wie stark ökonomische Prämissen die Naturlandschaft des Alpenraums zu dominieren wissen, sie verändern oder gar nachhaltig beschädigen, analysiert die *Ladiz*-Serie aus gebotener Distanz. Mit dem Buchprojekt reüssiert Sailer in der deutschsprachigen Fotoszene, eine multimediale Installation wird folgen.

Der Fotograf dokumentiere „eine durch fortschreitende Technisierung und touristische Erschließung versehrte und zerstörte Bergwelt, deren alter Zauber und Mythos mit enormem Aufwand und massiven Eindrücken wie etwa den Vliesabdeckungen der Gletscher in den Ötztaler und den Zillertaler Alpen in die Gegenwart hinübergerettet werden sollen", heißt es in einer Besprechung.[6] Wer den Fotoband durchblättert, mag sich vielleicht noch einmal an die Ausrichtung des strengen Becher-Dokumentarismus erinnern. Denn längst ist auch in Sailers Farbaufnahmen die Transformation der Gebirgslandschaft um Ladiz zu einem „industriellen Hochgebirge" abgeschlossen. Die technoide Überformung des heimatlichen Terrains erfasst der Fotograf beispielhaft im Hightechdesign einer Skiliftanlage, aber auch über eine nächtlich erstrahlende Megabühne, die auf rund 3.000 Meter Höhe eigens für ein „mars-event" errichtet worden ist. In welch befremdliche Territorien ist das Auge vorgedrungen? Paradox genug bewahren die Aufnahmen einen Moment von Erhabenheit und Ruhe. Immer wieder stößt der Blick dabei auf eigentümliche, vom Menschen ersonnene Texturen der Aneignung: Gatter, Planen, Verstrebungen. Eingebettet in die alpine Naturkulisse wirken sie so real wie absurd, so funktional wie fehlplatziert. Die Fallhöhe, die mit dem aberwitzigen Perfektionismus der Höhenregionen um Ladiz einhergeht, scheint enorm. Einem solchen Außen ist schlicht nicht zu trauen.

this day, Sailer and his family call the Tyrolean locale, Vomp, their home; in these environs, he states, he replenishes strength for his ventures; here is his place of retreat and privacy. His father runs an architect's office in the region; his youngest brother, who assists him occasionally on travels, earns his crust in IT at an optical company. Existences like these are seriously at odds with those romantic notions that persist to this day in the collective alpine cliché of longing. From a due distance, the *Ladiz* series offers an analysis of how strongly economic premises can dominate, change, or even lastingly damage the natural alpine landscape. Sailer garners acclaim with his book in the German-speaking region; a multimedia installation is to follow.

One review has it that the photographer documents "a mountain world damaged and destroyed by advancing technologisation and tourism development, where there are attempts to preserve its former magic and myth in the present day at enormous expense and with grand impressions, such as the fleece coverings on glaciers in the Ötztaler and Zillertaler Alps."[6] Browse through the photobook, and one may be perhaps, once again, reminded of the stringent documentary style of Becher. For, in Sailer's colour shots, the morphing of the mountain landscape around Ladiz into an "industrial highland" was complete a long time ago. The photographer exemplarily captures the technoid transformation of the homeland terrain in the high-tech design of a ski lift; and not only there, but also in a nocturnally gleaming megastage, set up specially for a "Mars event" at about 3,000 metres. Into what outlandish territories has the eye pressed forward? Paradoxically enough, the shots preserve a circumstance of loftiness and serenity. Over and over, the gaze encounters quaint, man-concocted textures of appropriation: enclosures, tarpaulins, struts. Embedded in the natural alpine backdrop they look equally real and absurd, equally functional and misplaced. The drop height, which is accompanied by the ludicrous perfectionism of the highland regions around Ladiz, seems vertiginous. There is simply no trusting an Outside like this.

6
Daniel Hess, „Zwischen Schwindel und Gottesnähe: Der Blick vom Berg", in: *Von oben gesehen: Die Vogelperspektive,* Ausst.-Kat. Nürnberg 2014, S. 167.

Daniel Hess, "Zwischen Schwindel und Gottesnähe: Der Blick vom Berg," in *Von oben gesehen: Die Vogelperspektive,* exh. cat. (Nuremberg 2014), 167.

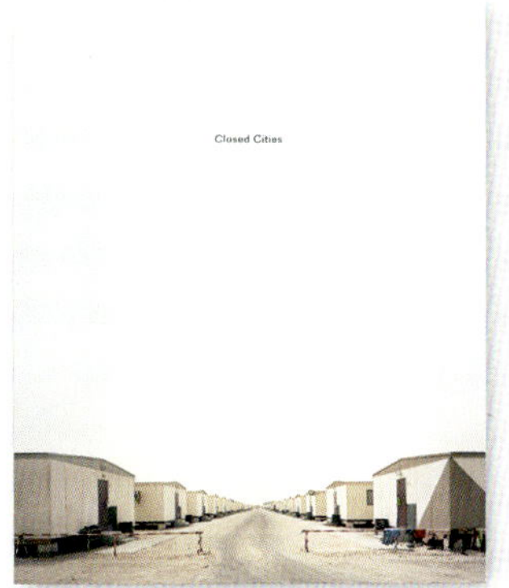
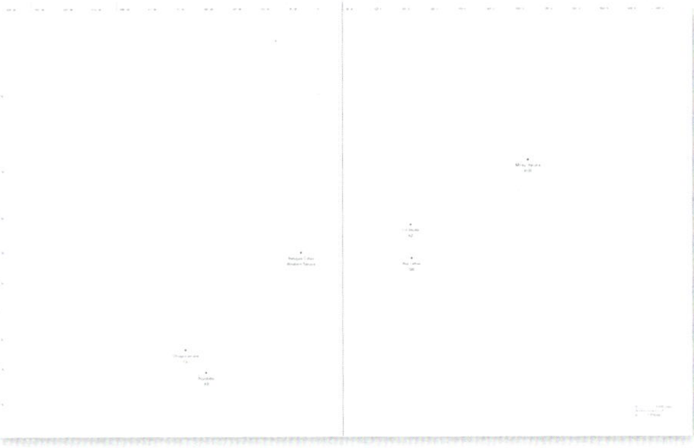
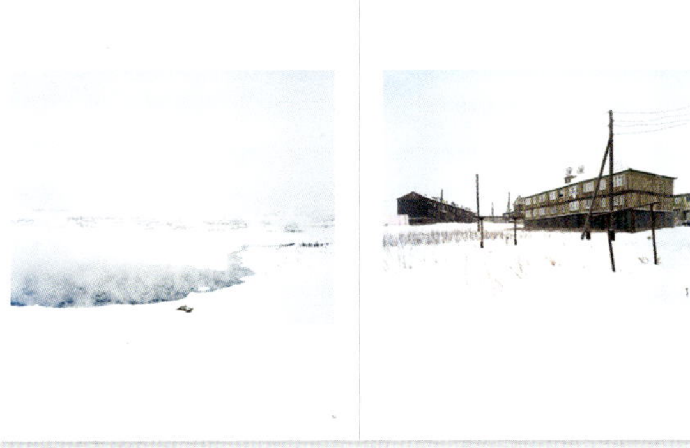

Closed Cities, Cover　　　　*Closed Cities*

Closed Cities

Vielleicht lässt sich in dem skeptischen Gedanken die Essenz der fotografischen Bildarbeit von Gregor Sailer verorten. Jedenfalls widmen sich die drei extrem aufwendigen Langzeitprojekte, die er in der nächsten Dekade realisieren wird, immer radikaler den peripheren Lebenszonen der Zivilisation, in denen Architekturen und die sie umgebenden Räume ihre eindeutige Codierbarkeit verloren haben. Die Broschur *Closed Cities,* die 2012 ebenso wie die beiden Folgebände im Verlag von Klaus Kehrer erscheint, wartet auf dem Umschlag mit dem Farbmotiv einer Straßenflucht auf, die beiderseits von uniformen Baracken gesäumt wird. Der Informationswert rückt gegen null, der Blick flutet unweigerlich ins Leere. „Gregor Sailer visiert Bezirke menschlichen Lebens und Arbeitens an, die sich durch Hermetik und Abgeschlossenheit auszeichnen", schreibt Margit Zuckriegl. „Orte, Plätze, Gegenden, an denen Menschen den unglaublichsten Bedingungen und Strapazen ausgesetzt werden – allen voran der unerschütterlichen Isolation von allem anderen."[7]

Die oftmals temporär errichteten Siedlungsformen der sogenannten Closed Cities dienen unterschiedlichsten Zwecken, sei es zur Rohstoffförderung oder militärischen Nutzung, als Flüchtlingslager oder auch als Rückzugsresidenz wohlhabender Gated Communities, die unter allen Umständen autark bleiben wollen. Sailer spürt die geschichts- wie gesichtslosen „Unorte", die sich nach Marc Augé mit Kalkül allen identitätsstiftenden Prämissen verweigern, in den entlegensten Gegenden dieser Welt auf, er findet sie in Algerien, Argentinien, Aserbaidschan, Chile, Katar und Russland. Man merkt der Serie an, wie viel Kraft und Beharrlichkeit sie auf Autorenseite gekostet haben muss. Neben der akribischen Recherche galt es, im Vorfeld über Botschaften und Ministerien Genehmigungen und Beglaubigungen einzuholen, um überhaupt Zugang zu den abgeschiedenen Territorien zu bekommen. Mehrere Male musste von Sailer auch der Vorwurf möglicher Spionage oder investigativer Umtriebe ausgeräumt werden. Es verwundert kaum, dass die hermetisch abgeriegelten Areale allesamt von Zeichen der Abweisung durchsetzt sind, die signalisieren: Hier darf und sollte man nicht sein.

Closed Cities

Perhaps this sceptical thought is where we can pinpoint the essence of Gregor Sailer's photographic pictorial work. At any rate, the three extremely elaborate long-term projects that he is about to produce in the decade to come are dedicated, ever more radically, to the peripheral life zones of civilisation, in which architectures and the spaces surrounding them have lost their clear codability. The brochure *Closed Cities,* which appears — like the two subsequent volumes — at Klaus Kehrer's publishing house, bears on its cover the colour motif of a streetscape lined with uniform shacks on both sides. The information value drops to about zero, the gaze surges ineluctably into the void. "Gregor Sailer takes aim at areas of human life and work that are characterised by hermetics and seclusion," writes Margit Zuckriegl. "Locations, places, regions where people are exposed to the most unbelievable conditions and stresses — above all, to insurmountable isolation from everything else."[7]

The often temporarily erected settlement forms of the so-called Closed Cities serve the widest variety of purposes, be they for raw material conveyance or military use, for refugee camps or prosperous gated communities who are determined to stay self-contained. Sailer tracks down the equally faceless and unstoried "non-places," which, according to Marc Augé, calculatedly refuse any identity-establishing premisses, in the remotest regions of this world: he finds them in Algeria, Argentina, Azerbaijan, Chile, Qatar, and Russia. One can see by the series how much strength and perseverance it must have cost its author. Besides the painstaking research, approvals and accreditations had to be obtained via embassies and ministries in advance, so that access could be gained to the isolated territories in the first place. Several times, Sailer found himself having to refute the accusation of potential espionage or investigative activities. It comes as almost no surprise that the hermetically sealed-off areas are all interspersed with signs of dismissal, which signal: people must not and should not be here. As an image

7
Margit Zuckriegl, „Fotografie als investigativer Akt – Zu den fotografischen Serien von Gregor Sailer", in: *Gregor Sailer. Closed Cities,* Heidelberg 2012, S. 273.

Margit Zuckriegl, "Fotografie als investigativer Akt — Zu den fotografischen Serien von Gregor Sailer. Closed Cities* (Heidelberg 2012), 273.

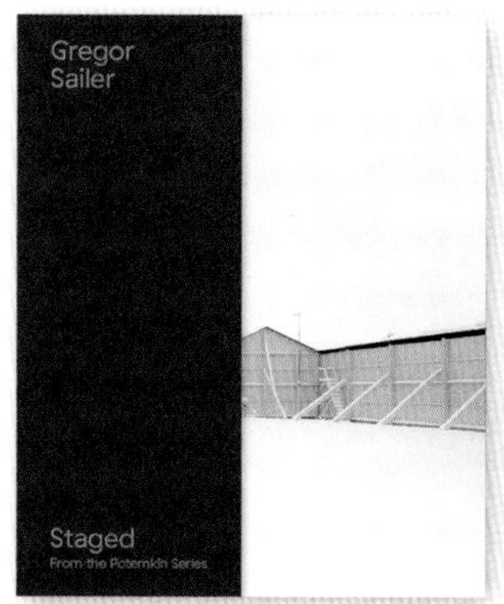

Staged, Cover

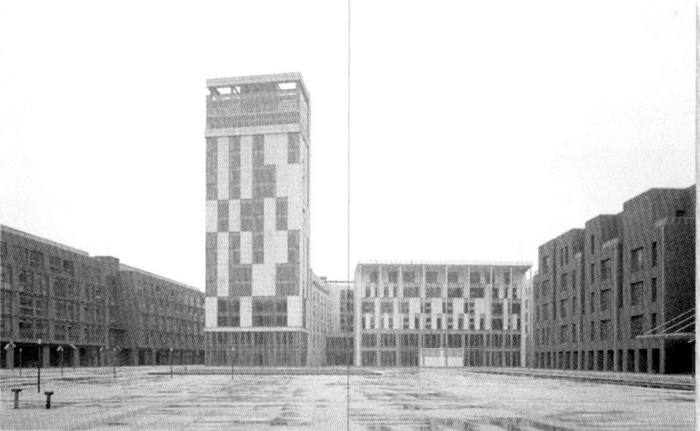

Staged

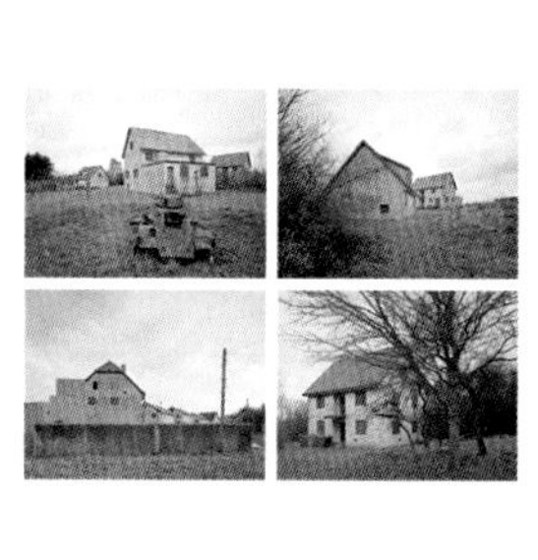

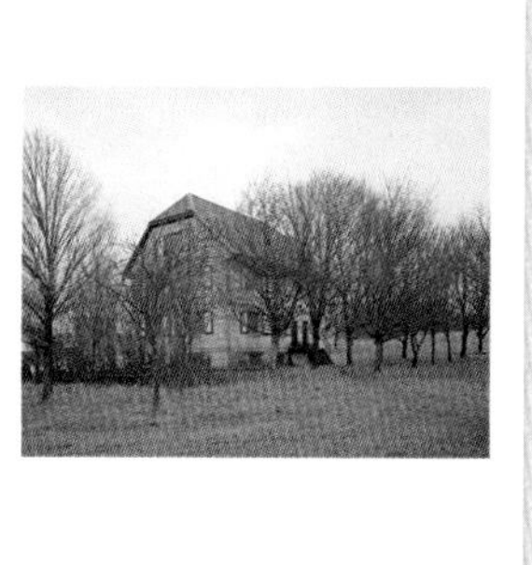

Als ein Bilderkorpus, der in der vergleichenden Betrachtung eine globale Analyse auf die Spezies der Closed Cities eröffnet, verstört Sailers Sichtung umso mehr, weil eine Erkenntnis nicht außen vor bleibt: Der Mensch, der in den lebensfeindlichen und unwirtlichen Anlagen stets abwesend und dennoch merkwürdig gegenwärtig ist, bildet die unheimlichste Konstante.

corpus that forms the opener to the comparative examination, a global analysis of the Closed Cities species, Sailer's inspection is all the more unsettling, because there is one insight that cannot be ignored: the eeriest constant — always absent and yet remarkably present in the inhospitable facilities — is humankind.

The Potemkin Village

Ohne Abstriche lässt sich das auch für das Folgeprojekt *The Potemkin Village* sagen, das fünf Jahre später in Buchform veröffentlicht wird. Die Referenz auf den berühmten russischen Feldmarschall, der seine Zarin angeblich mit bemalten Dorfkulissen zu blenden wusste, lenkt auf ein tradiertes Motivfeld der Fotografie. Schließlich bildet der Fragenkatalog über Schein und Sein, Wahrheit und Lüge, Oberfläche und Tiefe bis heute einen probaten Ausgangspunkt fotografischer Unternehmungen, die einer sich entziehenden und von Widersprüchen geprägten Welt auf die Schliche kommen wollen. Vom Vorwurf der Fassadenhaftigkeit, wie sie in der Denkfigur der Potemkinschen Dörfer zutage tritt, ist indes auch die Fotografie selbst in ihrer medialen Hinterlegung nicht unberührt geblieben. Gregor Sailer aktiviert die mythische Folie des Fürsten Potjomkin auf überraschend buchstäbliche Weise, um im Sinne eines Panoptikums die grassierenden Auswüchse von Fake-Architekturen unserer Epoche aufzuzeigen. Abermals ist die Sichtung global angelegt, abermals sind die vorgefundenen Ausprägungen in Sailers Farbabzügen so facettenreich und bizarr, dass das begleitende Druckwerk in der Kritik gar als „Märchenbuch des Unglaublichen"[8] beschrieben wird. Bei der Bildlektüre sieht man sich etwa konfrontiert mit arabisch anmutenden Dörfern, die in der Mojave-Wüste von Kalifornien errichtet worden sind und als Trainingscamp für fiktive Kriegshandlungen des US-Militärs dienen. In China mutieren retortenartige Modellstädte unter dem Label „German Town", „Swedish Town", „Holland Town" und „Thames Town" zu einer atemberaubenden Kulturaneignung des Westens. Und in der russischen Kleinstadt Suzdal warten Hausruinen, die

The Potemkin Village

Without subtractions, this can be said also for the subsequent project, *The Potemkin Village,* which is published as a book five years later. The reference to the famous Russian field marshal, who allegedly dazzled his Tsarina with painted village backdrops, brings to mind a traditional design field of photography. After all, to this day, the catalogue of questions concerning appearance and being, truth and lies, surface and depth, forms an appropriate starting point for photographic activities that try to get wise to an evasive world shaped by contradictions. Meanwhile, not even photography itself, in its media custodianship, remains untouched by the accusation of being façade-like as it comes to light in the Potemkin villages. Gregor Sailer activates the legendary foil of Prince Potemkin in a surprisingly literal way, in order to show, in the sense of a panopticon, the rampant excrescences of today's fake architectures. Again, the inspection takes a global approach; again, the found characteristics in Sailer's colour prints are so richly faceted and bizarre that the accompanying printed work is even critiqued as being a "fairy-tale book of the unbelievable."[8] When looking at the pictures, one finds oneself confronted, for instance, with Arabic-looking villages, which have been built in the Mojave desert in California and serve as a training camp for fictitious acts of war by the US military. In China, synthetic-looking model cities mutate under the labels "German Town," "Swedish Town," "Holland Town," and "Thames Town" into a breathtaking cultural appropriation of the West. And in the small Russian town, Suzdal, ruined

8
Margit Zuckriegl, „Gregor Sailer: The Potemkin Village (Rezension)", in: *Eikon. Internationale Zeitschrift für Photographie und Medienkunst*, Nr. 100, 2017, o. S.

Margit Zuckriegl, 'Gregor Sailer: The Potemkin Village,' in *Eikon. Internationale Zeitschrift für Photographie und Medienkunst,* no. 100 (2017), n. p.

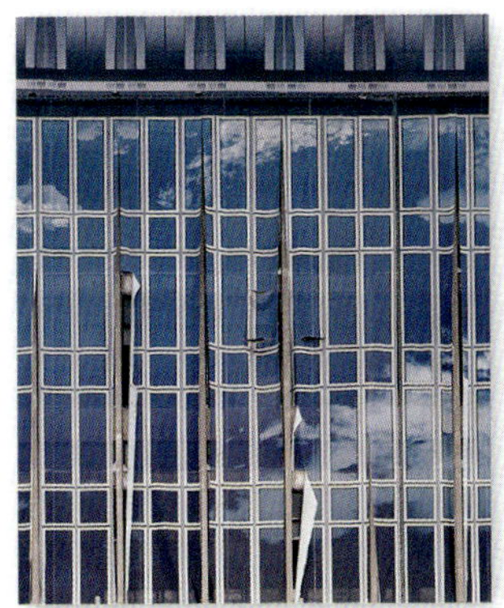
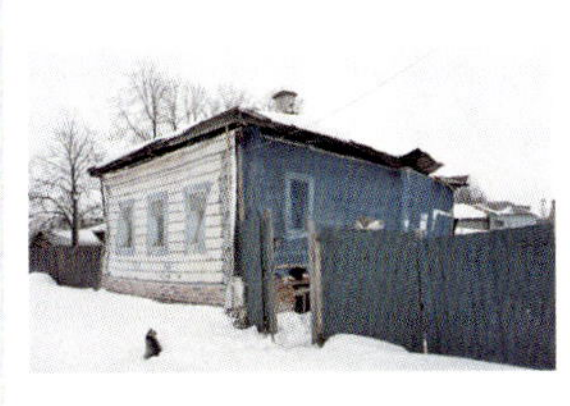
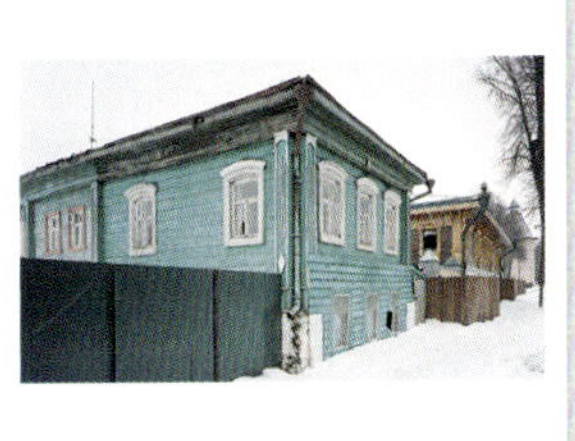
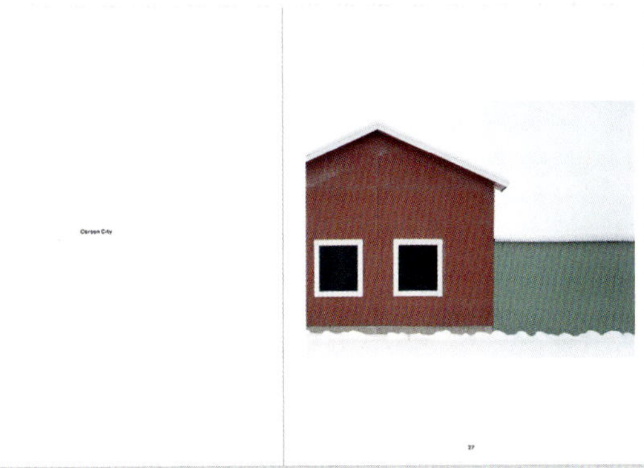

The Potemkin Village, Cover   *The Potemkin Village*

eigens für einen Putin-Besuch durch Bauplanen verblendet worden sind, mit Fake-Architekturen auf. Das Umschlagbild des Bandes zeigt ein Detail einer solchen Scheinfassade. Sie verspricht im Prospekt einen ungetrübten blauen Himmel, weist aber schon Risse auf. Einmal mehr mag man seinen Augen nicht trauen.

Der bilddokumentarische Skeptizismus von Sailer lässt sich gewiss im Sinne der Aufklärung begreifen. Hierzu passt, dass er mit der konsistenten Form des Fotobuchs agiert. „Ein Fotobuch ist ein perfektes Medium, um meine Arbeit zu transportieren", merkt er in einem Interview an. „In einem Buch kann man seinen Bildern eine andere Dramaturgie hinzufügen. Deshalb denke ich im Vorfeld oft in Buchform."[9] Neben einer genau austarierten Bilderfolge enthalten Sailers jüngere Buchwerke oftmals kartografisches Material und einen Reigen fachkundiger Textbeiträge, die weitere Zugänge zu dem komplexen Themenfeld gewähren. Dennoch bleibt wohl nach der Lektüre die irritierende ikonische Qualität des Bilderkorpus im Gedächtnis haften. In der Summe bedeutet Sailers Motivarsenal von *The Potemkin Village* nicht weniger als ein beklemmendes Sinnbild der Gegenwart.

houses await specifically for a visit by Putin with fake architectures and concealed with tarpaulins. The volume's cover illustration shows a detail of one such façade. In the backdrop, it promises a dazzling blue sky, but it is already showing cracks. Once more, one is hesitant to trust one's eyes.

Certainly, Sailer's scepticism about visual documents can be grasped in the concept of the enlightenment. It suits that purpose that he consistently employs the photobook form. "A photobook is a perfect medium for conveying my work," he comments in an interview. "In a book, you can add another dramaturgy to your pictures. That is why I often think in book form beforehand."[9] Besides a precisely balanced succession of images, Sailer's more recent books often contain cartographic material and a round of expert text contributions, which grant further insights into the complex thematic field. Yet, after reading, the disconcerting iconic quality of the image corpus is what is likely to be retained in the memory. In sum, Sailer's arsenal of motifs from *The Potemkin Village* means nothing less than a nightmarish allegory of the present day.

The Polar Silk Road

In seinem jüngsten, 2021 erschienenen Fotoband *The Polar Silk Road* weitet sich Gregor Sailers Fokus erstmals auf eine zukünftige Perspektive. Mit dem Etikett einer polaren Seidenstraße ist jener imperiale Traum einer See- und Handelsroute über die Nordwestpassage bezeichnet, der im Zuge der Klimaerwärmung zu einer Realität werden könnte. Prognosen zufolge soll die Route schon Mitte dieses Jahrhunderts ganzjährig befahrbar sein. Damit einher geht ein national dominierter Kampf zwischen den Anrainerstaaten um materielle und geopolitische Ressourcen, der im Stillen längst begonnen hat. Sailer greift mit *The Polar Silk Road* die hochprekäre Folie in all ihren sozialen, wirtschaftlichen und militärischen Verwebungen auf. Über fünf Jahre hinweg bereist er auf ausgedehnten Expeditionen

The Polar Silk Road

In his latest volume of photos, *The Polar Silk Road,* published in 2021, Sailer's focus widens to a future outlook for the first time. The label of a polar silk road is worn by that imperial dream of a sea and trade route via the Northwest Passage, which could become a reality as global warming continues. According to forecasts, the route is expected to be navigable all year round as early as the middle of this century. Associated with this is a long-running, tacit tussle among neighbouring states over material and geopolitical resources. With *The Polar Silk Road,* Gregor Sailer takes up the highly precarious setting in all its interwoven aspects — social, economic, and military. For five years, he undertakes extended expeditions to geothermal power stations and production

9
Michael Braunschädel, „The Potemkin Village. Special Interview with Gregor Sailer", in: *Lens Magazine,* Nr. 46, Juli 2018, S. 66.

Michael Braunschädel, "The Potemkin Village. Special Interview with Gregor Sailer," in *Lens Magazine,* no. 46 (July 2018), 66.

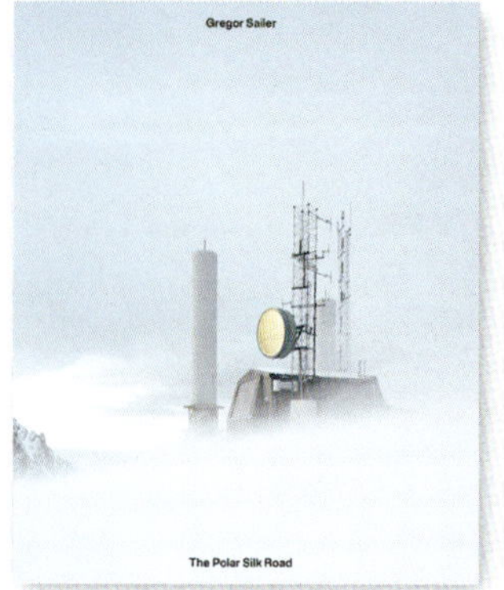

The Polar Silk Road, Cover

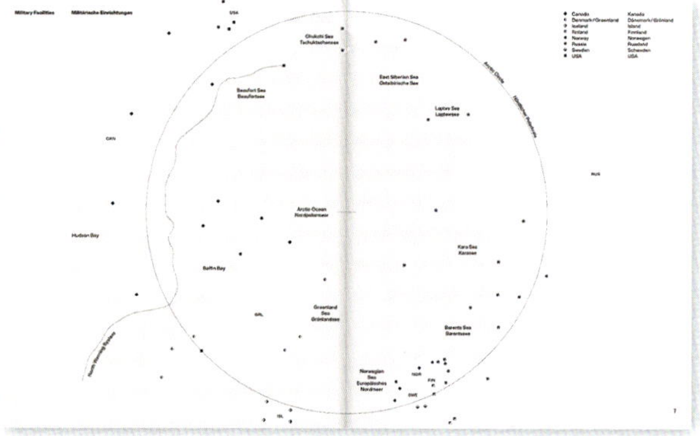

The Polar Silk Road

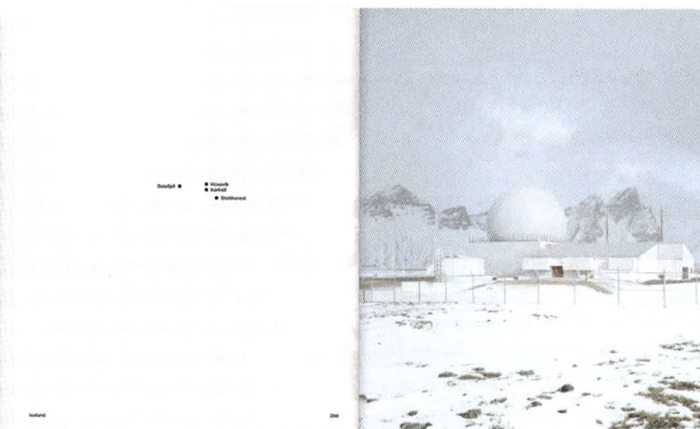

Geothermalkraftwerke und Produktionsstätten, Sendeanlagen und Bohrinseln, Forschungslabore und militärische Abhörstationen. Was sich in der lautlosen Abgeschiedenheit der Arktis unbemerkt von der Weltöffentlichkeit vollzieht, erfasst Sailers Kamera so nüchtern wie ein Seismograf. Formstrenge Architekturen behaupten sich inmitten eisiger Lebenswelten und schälen sich wie bizarre Skulpturen aus einer milchig weißen Umgebung sanft heraus. Einmal mehr ist die sachliche Bildrhetorik von Ambivalenzen geprägt, sie zeugt gleichermaßen von Dynamik und Stagnation.

Man spürt, die robusten Architekturgebilde entziehen sich jedwedem Zugriff, sie verharren seltsam entrückt und sind doch auf unheimliche Weise präsent. Derart rücken sie in der Anschauung mehr zu Leibe, als einem lieb sein kann. „Weil dort Dinge passieren, die wirtschaftspolitische und gesellschaftliche Auswirkungen auf uns haben", merkt Sailer an.[10]

Wie lässt sich sein bisheriger Werkbegriff im Rückblick benennen? Sicher darf man festhalten, dass mit den drei Bänden *Closed Cities, The Potemkin Village* und *The Polar Silk Road* nun ein spektakulärer Fotobuchkorpus vorliegt, eine Trilogie, die eine verstörende Diagnose für unsere Zeit bereithält. Mit Vehemenz erwehrt sich die Gegenwart ihrer Dechiffrierung. Umso kenntlicher wird, wie die vorliegende Retrospektive im KUNST HAUS WIEN zeigt, im Gegenzug die Autorenposition. Mit nur 42 Jahren zählt Sailer bereits zu den Protagonisten der europäischen Fotoszene. Sicher ließe sich seine fotografische Entwicklung im Sinne einer doppelten Wendung interpretieren. Diese würde nicht nur die Fotografie, jene eigentümliche Apparatur der Welterkennung, sondern auch ihren Autor betreffen. Denn je weiter Gregor Sailer mit seiner analogen Großbildkamera in das Außen unserer Zivilisation vordringt, desto mehr scheint er ein Innen vorzufinden.

sites, broadcasting facilities and drilling platforms, research laboratories and military listening stations. As soberly as a seismograph, Sailer's camera captures what takes place, unnoticed by the global public, in the Arctic's soundless seclusion. Stringently contoured architectures hold their own amid icy habitats, and gently peel themselves, like bizarre sculptures, out of milky-white surroundings. Once again, the objective visual rhetoric is characterised by ambivalence; it testifies dynamism and stagnation to equal degrees.

One feels it: the robust architectural structures elude access, they remain oddly enraptured and, nevertheless, in an eerie way, present. Thus, they bear down upon us onlookers more than can be comfortable. "Because things happen there that have economic policy and social impacts on us," notes Sailer.[10]

What can we call Sailer's concept to date? Certainly, we may establish that, with the three volumes, *Closed Cities, The Potemkin Village,* and *The Polar Silk Road,* we now have a spectacular corpus of photobooks, a trilogy that has in store for us a disturbing diagnosis of our day. The present is defying its decryption with vehemence. All the more discernible, conversely, as this retrospective at KUNST HAUS WIEN shows, is the author's position now. At just 42, Sailer is already one of the protagonists of the European photo scene. Certainly, his photographic evolution would allow itself to be interpreted in the sense of a double take. This would concern not only photography, that idiosyncratic apparatus for recognising the world, but its author as well. For, the more Gregor Sailer makes inroads, with his large-format analogue camera, into the Outside of our civilisation, the more he seems to discover an Inside.

10
Jelčić 2021
(wie Anm. 3), S. 25.

Jelčić 2021
(see note 3), 25.

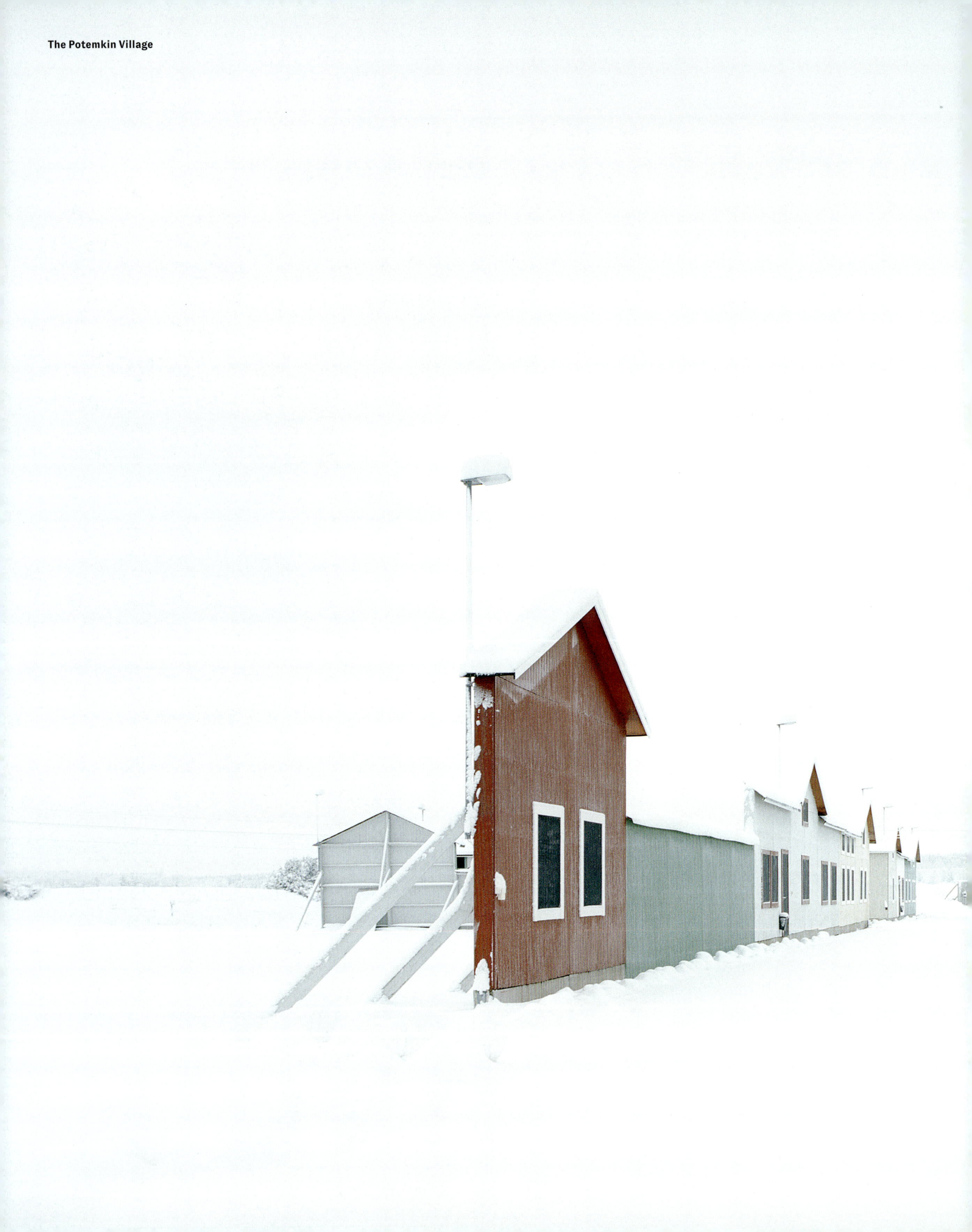

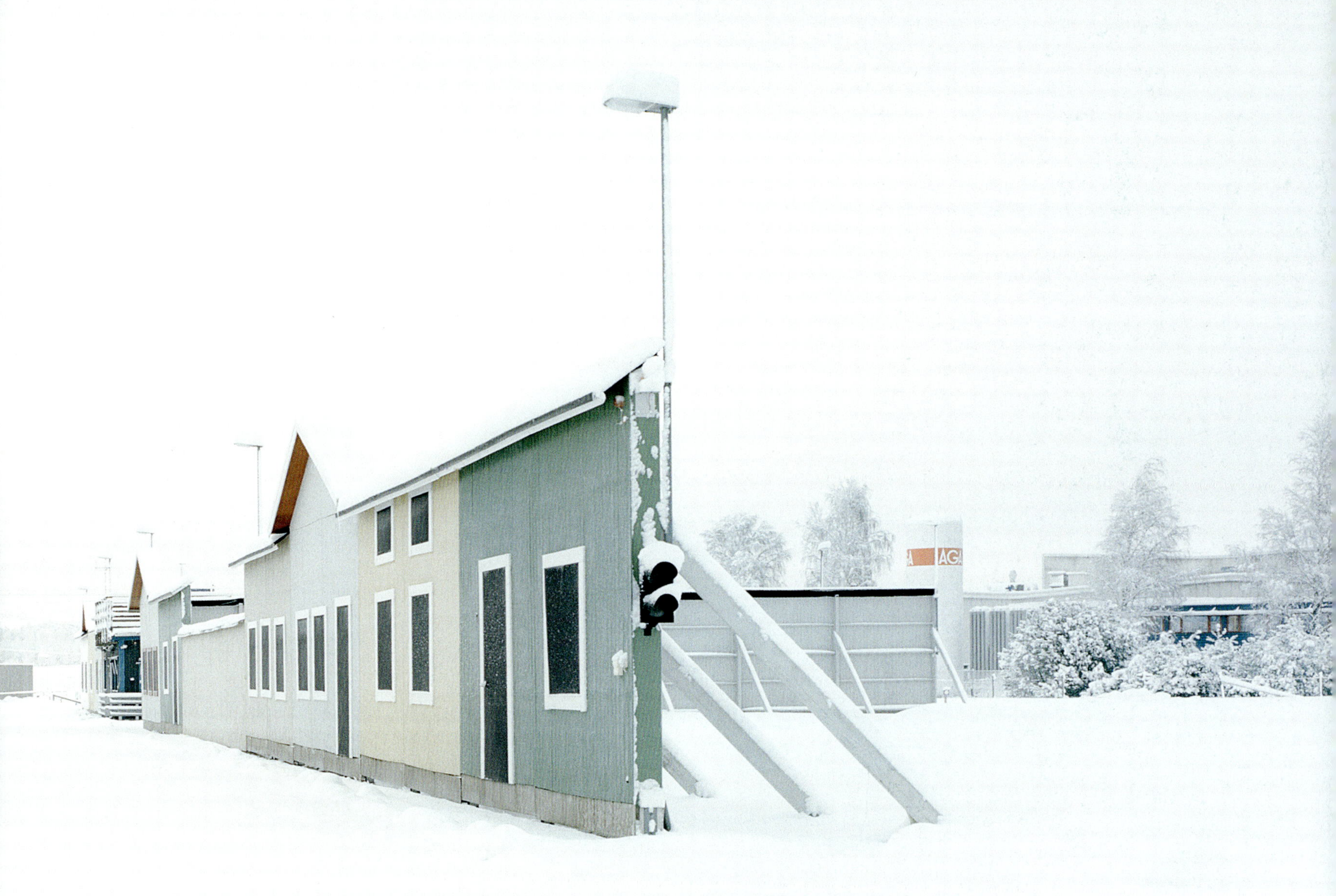

The Potemkin Village

Der Begriff des Potemkinschen Dorfes geht auf den russischen Feldmarschall Grigori Alexandrowitsch Potjomkin zurück. Der Legende nach ließ der Fürst im Jahr 1787 Dorfattrappen im neu eroberten Krimgebiet aufbauen, um der Zarin Katharina der Großen während ihrer Durchreise große Fortschritte in der Besiedelung vorzuspiegeln.

Gregor Sailer hat sich über zwei Jahre hinweg mit zeitgenössischen „Potemkinschen Dörfern" auseinandergesetzt. In sieben Ländern fotografierte er Scheinarchitekturen, Kulissenbauten und illusionistische Modelldörfer, darunter Stadtimitate nach europäischem Vorbild – Holland Town oder German Town – im Umland von Schanghai, rudimentäre Stadtarchitekturen für militärische Übungszwecke in Frankreich und den USA sowie Stadtkulissen für Fahrzeugtests in Schweden. Sailers Perspektive ist immer nüchtern, geradlinig und unprätentiös. Nichtsdestotrotz transportieren die Aufnahmen ganz unterschiedliche Stimmungen – sie wirken erschreckend oder brutal, bisweilen aber auch komisch, skurril oder tragisch. Allesamt sind sie zeitgenössische Bühnen für ebensolches menschliches Tun.

The notion of the Potemkin village can be traced back to the Russian field marshal, Grigory Aleksandrovich Potemkin. Legend has it that in 1787, the prince ordered the building of fake villages in the newly conquered Crimea region to show off the tremendous progress that had been achieved with these settlements to Empress Catherine the Great as she passed through.

Gregor Sailer spent two years exploring contemporary instances of Potemkin villages. In seven countries he photographed mock architecture, backdrops, and illusionistic model villages, including replica towns and cities based on European models — Holland Town and German Town — in the environs of Shanghai, rudimentary urban architectural settings for military training purposes in France and the United States, as well as urban backdrops for vehicle testing in Sweden. Sailer's perspective is always sober, straightforward, and unpretentious. The moods conveyed by his photographs vary greatly nonetheless: their impact can be frightening or brutal, but also comical, bizarre, and even tragic. And yet they are all contemporary stages reflecting the associated human activities.

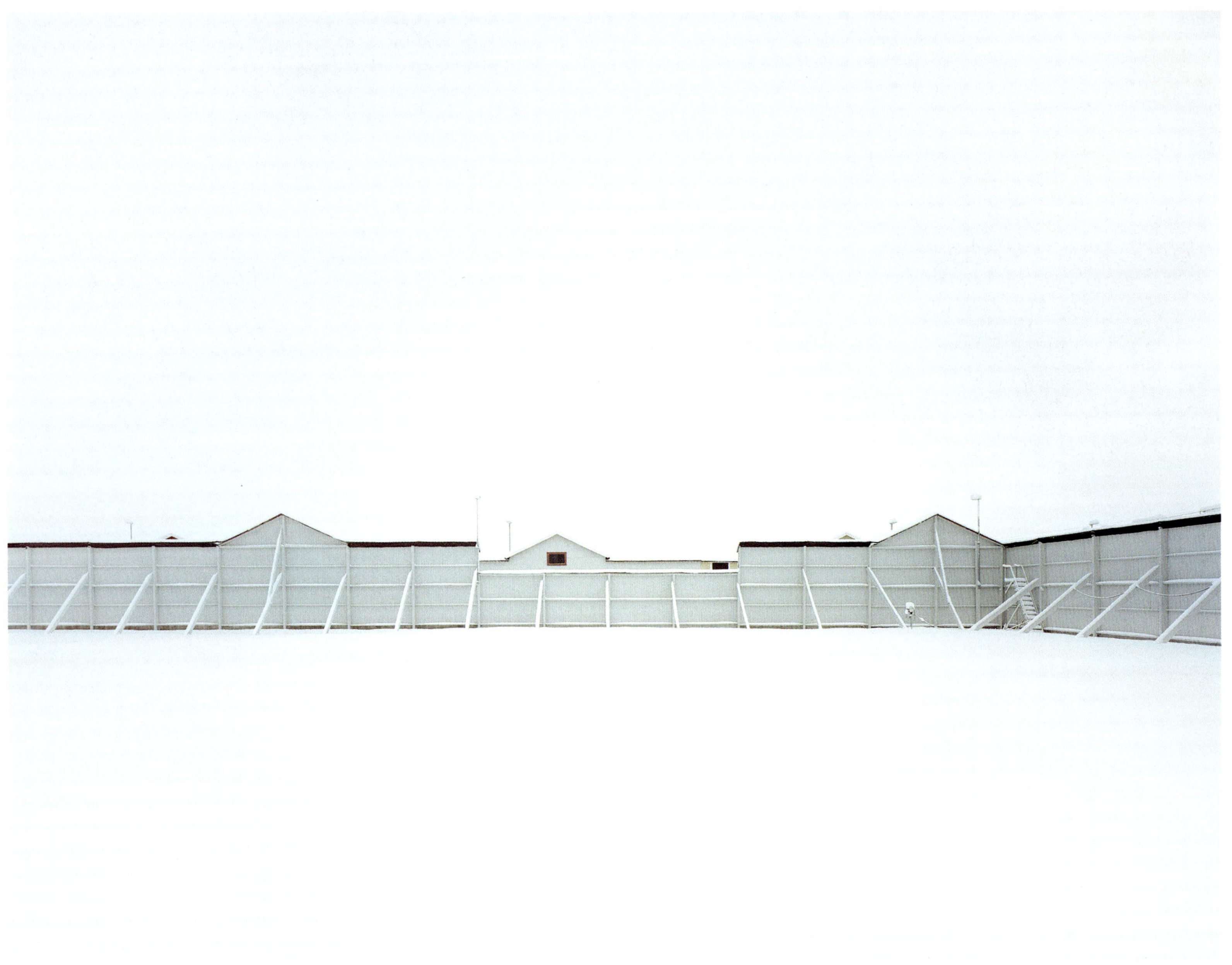

„Wo das Lügen zum tolerierten Handwerkszeug der Politik geworden ist, sind seine Bilder nicht weniger als Metaphern für den Allgemeinzustand unserer Kultur."

Hans-Michael Koetzle in: *Photo International* 1/2018, S. 24–25.

"Where lying has become the tolerated tool of politics, his images are nothing less than metaphors for the general state of our culture."

Hans-Michael Koetzle in *Photo International* 1 (2018), 24–25.

2
3

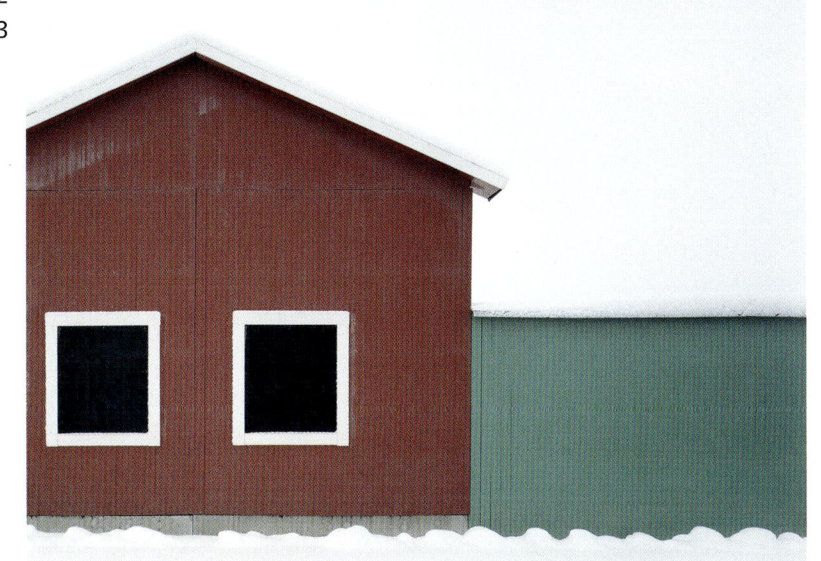
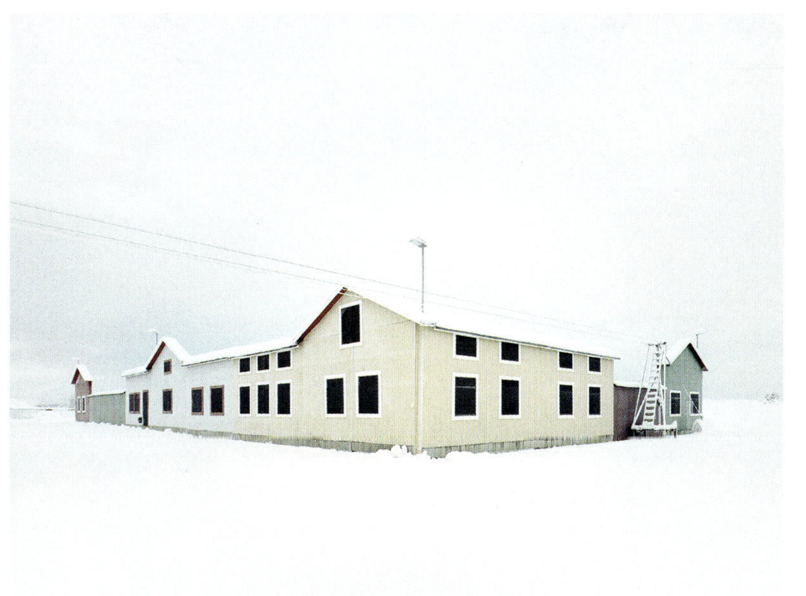

4
5

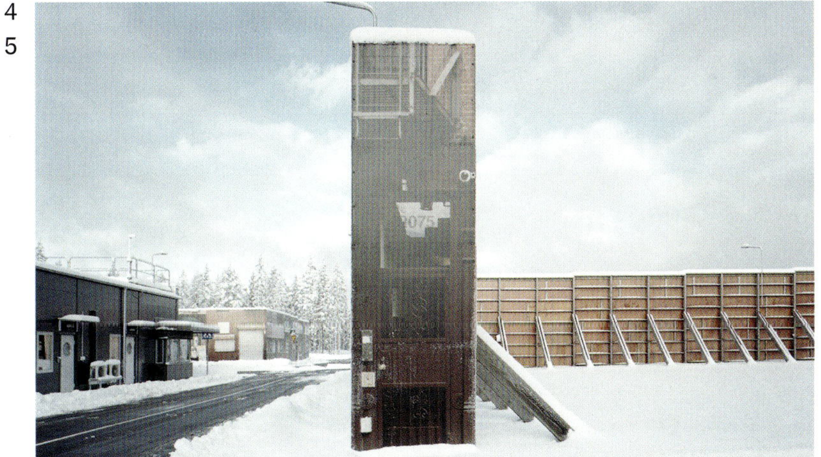
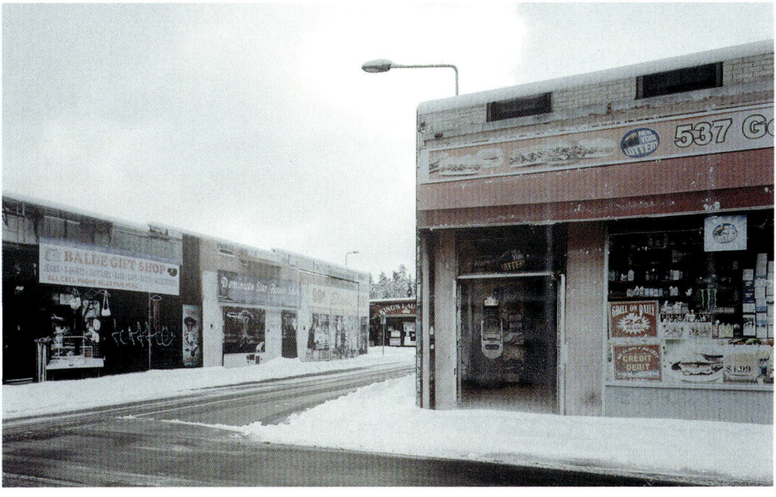

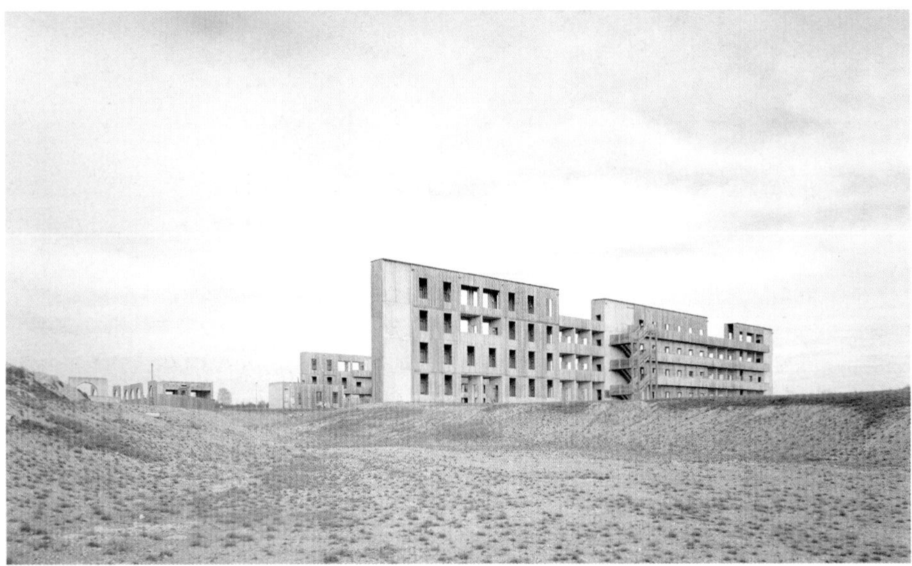

6

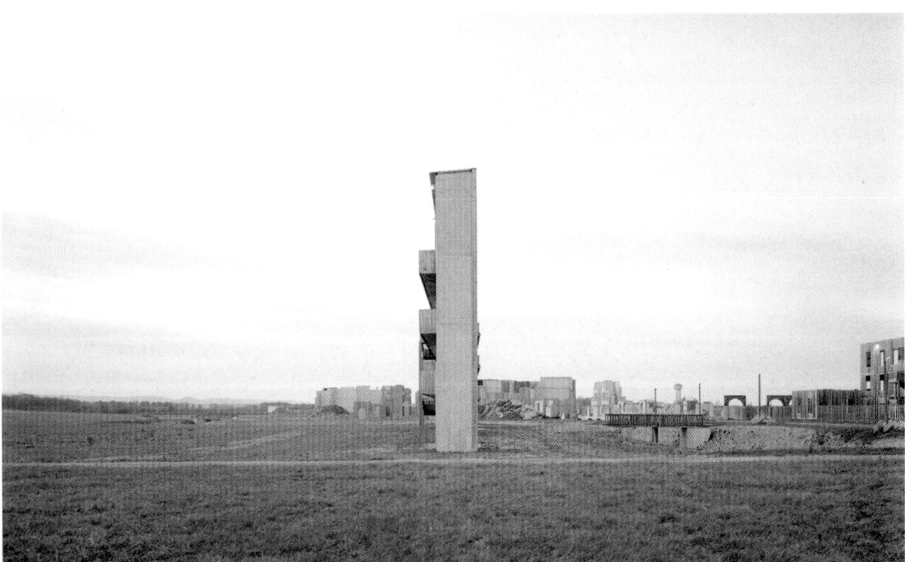

7

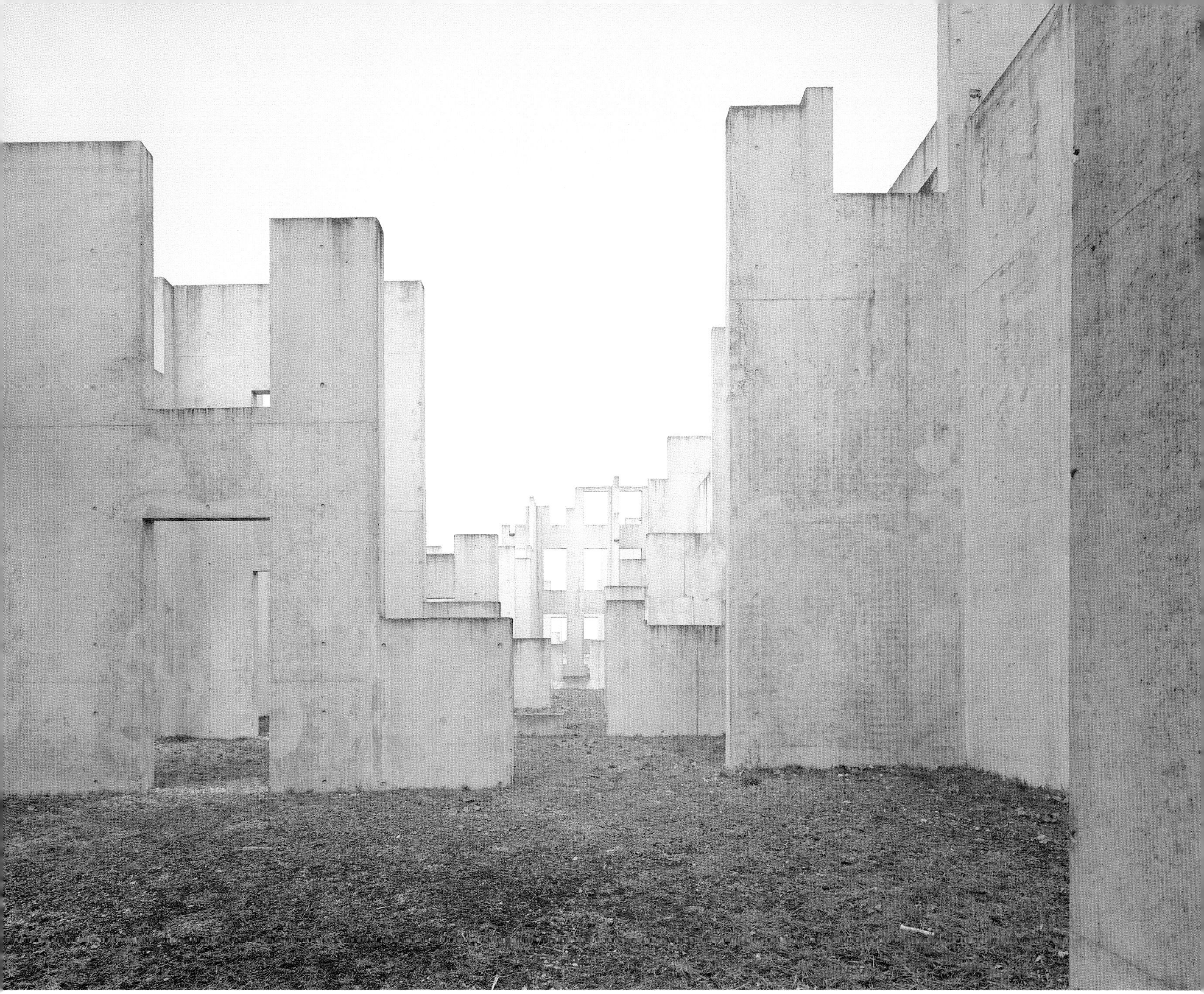

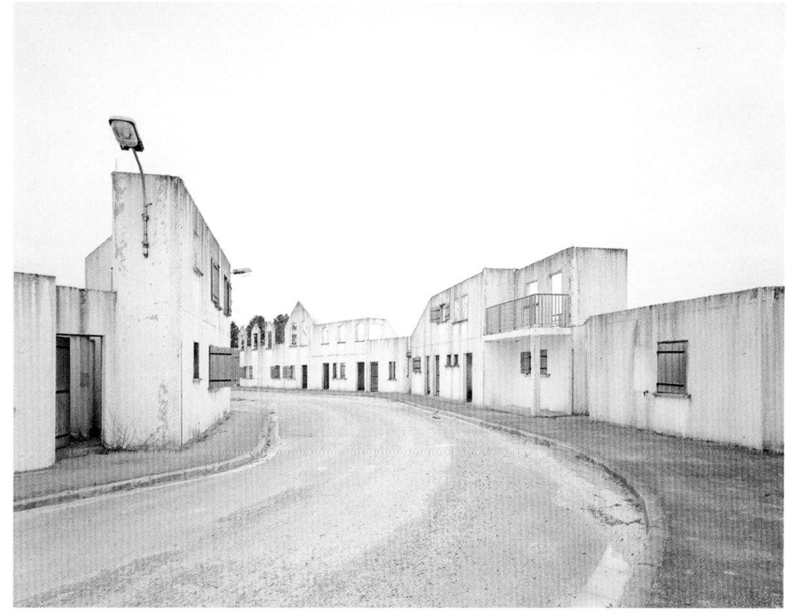

8

9

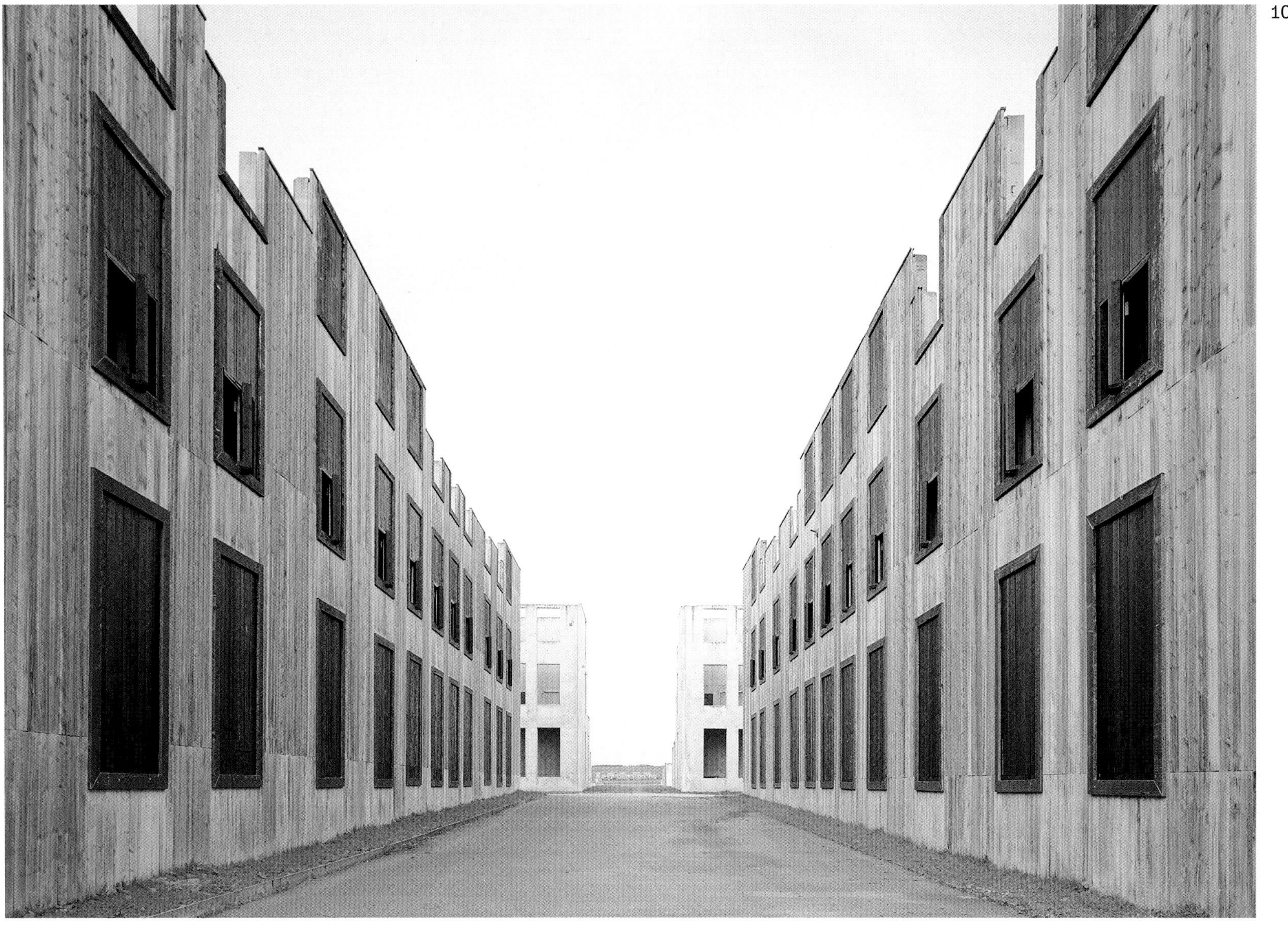

10

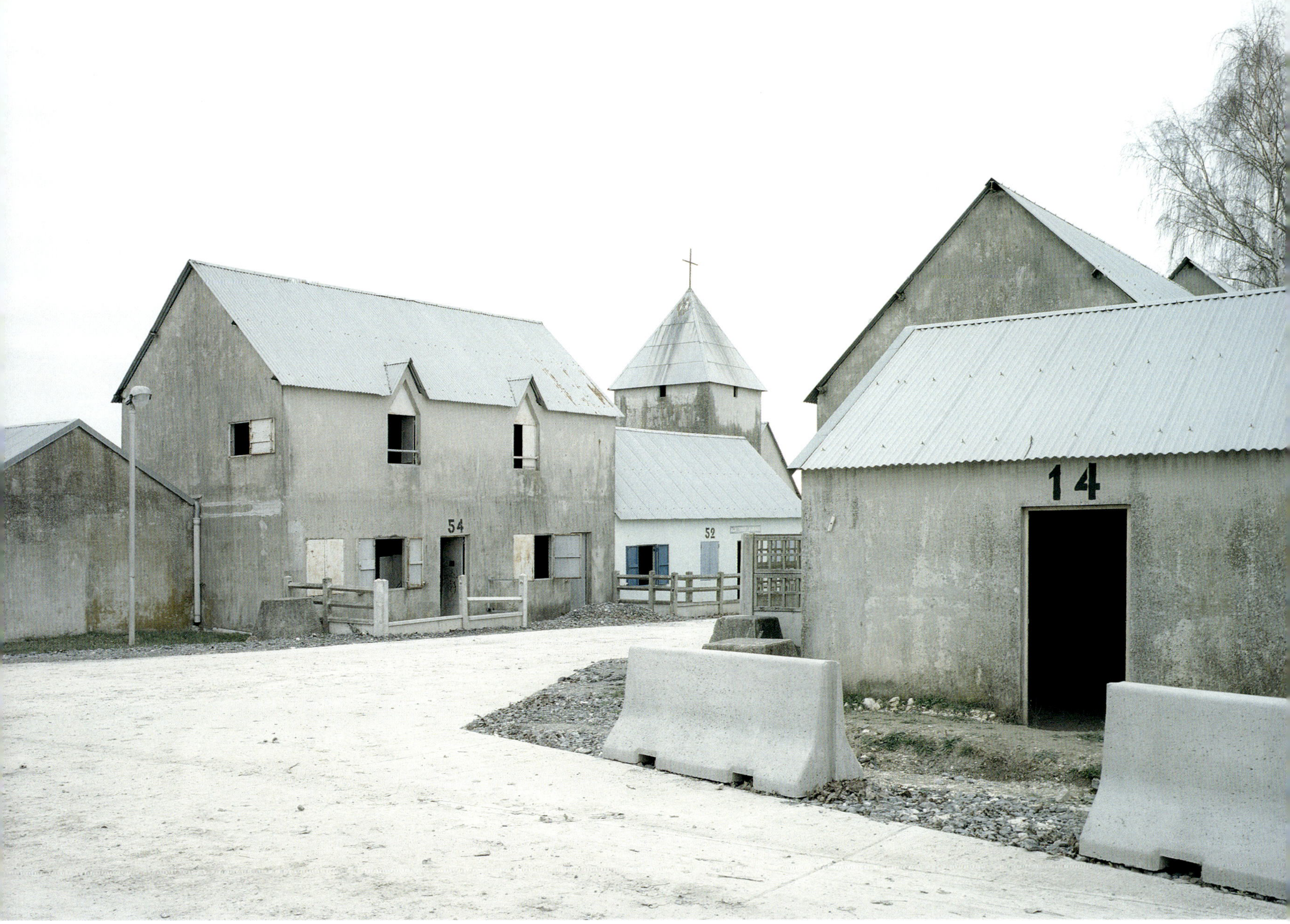

11

12

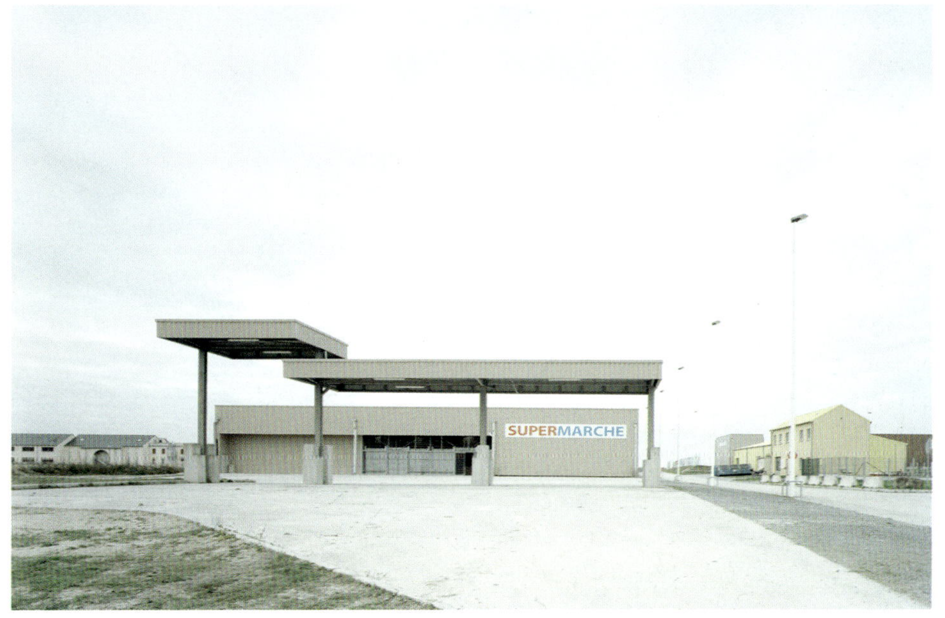

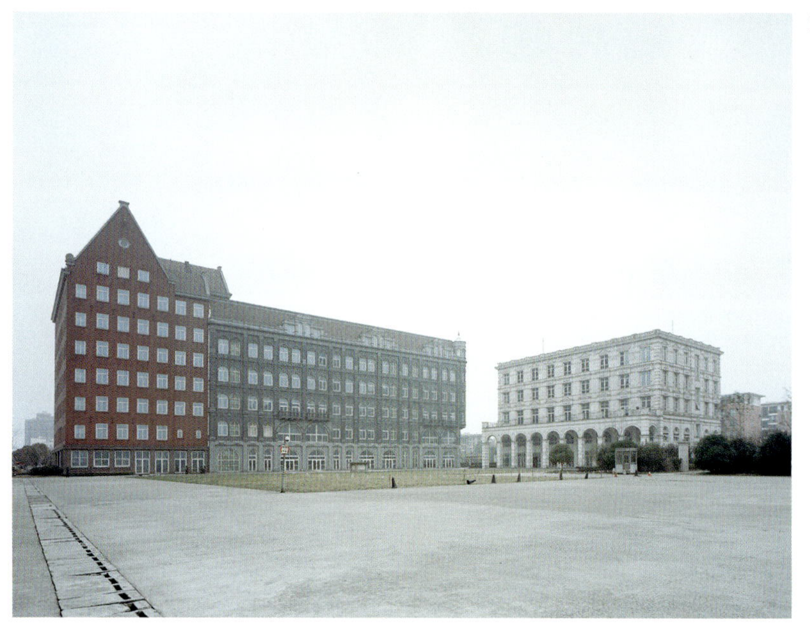

13

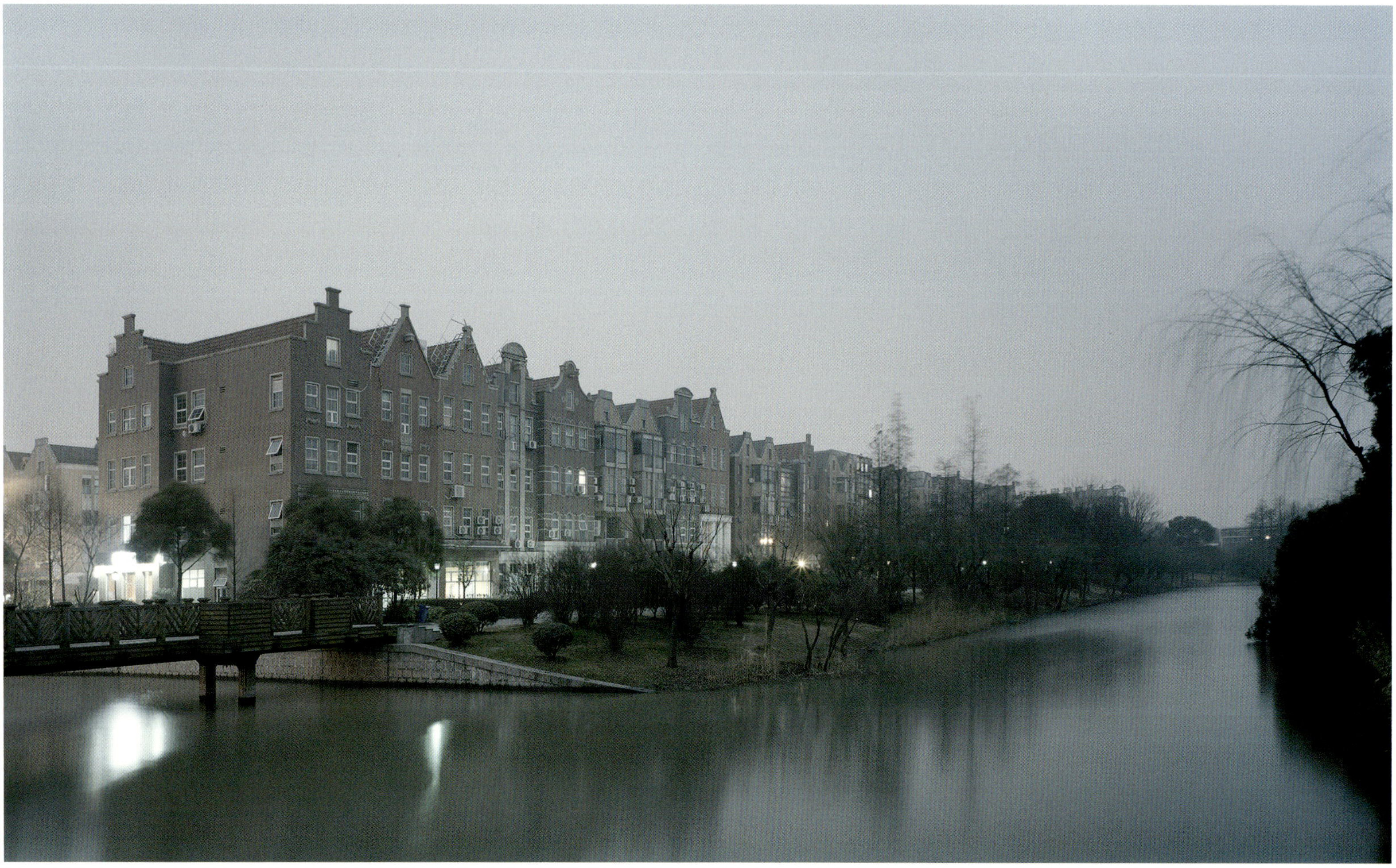

14

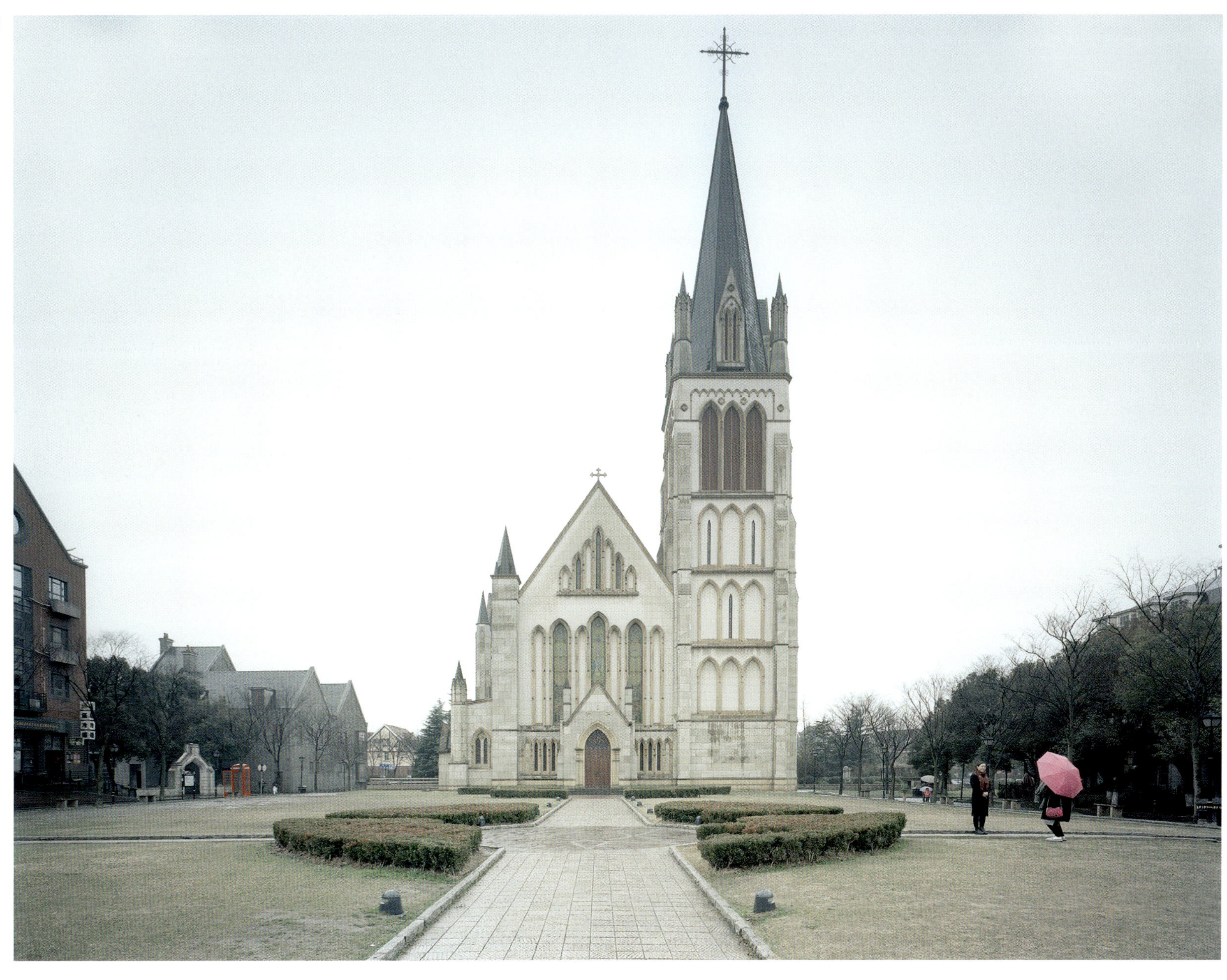

„Diese künstlichen Stätten erlauben es Sailer, die hermetischen, frappierenden Eigenschaften von ‚fake cities' zu vermessen, während er den Sinngehalt der Wahrheit hinter dem fotografischen Bild examiniert. Der Gegensatz zwischen Realem und Irrealem wird greifbar gemacht und beides untrennbar miteinander verbunden."

Linde B. Lehtinen, „Irreale Fotografie: Gregor Sailers Das Potemkinsche Dorf", in: *Gregor Sailer. The Potemkin Village*, Heidelberg 2017, S. 170.

"These artificial sites allow Sailer to survey the hermetic, uncanny qualities of fake cities while interrogating the very meaning of truth behind the photographic image. The opposition between real and unreal is made tangible and inextricably linked."

Linde B. Lehtinen, "Unreal Photography: Gregor Sailer's The Potemkin Village," in *Gregor Sailer: The Potemkin Village* (Heidelberg 2017), 153.

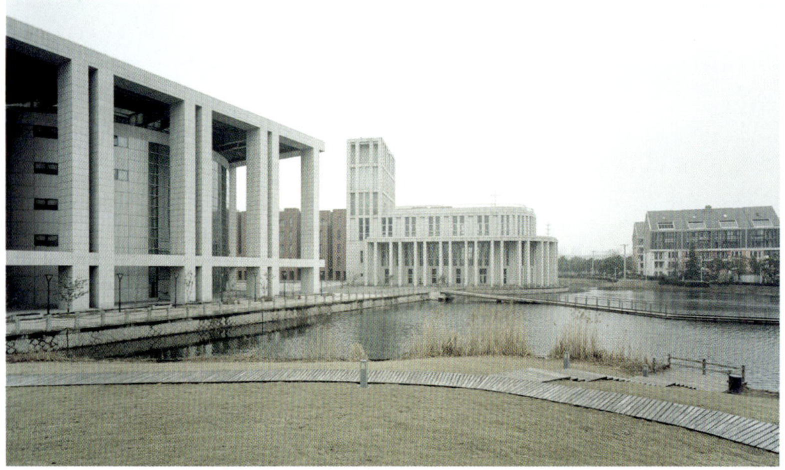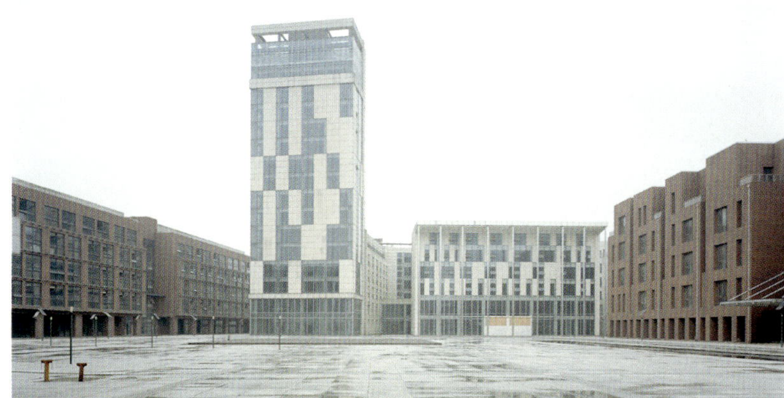

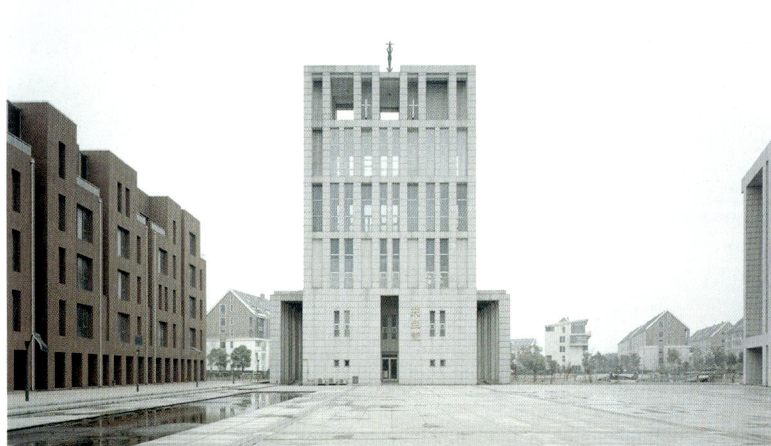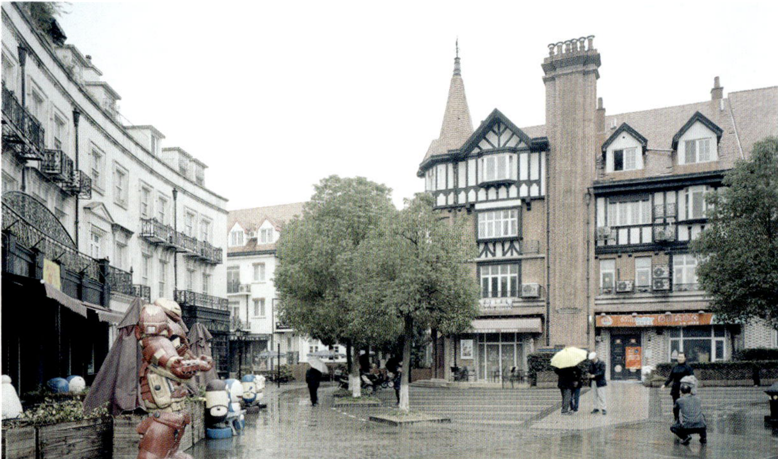

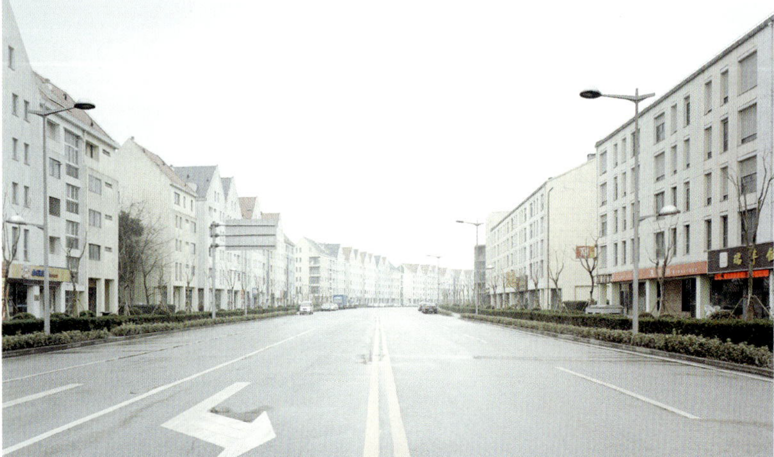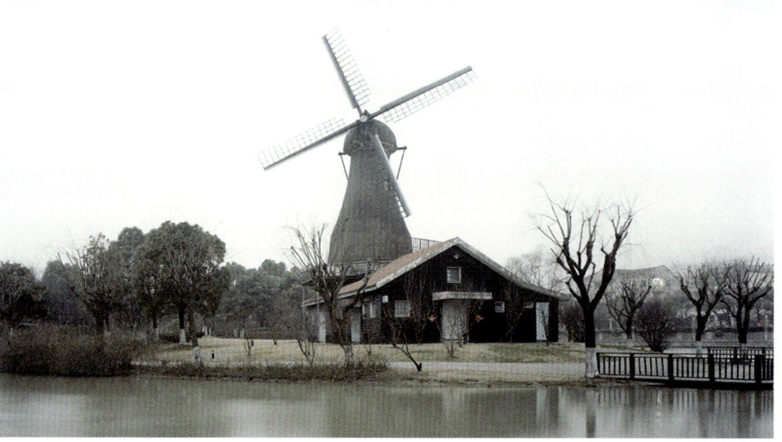

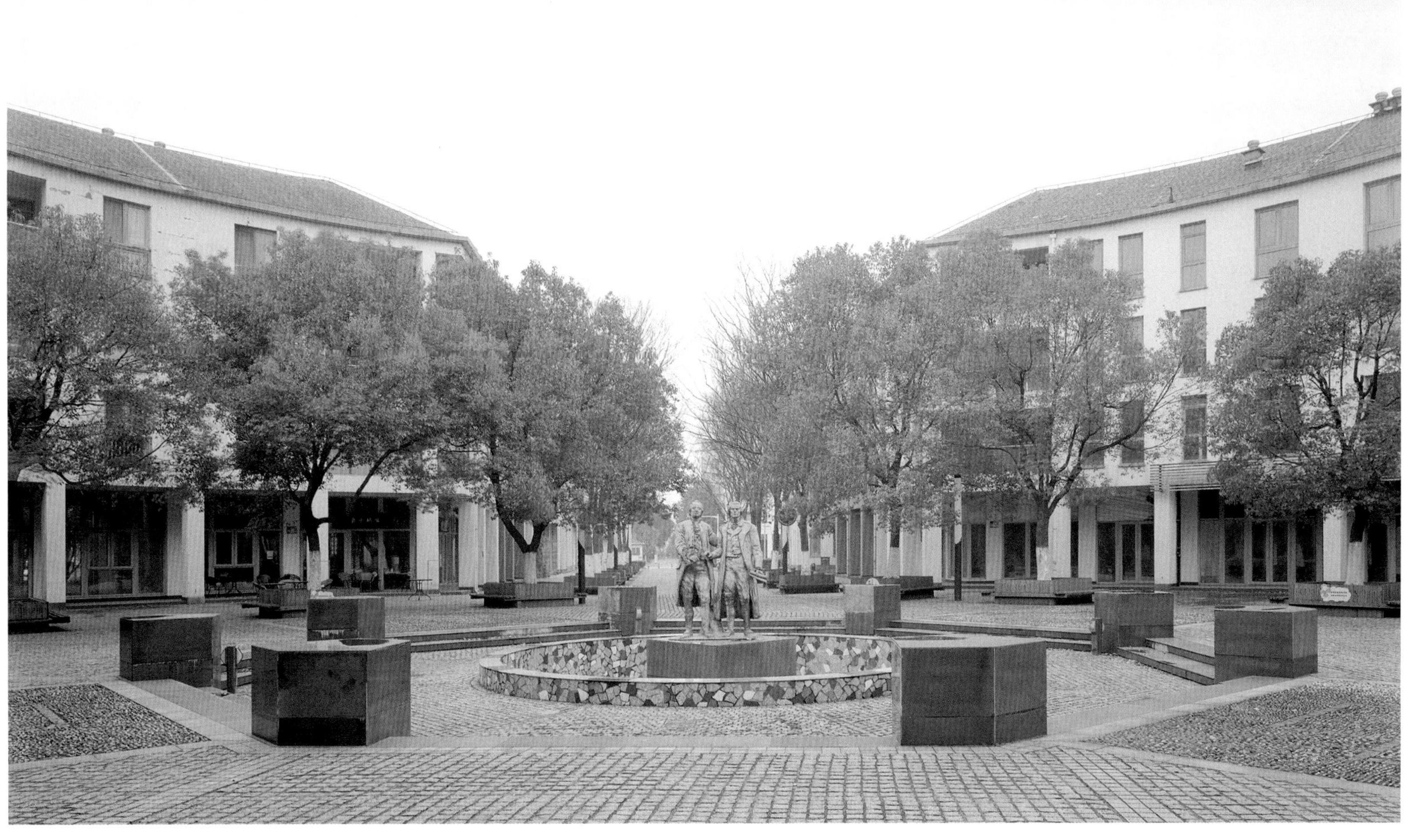

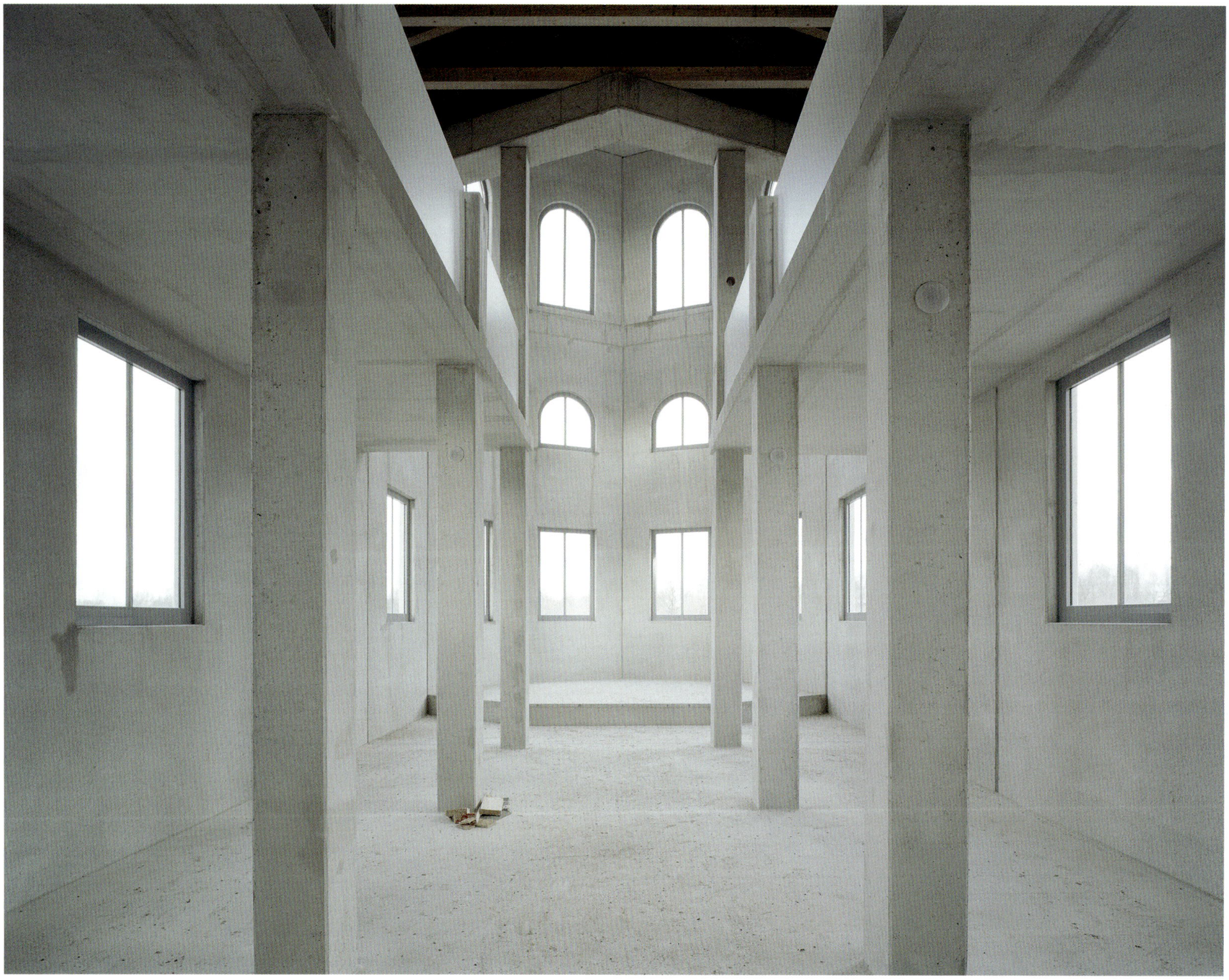

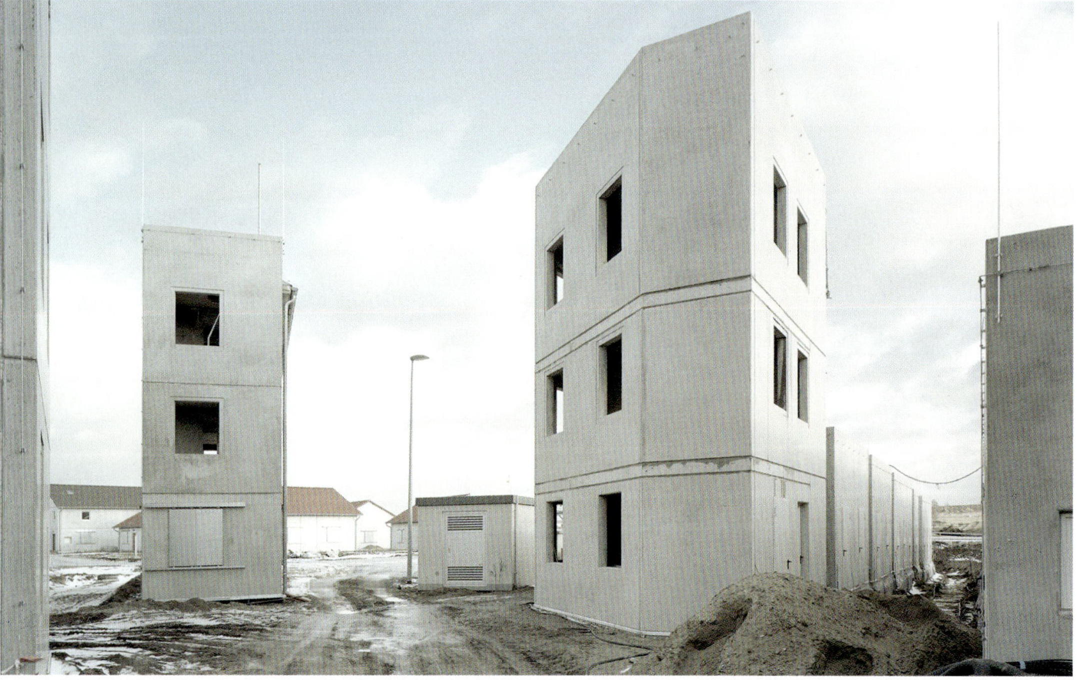

24

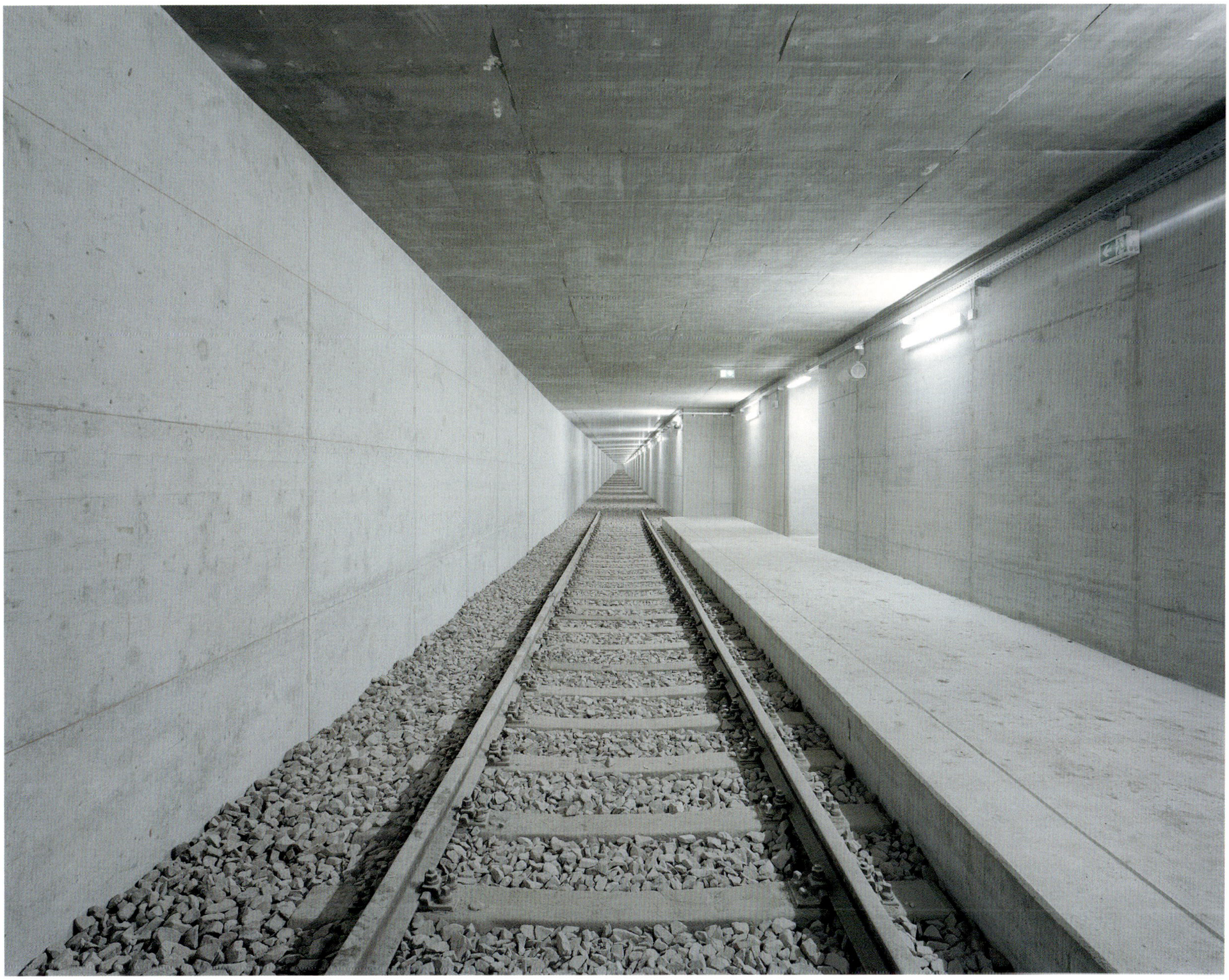

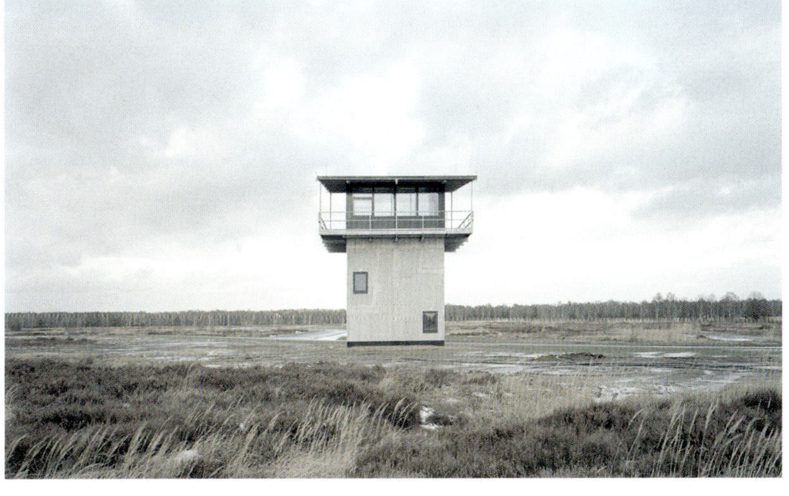

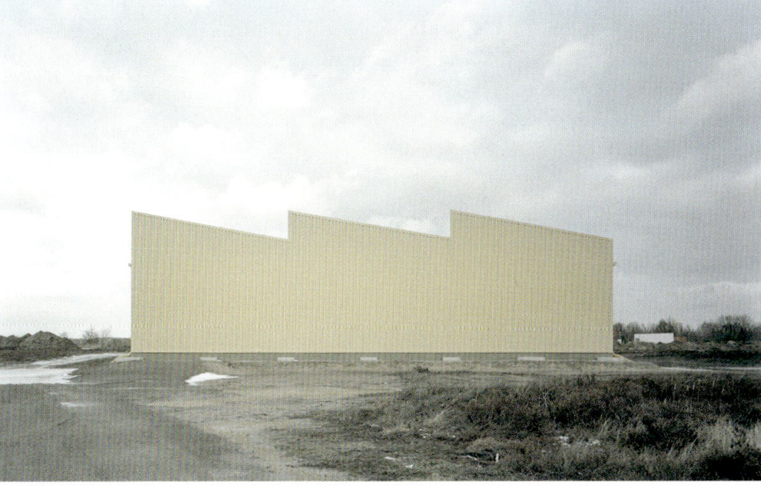

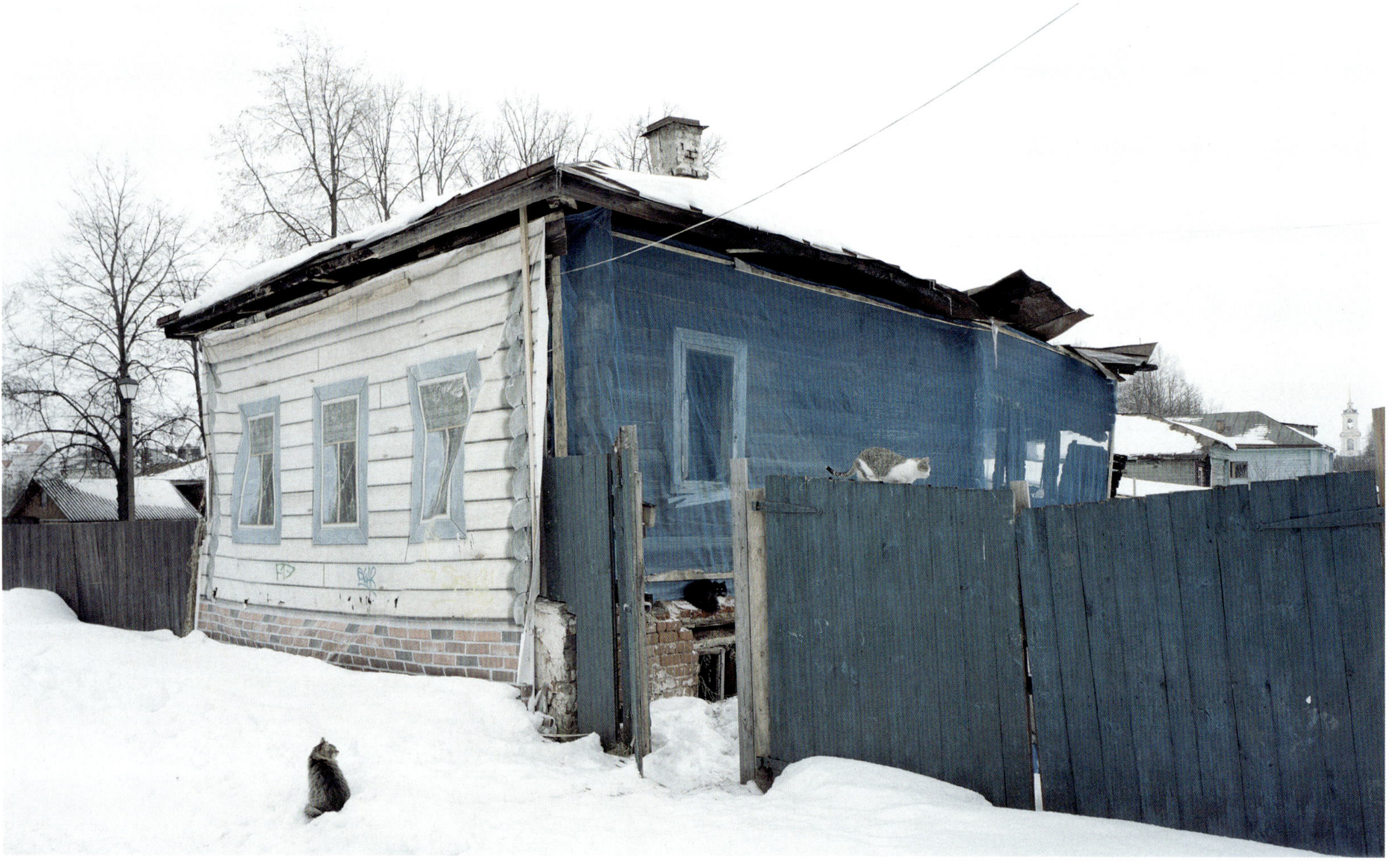

„Die von Gregor Sailer mit The Potemkin Village durchgeführte weltweite Studie enthüllt das neue herrschende System von Realität: Unsere Lebensräume werden nicht länger nur von Bildern eingenommen; sie bestehen in ihrer ganzen Wesentlichkeit aus Bildern.

Diese überdimensionalen Bilder, die aus ihren etablierten Rahmen herausgetreten sind, um die Realität zu durchdringen, überlagern jeden Bereich des täglichen Lebens. Sie treten an die Stelle dessen, was sie darstellen; sie verleihen dem, was nicht oder noch nicht existiert, Realität, wodurch die Realität selbst nichtig wird. In diesem Spiel der Täuschungen verlieren wir ungläubig den Halt angesichts der schleichenden Künstlichkeit der Welt. Mehr noch: Wir müssen an das glauben, was wir erleben. Und so akzeptieren wir das Falsche als wahr. Durch einen Überlebensreflex, nämlich unsere Anpassungsfähigkeit, bestätigen wir diese neue Version unserer Realität. Diese Simulation wird von der menschlichen Spezies auf eine andere Art und Weise akzeptiert als von nichtmenschlichen Spezies, die, von der Illusion getäuscht, deren Konstruktion nicht verstehen und buchstäblich mit ihr kollidieren. Wir menschlichen Tiere leben nun im Potemkinschen Dorf.“

Pascal Beausse, „Anthropology of the emptiness," in: *Staged — From the Potemkin Series,* Porto 2020, S. 12–15.

"The global survey conducted by Gregor Sailer with The Potemkin Village reveals the new regime of reality: our living environments are no longer only invaded by images; they are made up of images in their very materiality.

These images, oversized, taken out of their frames instituted to infuse reality, cover every aspect of daily life. They take the place of what they represent; they give force of reality to what doesn't exist, or doesn't exist yet, thus rendering reality itself useless. In this game of pretenses, incredulous, we lose our footing in the face of the creeping artificialization of the world. But much more: we need to believe in what we experience. And so, we accept the false for the real. We validate, by a survival reflex, which is our capacity to adapt, this new version of our reality. This simulation is accepted by the human species in a different way from non-human species, which, deceived by an illusion, do not understand its construction and come to bump into it, literally. We human animals now live in the Potemkin village."

Pascal Beausse, "Anthropology of Emptiness," in *Staged — From the Potemkin Series* (Porto 2020), 12–15.

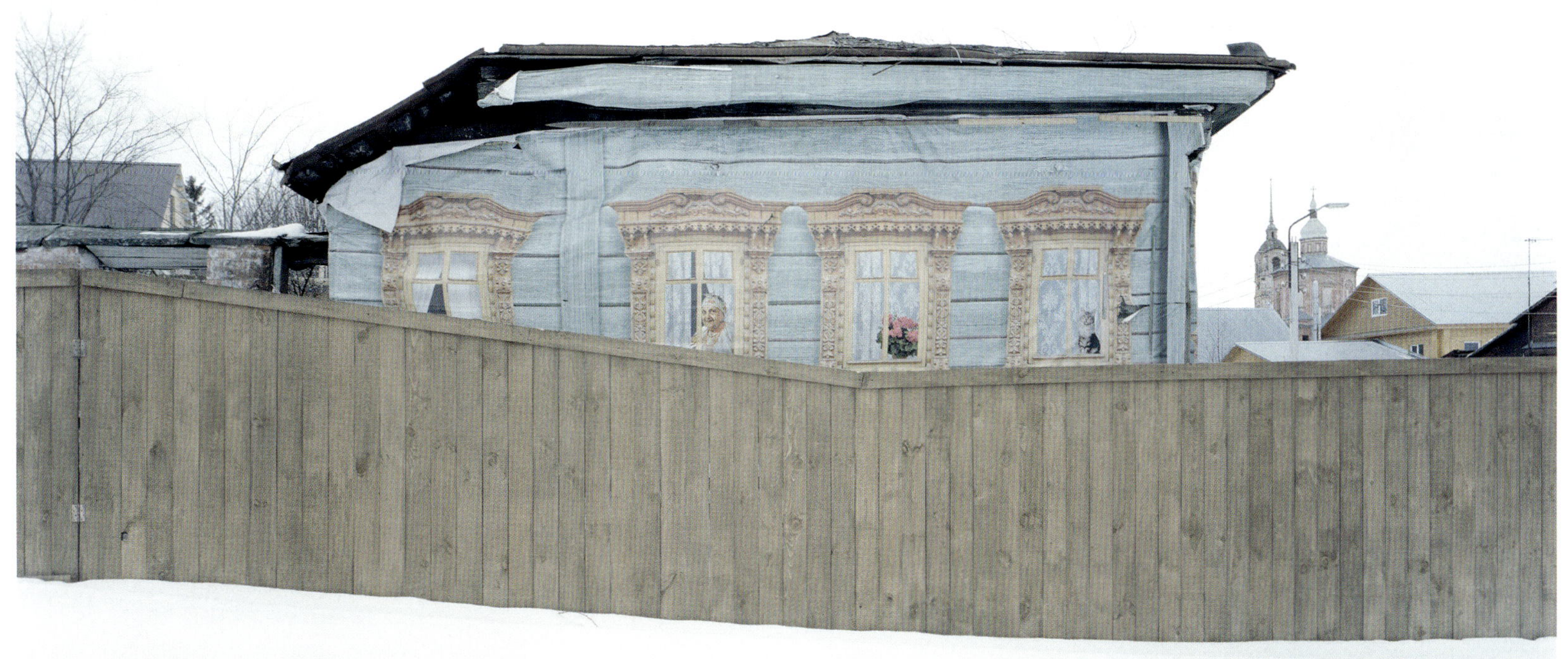

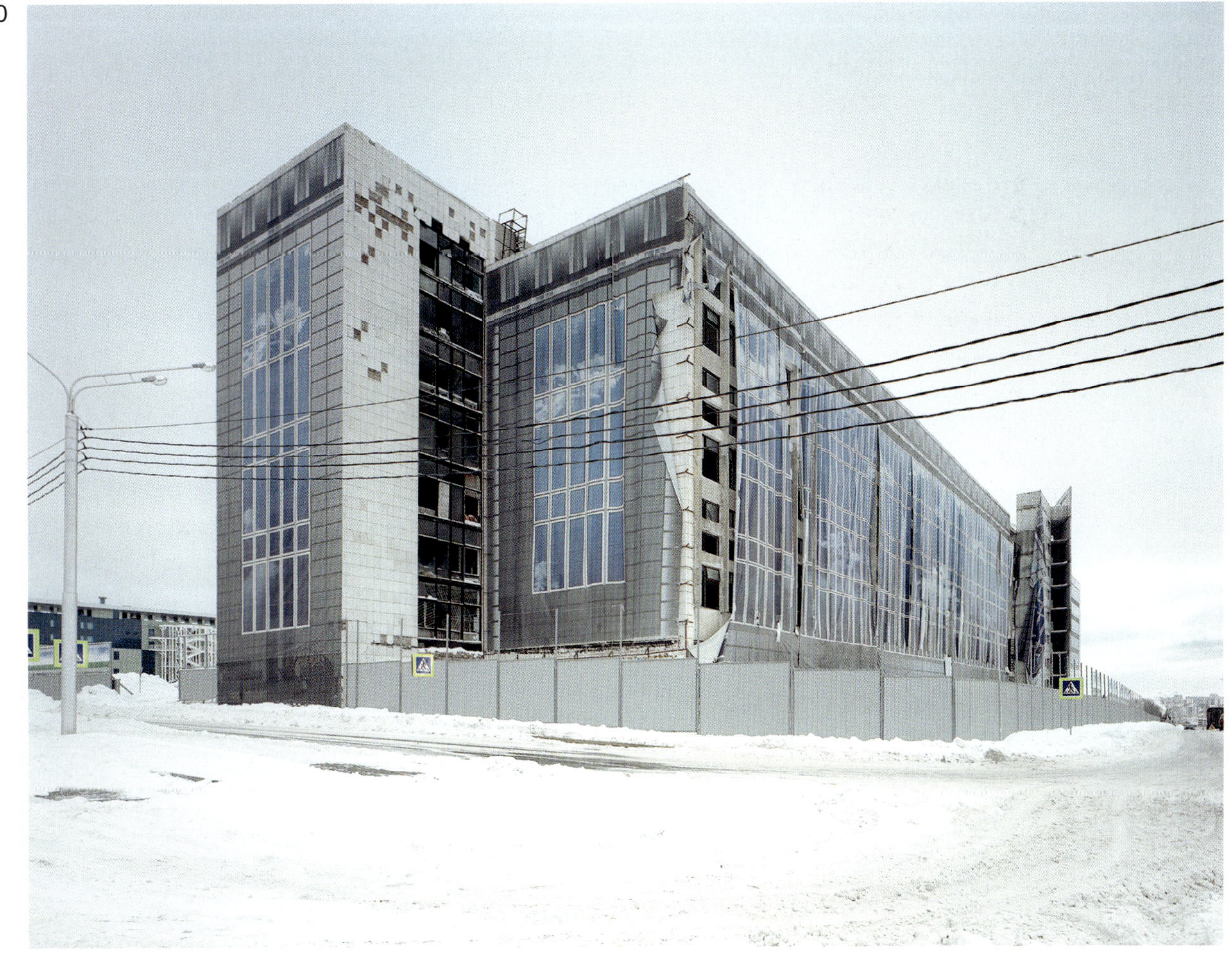

31
32

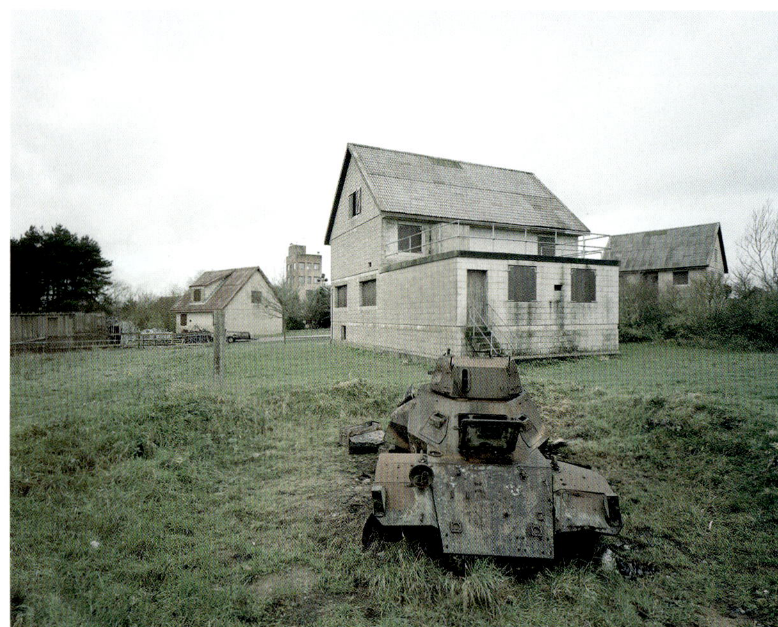
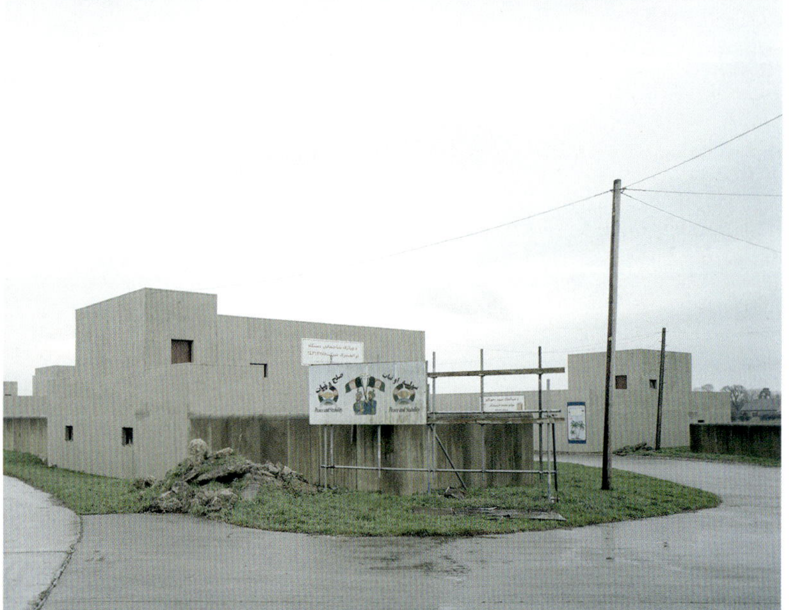

33

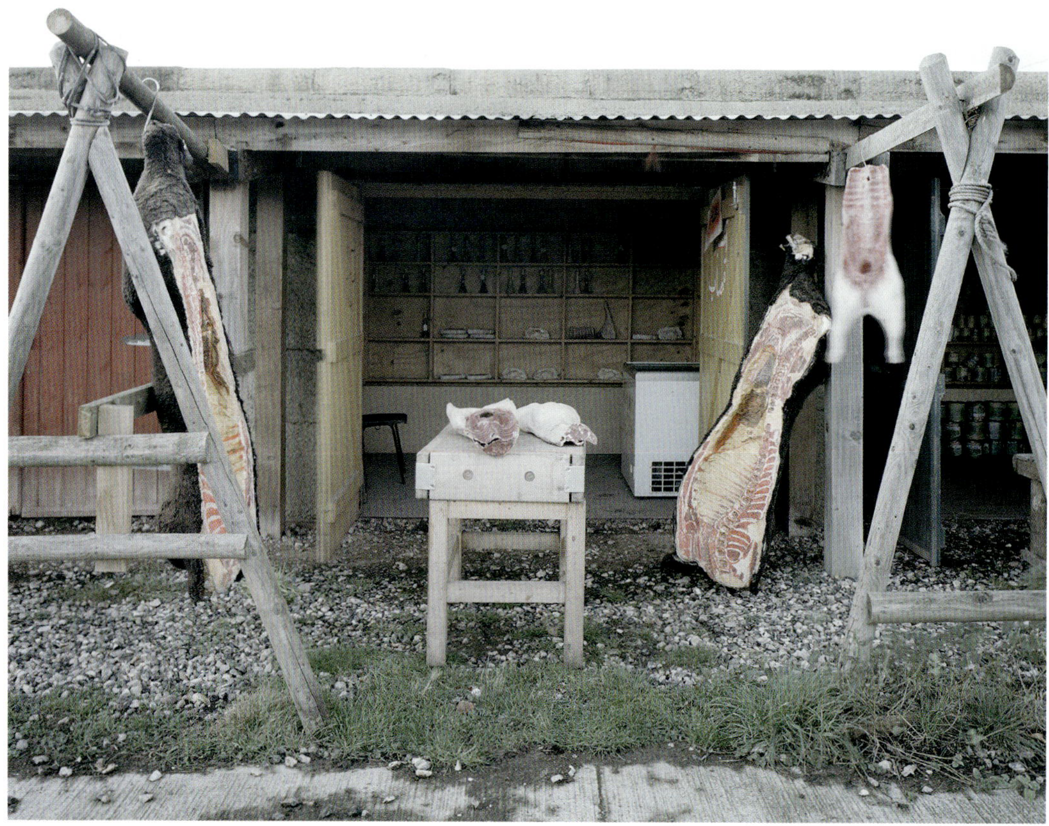

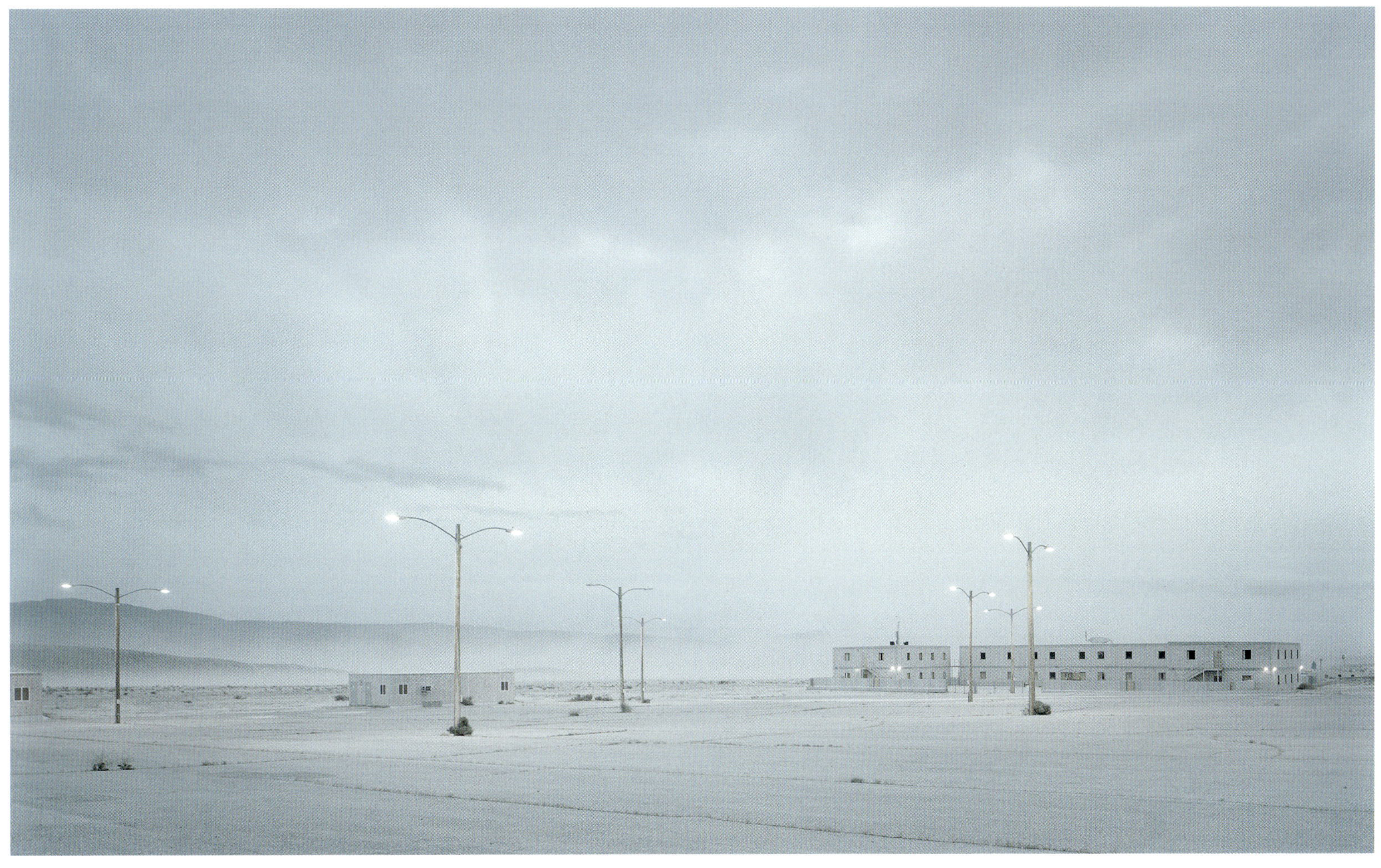

„Dies sind vergängliche Strukturen, die sich vor dem Betrachter verändern und den Anschein von Bühnenkulissen erwecken, die jeden Moment zusammenbrechen könnten. Die zarten Oberflächen, die nüchternen Linien und die verwaisten Elemente in Sailers Fotografien bieten eine Hinführung zu diesem Prozess der Gestaltung einer illusionären Umgebung, eines Theaters vermeintlicher Realität."

Linde B. Lehtinen, „Irreale Fotografie: Gregor Sailers Das Potemkinsche Dorf", in: *Gregor Sailer. The Potemkin Village,* Heidelberg 2017, S. 167.

"These are transitory structures that shift in front of the viewer and give the impression of stage sets that could collapse at any moment. The delicate surfaces, stark lines, and vacant elements of Sailer's photographs provide an introduction to this process of crafting an illusory environment, a theater of perceived reality."

Linde B. Lehtinen, "Unreal Photography: Gregor Sailer's The Potemkin Village," in *Gregor Sailer: The Potemkin Village* (Heidelberg 2017), 150.

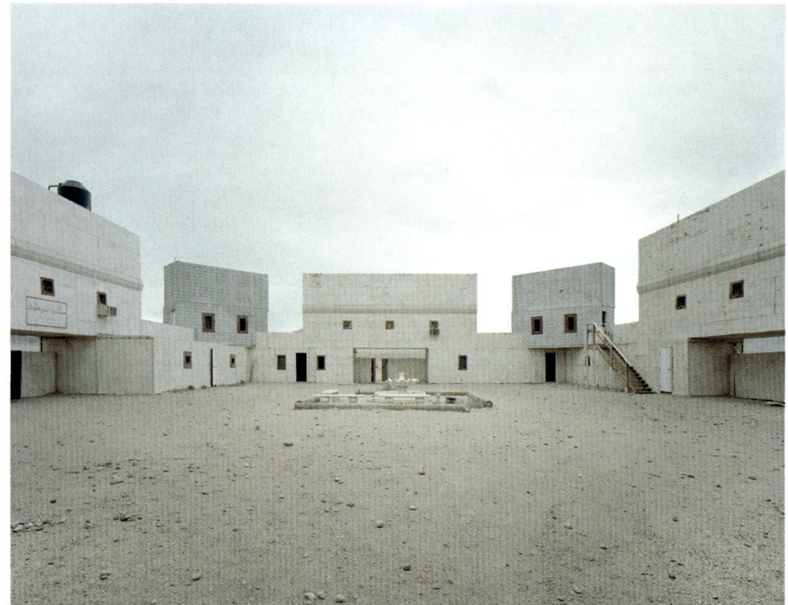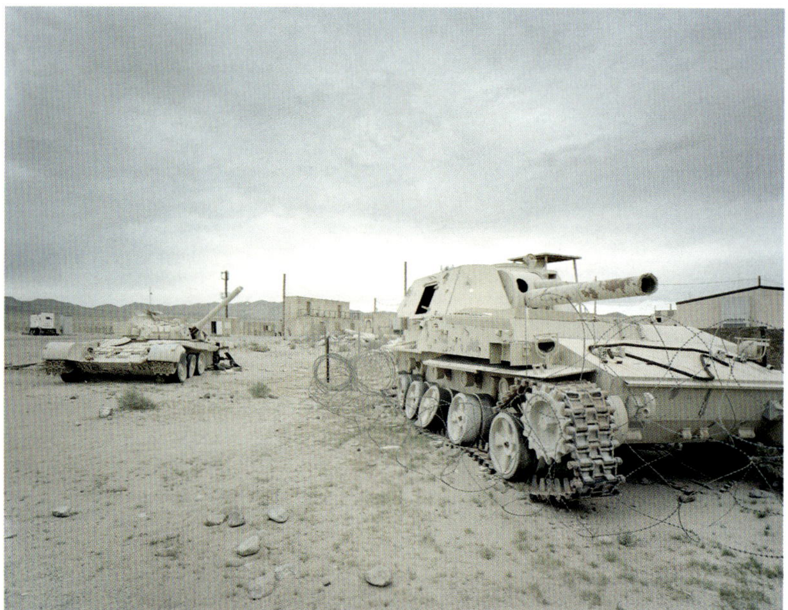

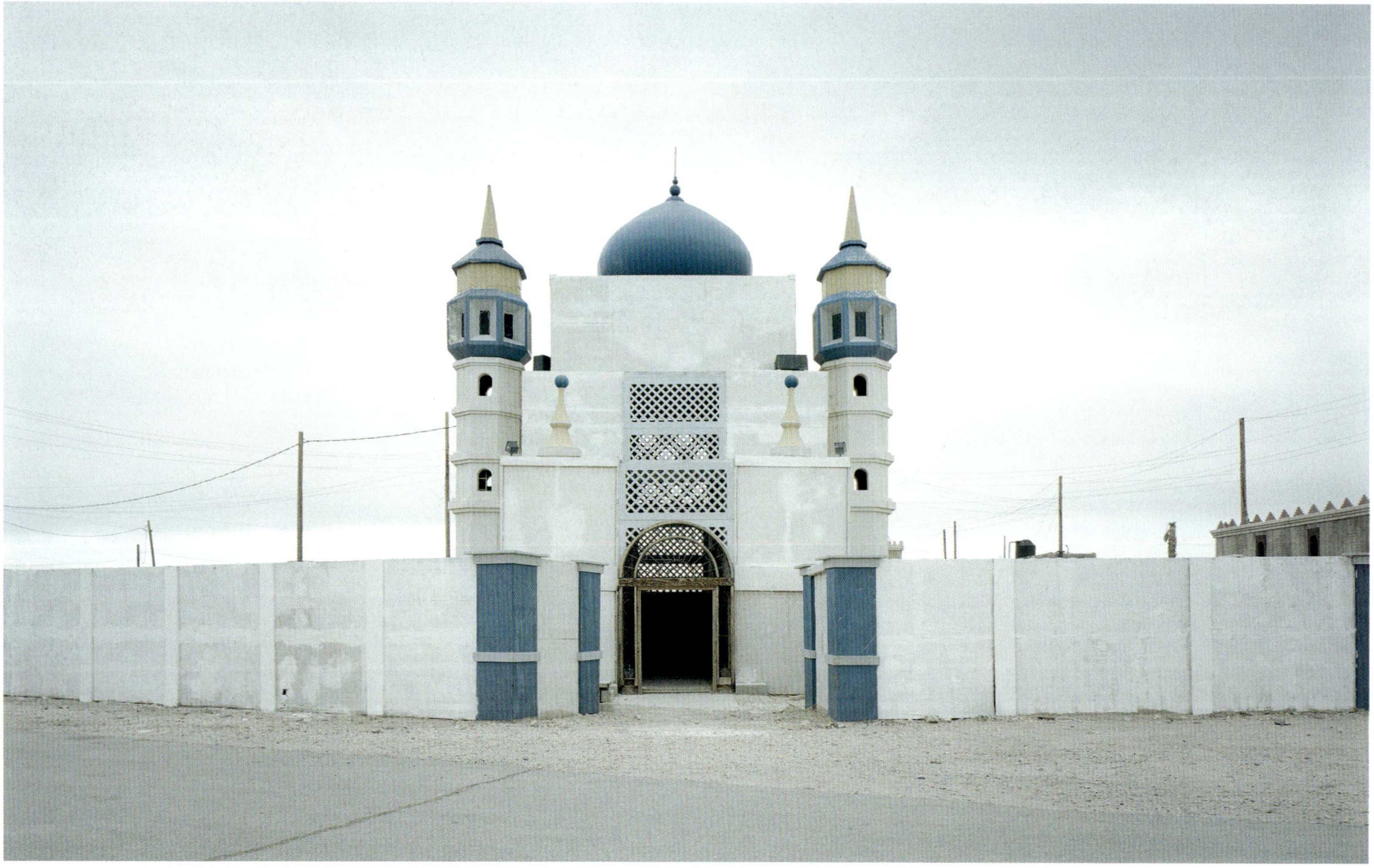

37

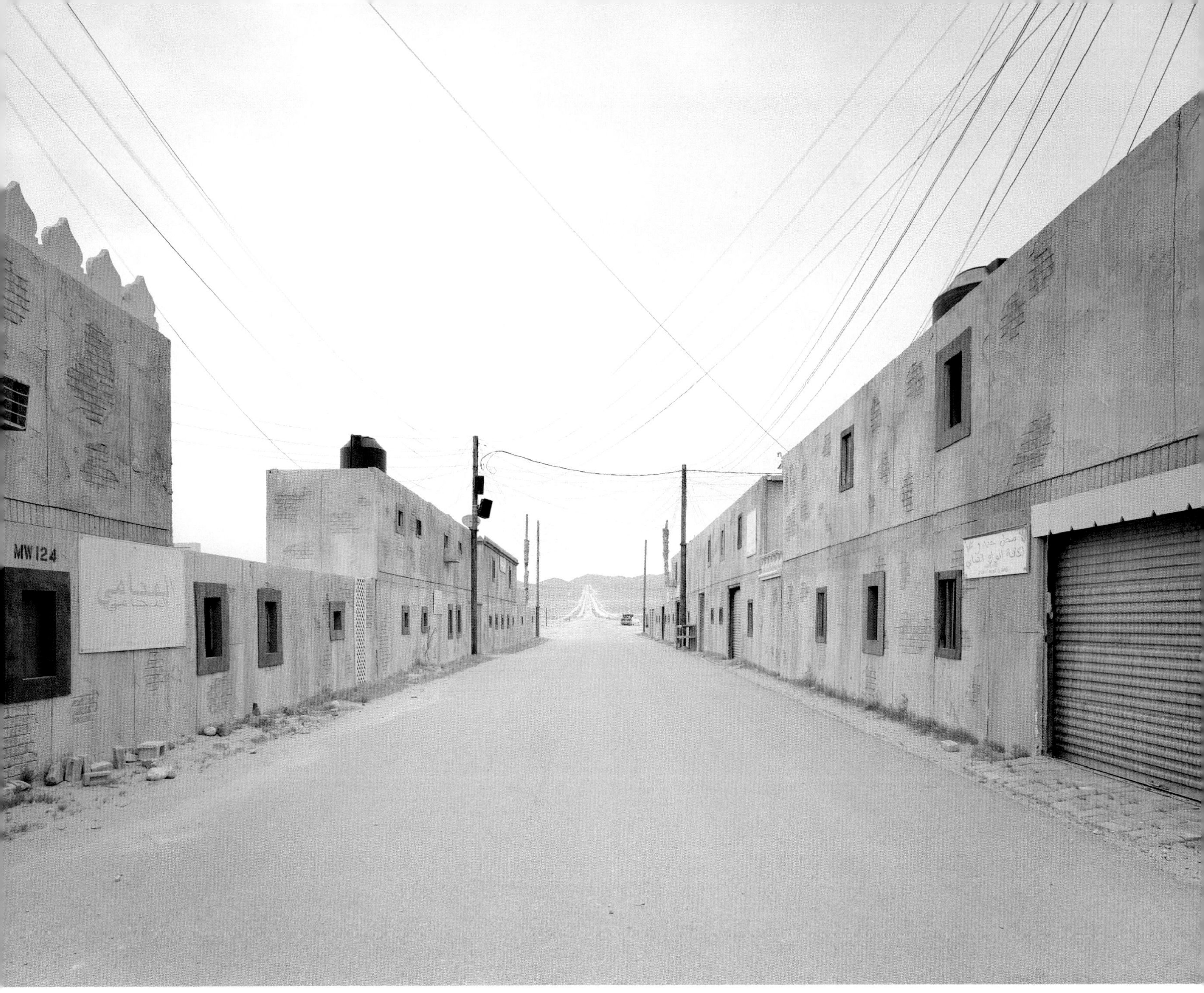

MW124
المحامي
المحامي

39

40

افران ومعجنات
كاظم
Afran wa moajanat Kadhem
Bakery and pastry kazim

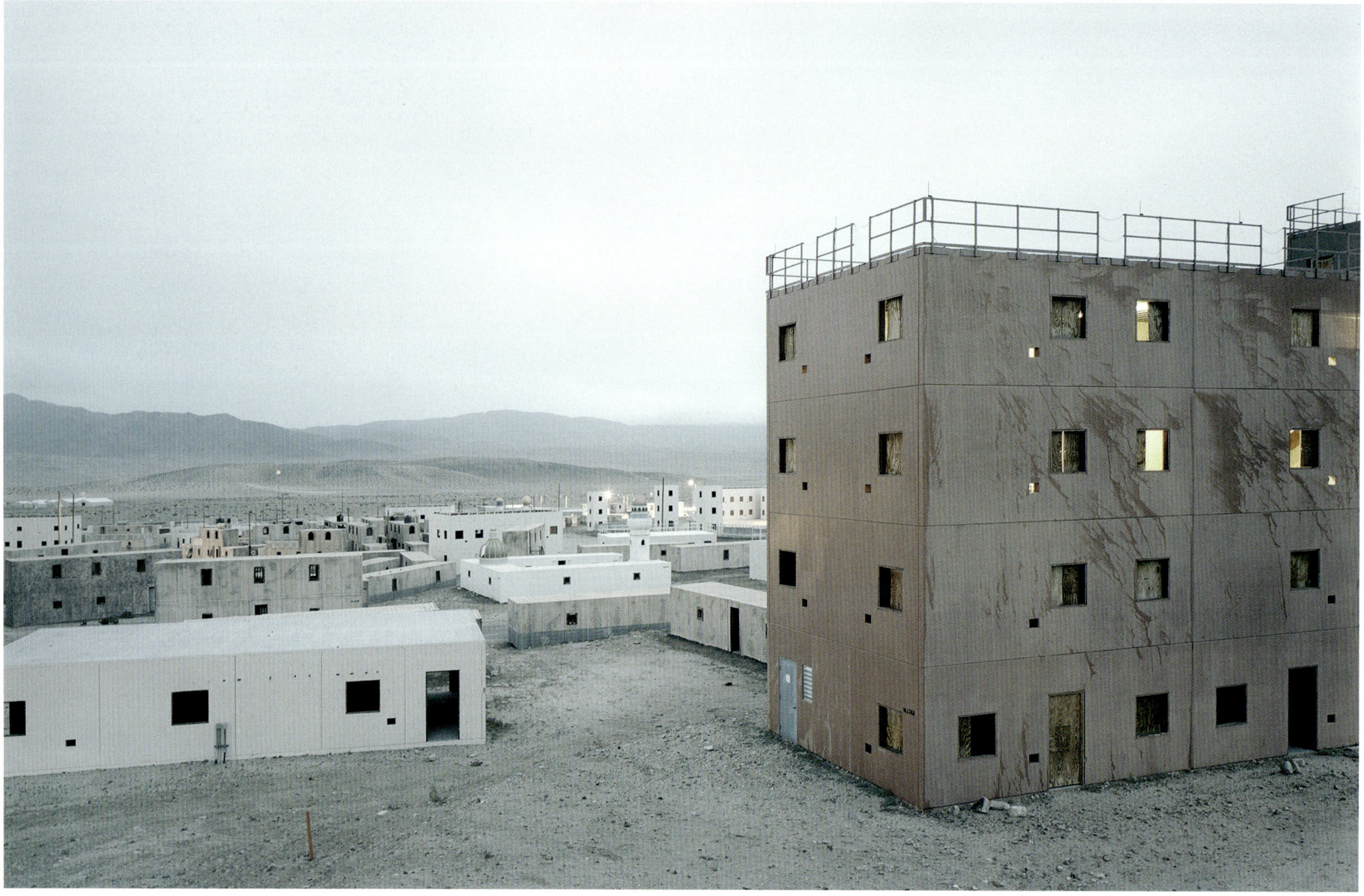

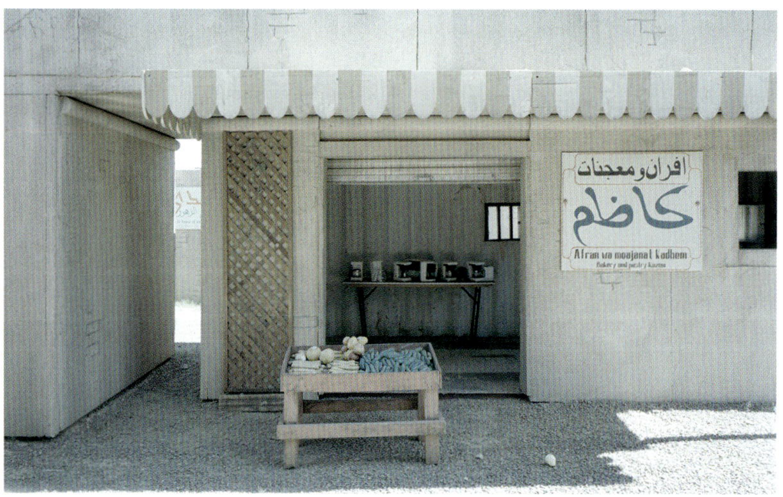

41

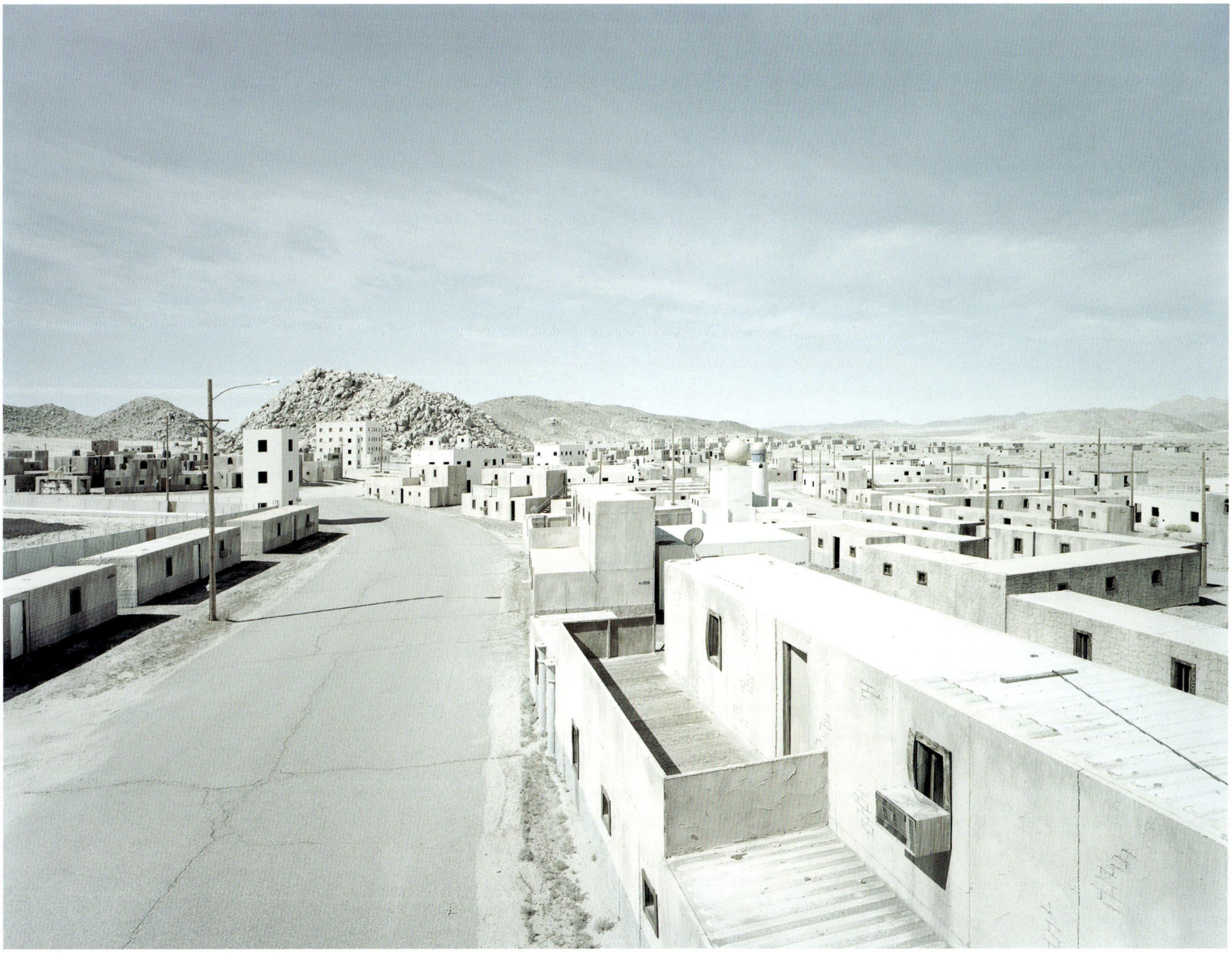

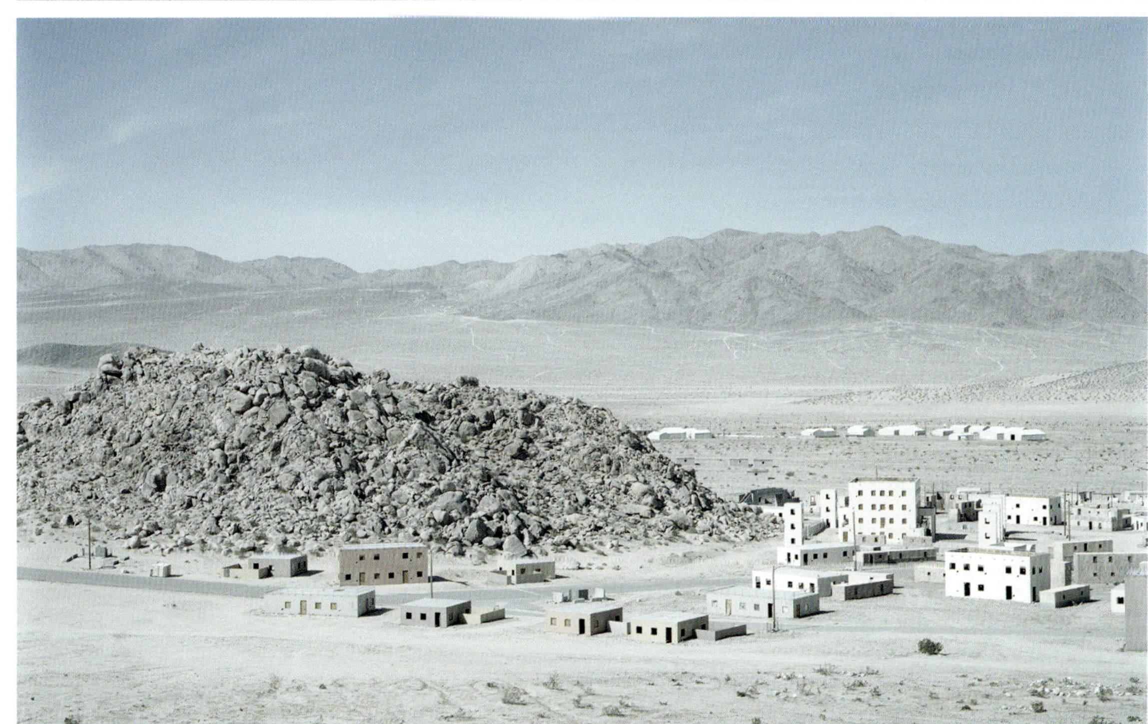

42

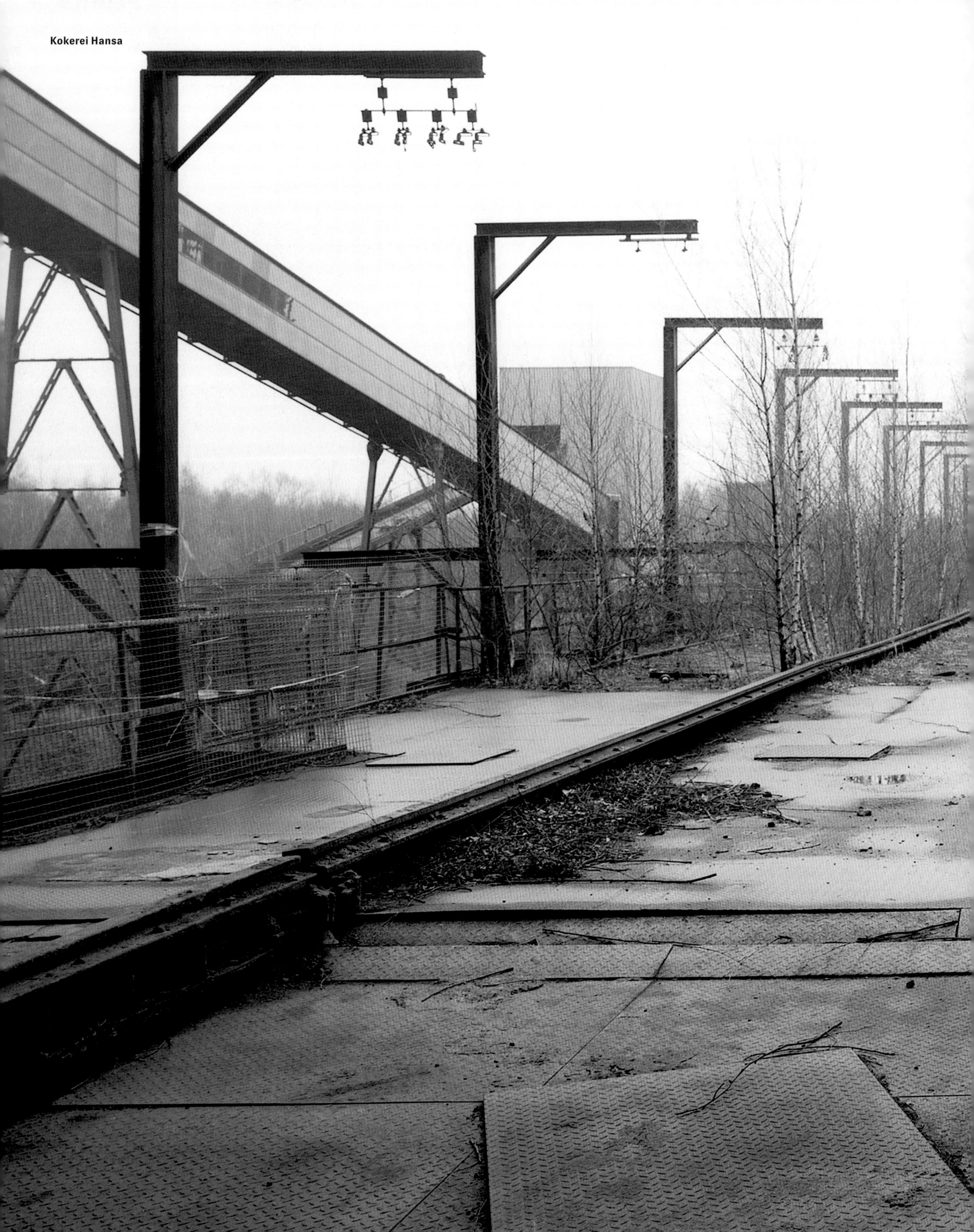

Kokerei Hansa

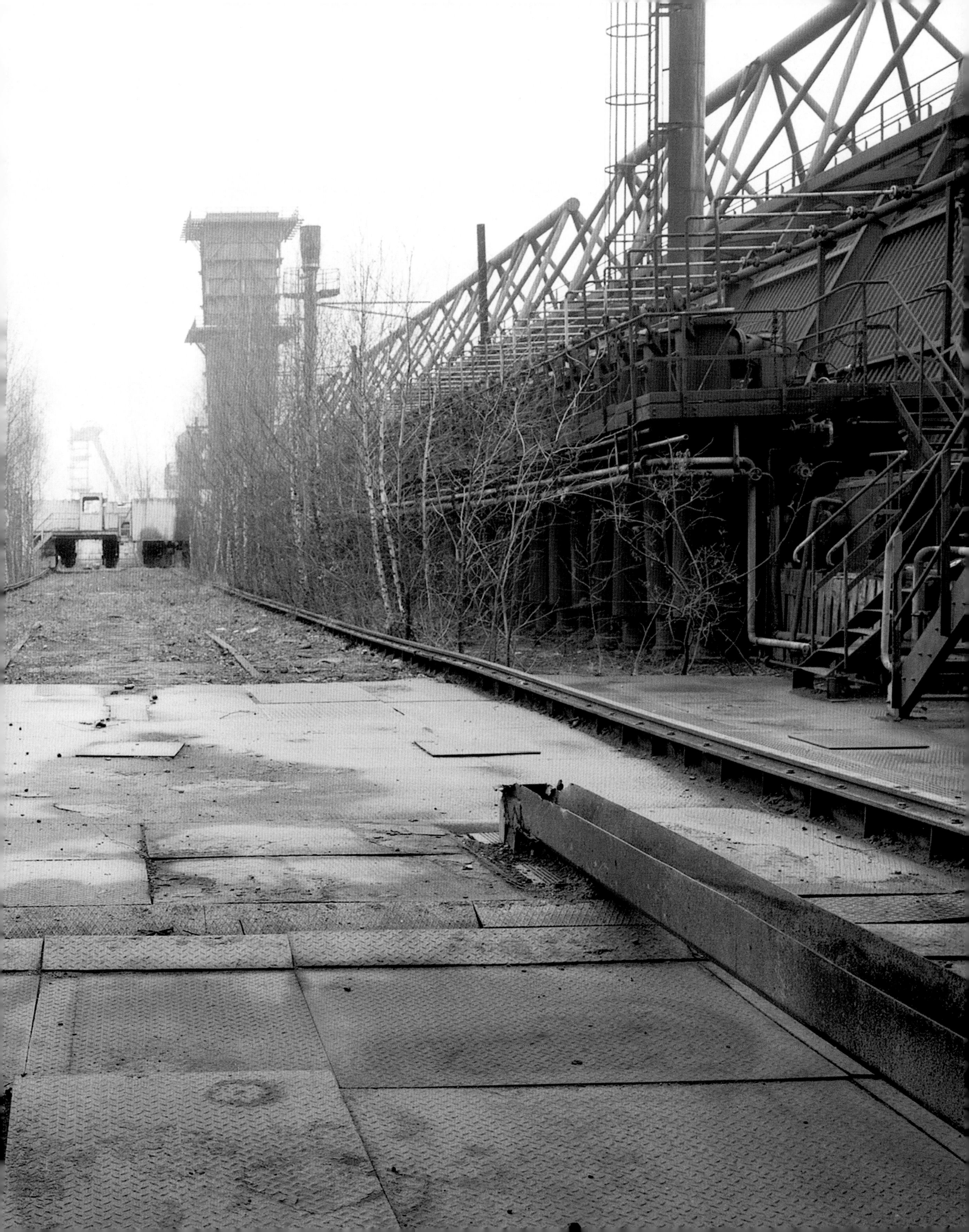

Kokerei Hansa

Auf Einladung der Stiftung Industriedenkmalpflege und Geschichtskultur näherte sich Gregor Sailer der Kokerei Hansa im Dortmunder Stadtgebiet fotografisch an. Ziel des Projekts war es, ein letztes fotografisches Dokument zu erstellen, welches den Gesamtzustand der Anlage zeigt. Sämtliche nicht unter Denkmalschutz stehenden Gebäude existieren bereits nicht mehr. 1992 wurde der Betrieb, an dem einst bis zu tausend Menschen im Schichtbetrieb Koks produzierten, eingestellt. In behutsamen Schwarz-Weiß-Aufnahmen, die in der Ausstellung als Slideshow gezeigt werden, zeichnet der Fotograf mit der Kamera den Weg der Kohle nach. Seine Bilder lassen die Industrieanlage aus den 1920er-Jahren als großen, von der Produktion gezeichneten Charakterbau auferstehen. Fast zärtlich porträtiert Sailer dieses Relikt der Schwerindustrie in diffusem, winterlichem Licht, wodurch die Formen aus Stahl ruhig, monumental und zeitlos erscheinen.

Der österreichische Musiker David Geretschläger hat eigens für die Präsentation als Slideshow ein Musikstück komponiert und eingespielt.

At the invitation of the Foundation for the Preservation of Industrial Monuments and Historical Culture, Gregor Sailer adopted a photographic approach to the Hansa coking plant in the city area of Dortmund. The aim of the project was to produce a definitive photographic document showing the overall condition of the plant. All the buildings with the exception of those under preservation order have since disappeared. The plant, which at its peak employed thousands of workers to produce coke in shift work, shut down in 1992. In delicate and sensitive black-and-white photographs, shown as a slideshow in the exhibition, the photographer retraces the story of coal with his camera. His pictures bring the industrial plant established in the 1920s back to life as a large-scale character-filled building complex moulded by its production remit. Almost tenderly, Sailer portrays this relic of heavy industry in diffuse, wintry light, the steel shapes rendered as calm, monumental, and timeless.

Austrian musician David Geretschläger composed and recorded a piece of music especially for this showcase.

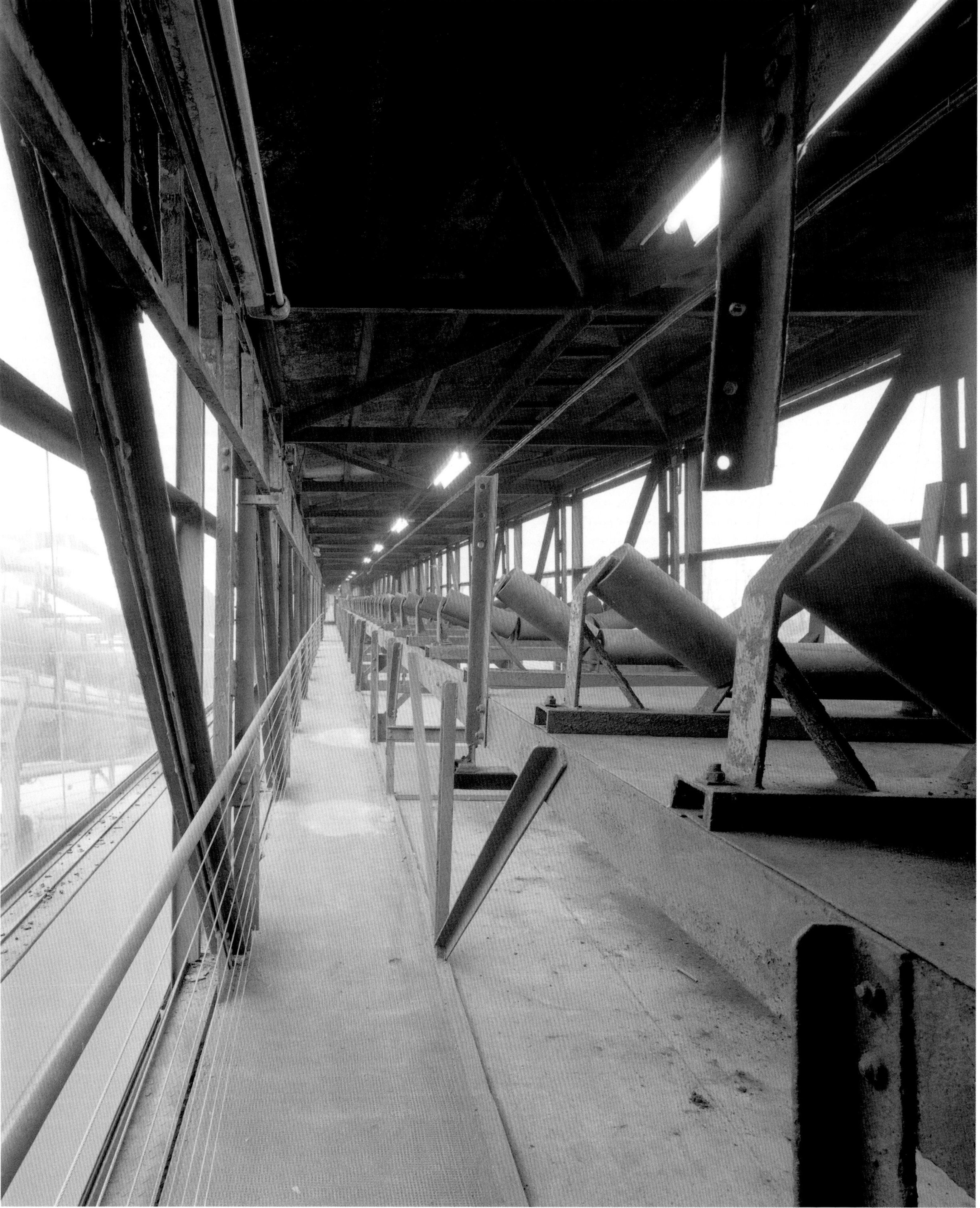

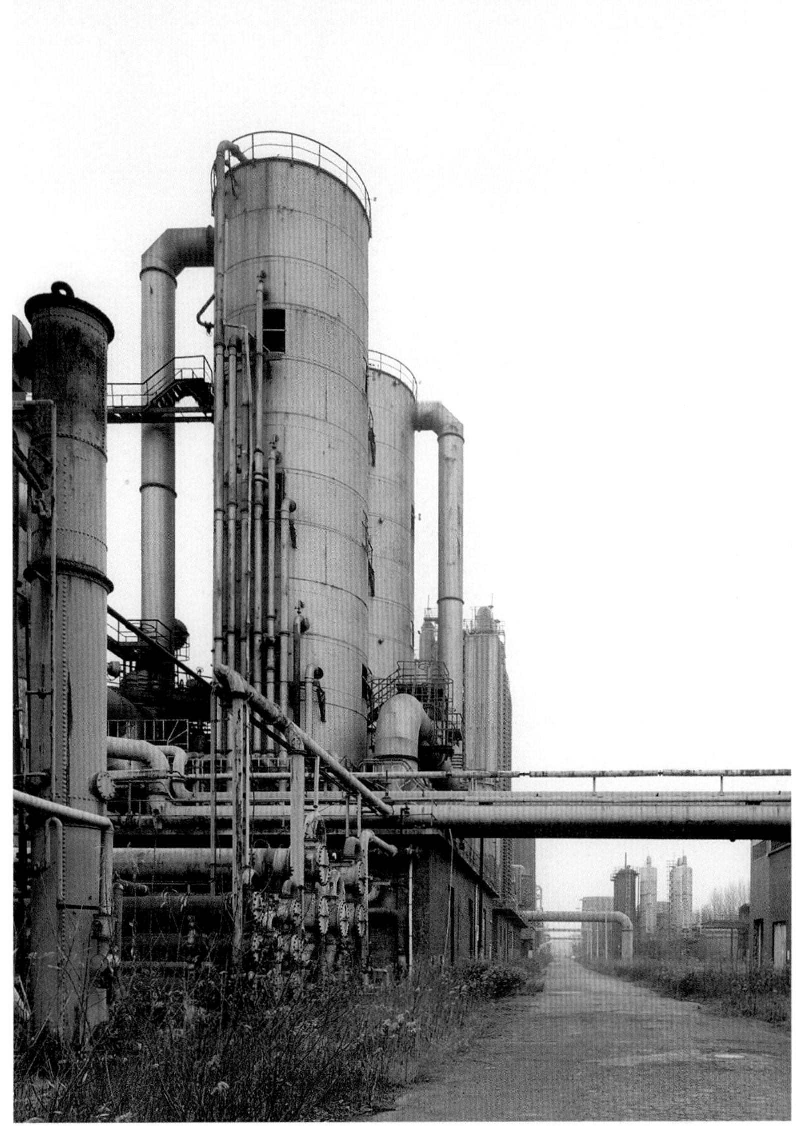

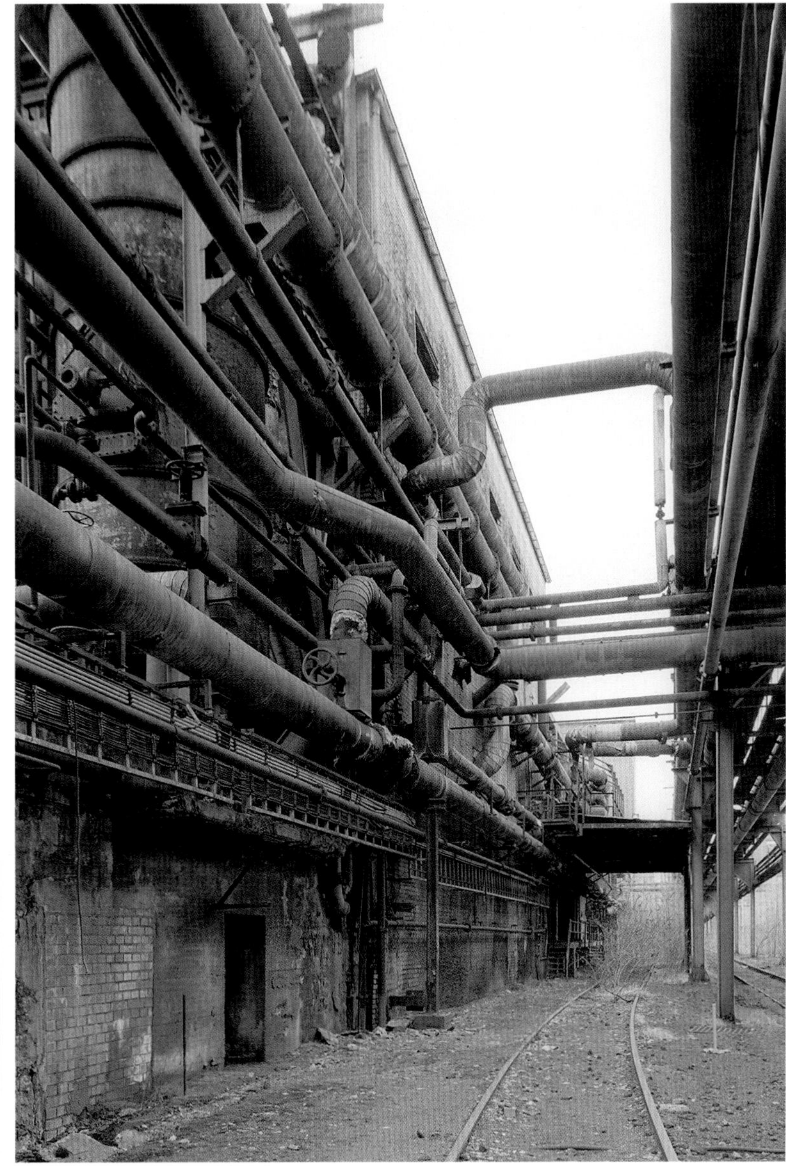

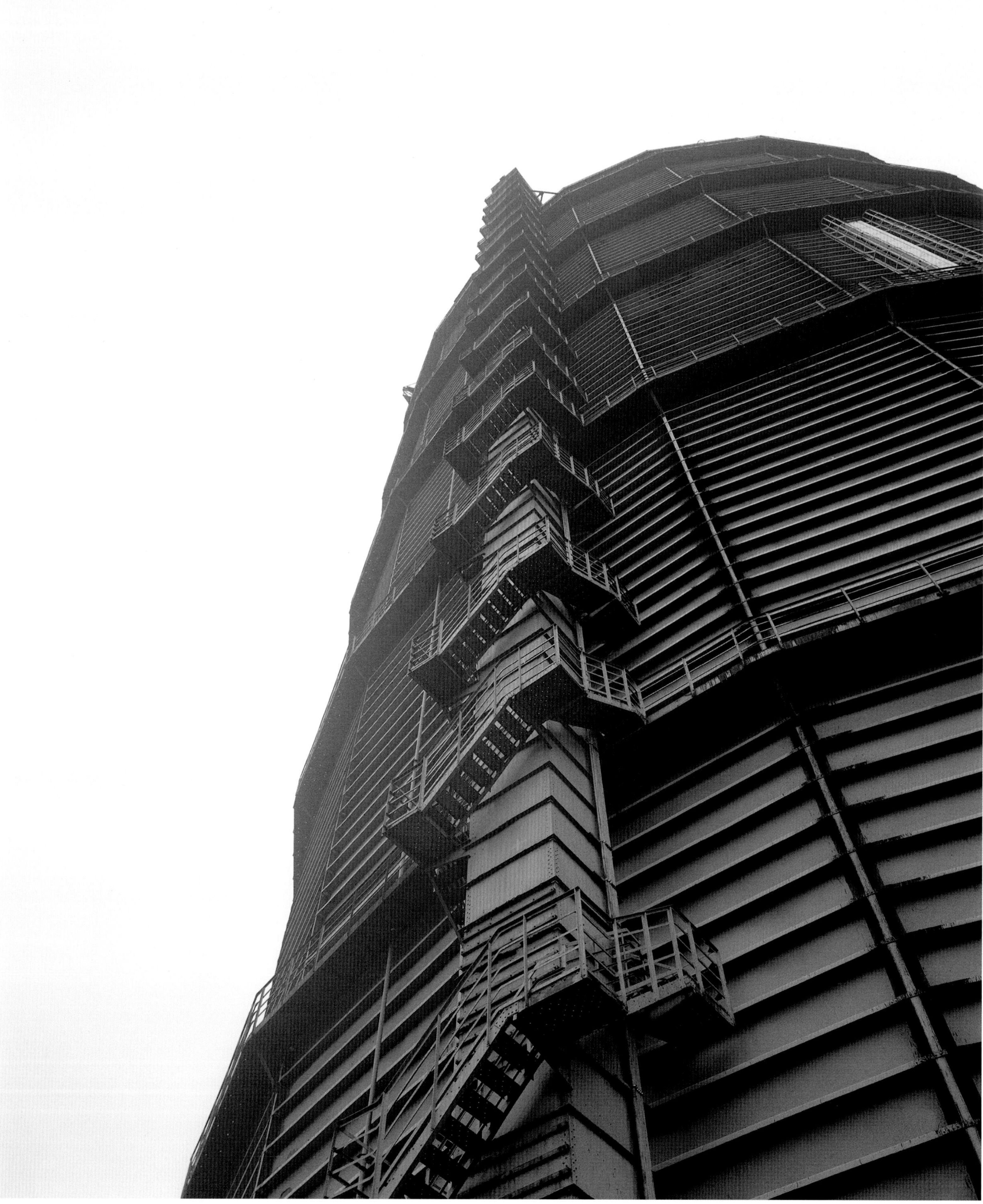

„Um die Linien und Kubaturen in ihrer Ordnung und Klarheit zu erfassen und eine Vorstellung von den Dimensionen der Anlage zu vermitteln, werden die Wintermonate für die Schwarz-Weiß-Fotografien ausgewählt. Die Industrienatur ruht, die laubfreien Bäume ermöglichen jetzt den Blick auf die Architekturen und in die Ferne. Er bewegt sich auf der schwarzen und der weißen Seite der Kokerei. Doch ist sein Interesse am historischen Produktionsablauf nur sekundär. Seine Aufmerksamkeit gilt der Architektur und der Technik als stille, ästhetische Größen."

Ursula Mehrfeld, „Vorwort", in: *Kokerei Hansa*. Gregor Sailer, hrsg. von der Stiftung Industriedenkmalpflege und Geschichtskultur, Dortmund 2005, S. 2–3.

"The winter months are the season of choice for these black-and-white photographs so that the lines and cubic volumes in their orderly arrangement and their clarity can be captured and an idea of the dimensions of the plant conveyed. With the industrial habitat now at rest and the trees freed of their leaves, views of the architecture and far horizons open up. He [Sailer] moves about the black side of the coking plant and the white. Yet his interest in the historical production process is merely secondary. His focus is trained on both the architecture and the technology as silent, aesthetic quantities."

Ursula Mehrfeld, "Foreword," in *Kokerei Hansa*. Gregor Sailer, ed. Stiftung Industriedenkmalpflege und Geschichtskultur (Dortmund 2005), 2–3.

5

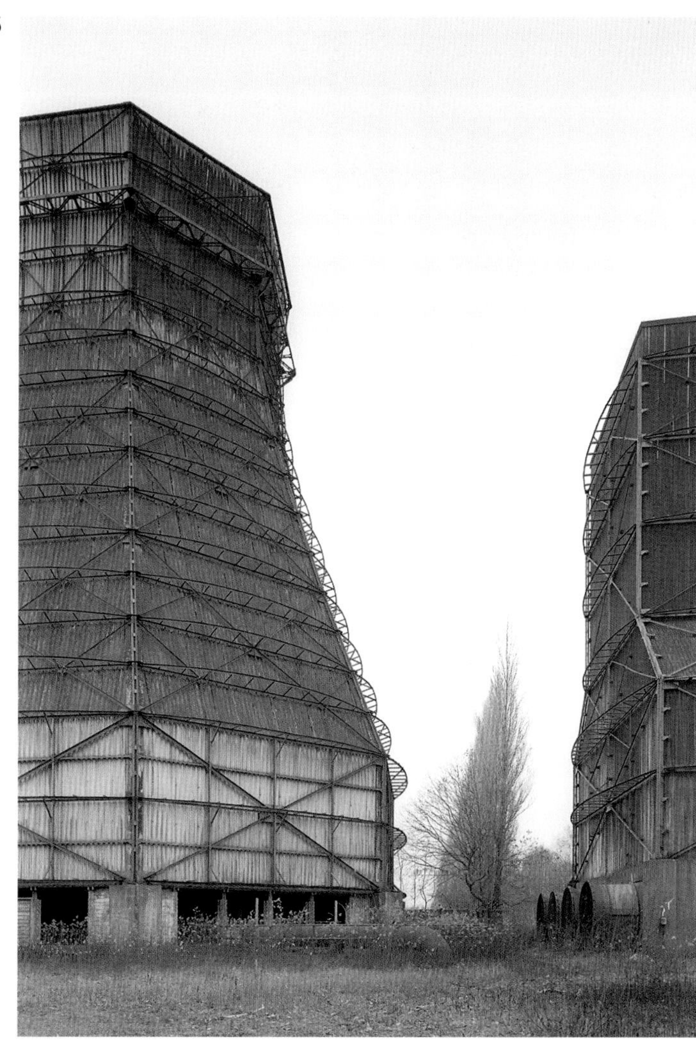

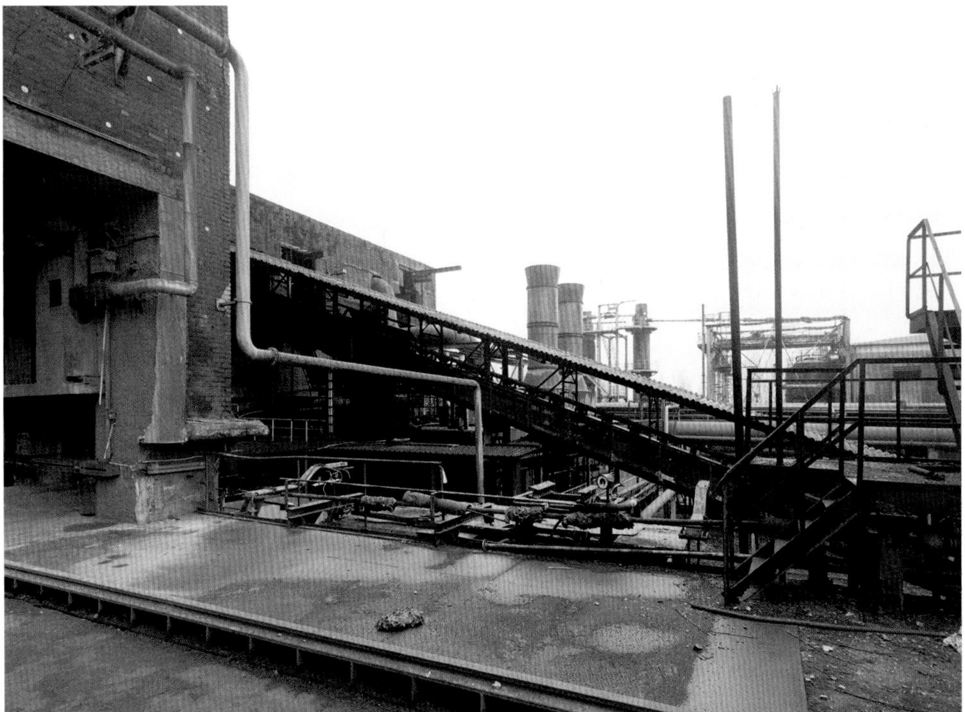

6

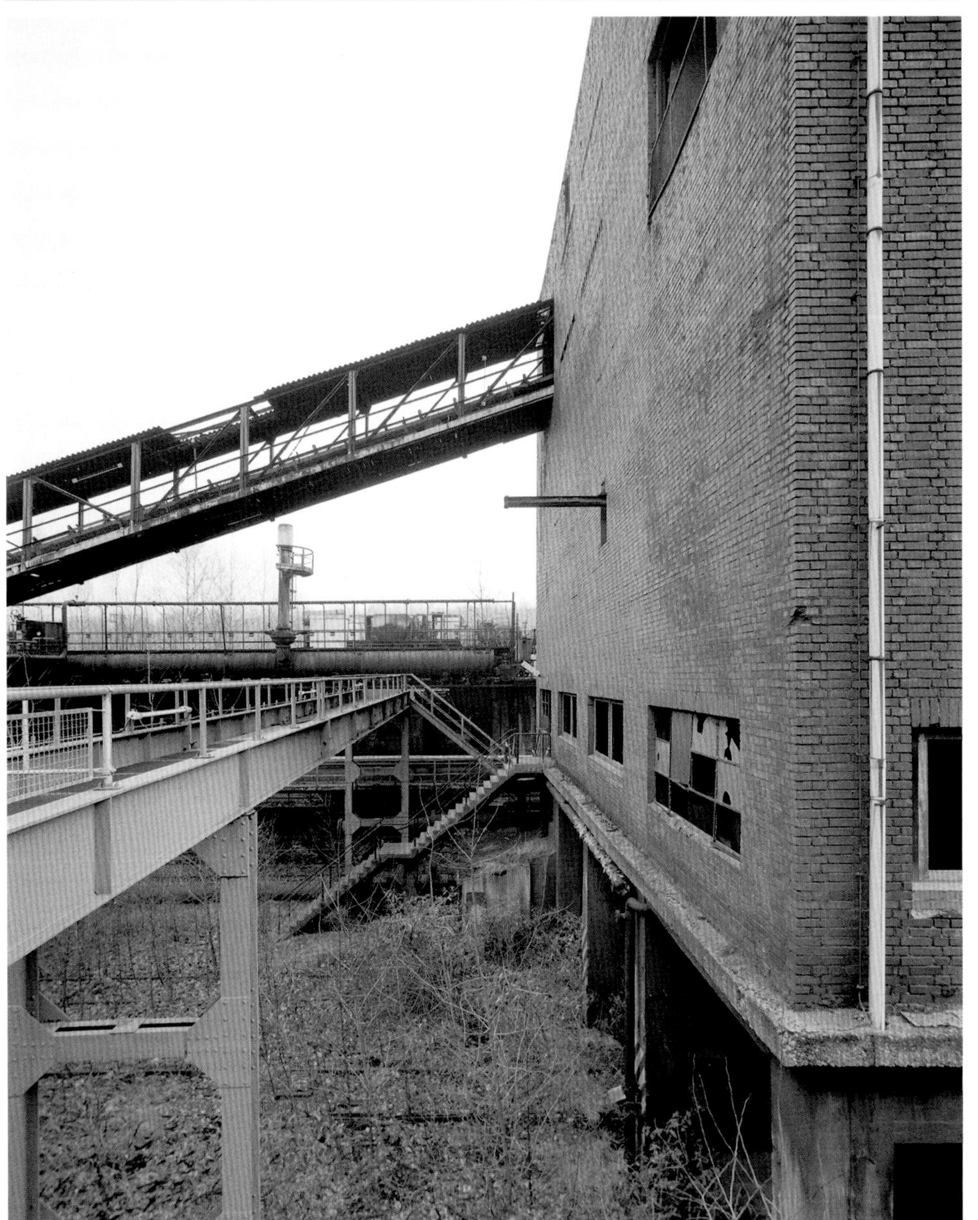

7

8

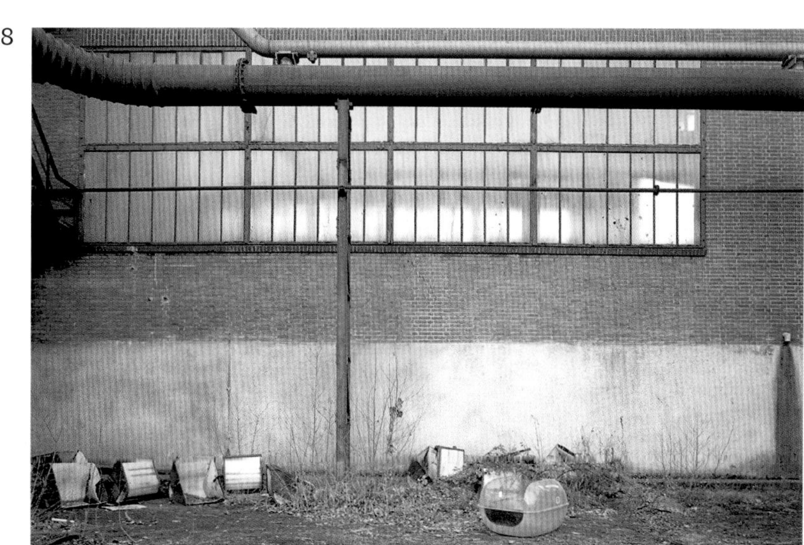

9

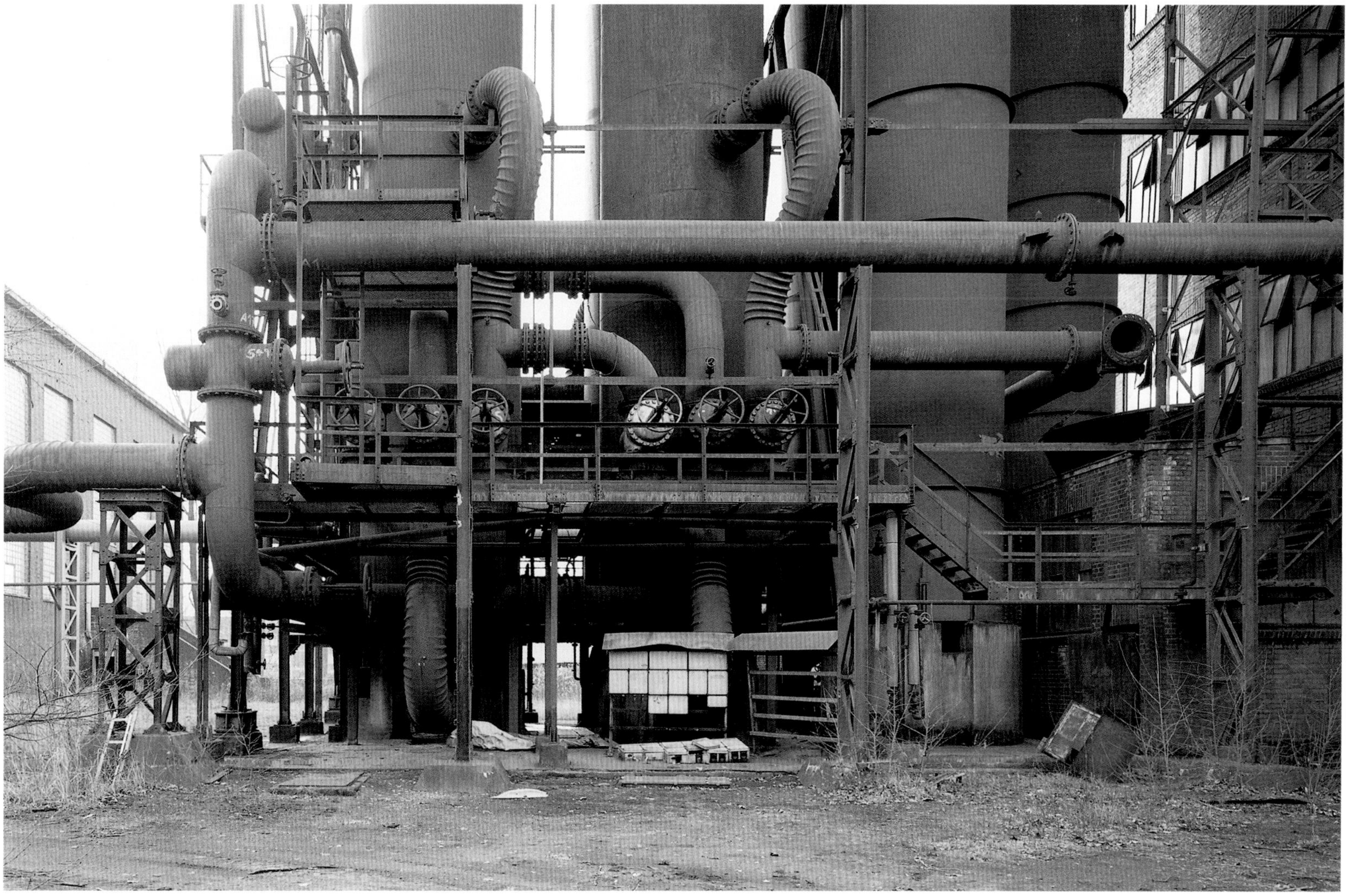

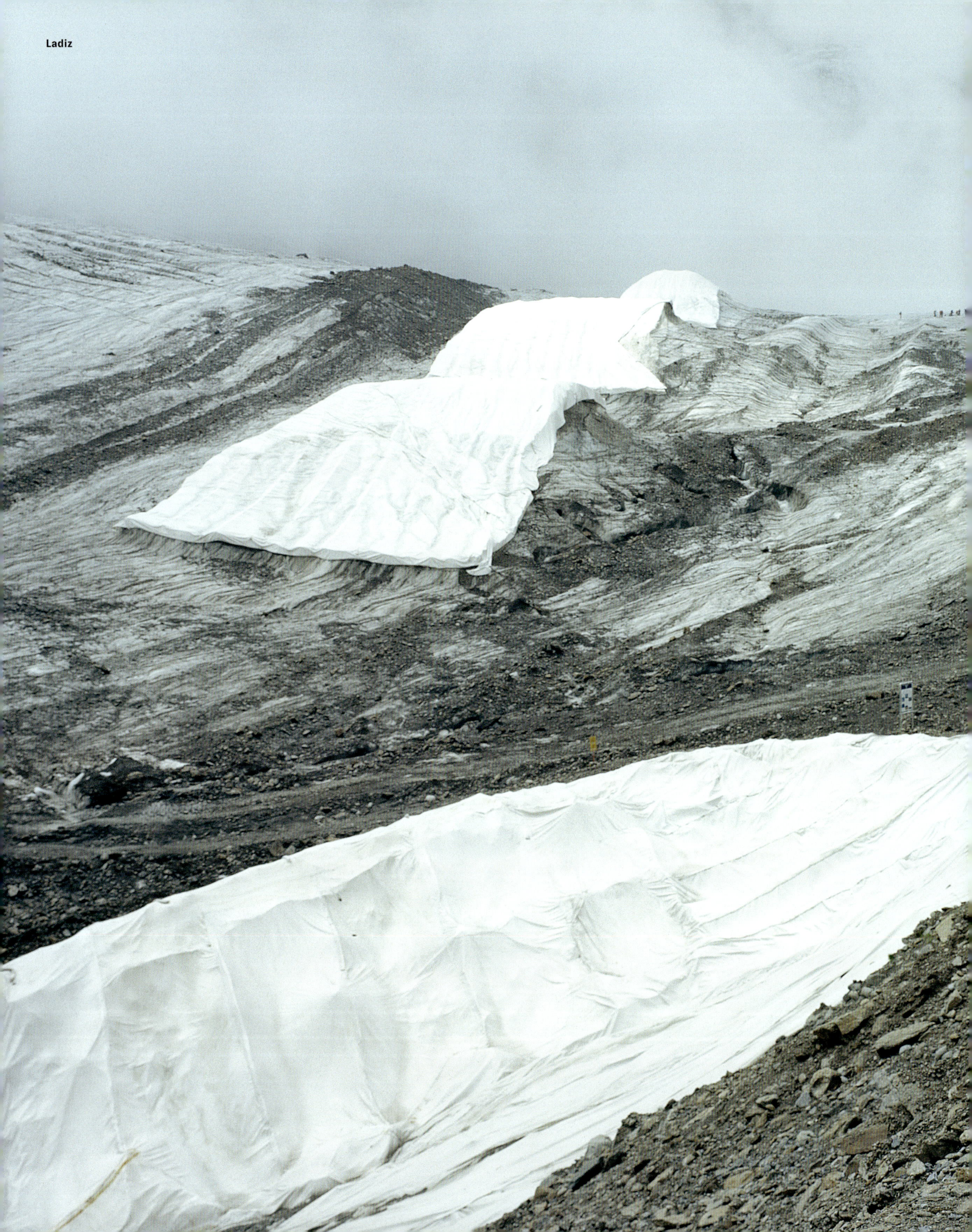

Ladiz

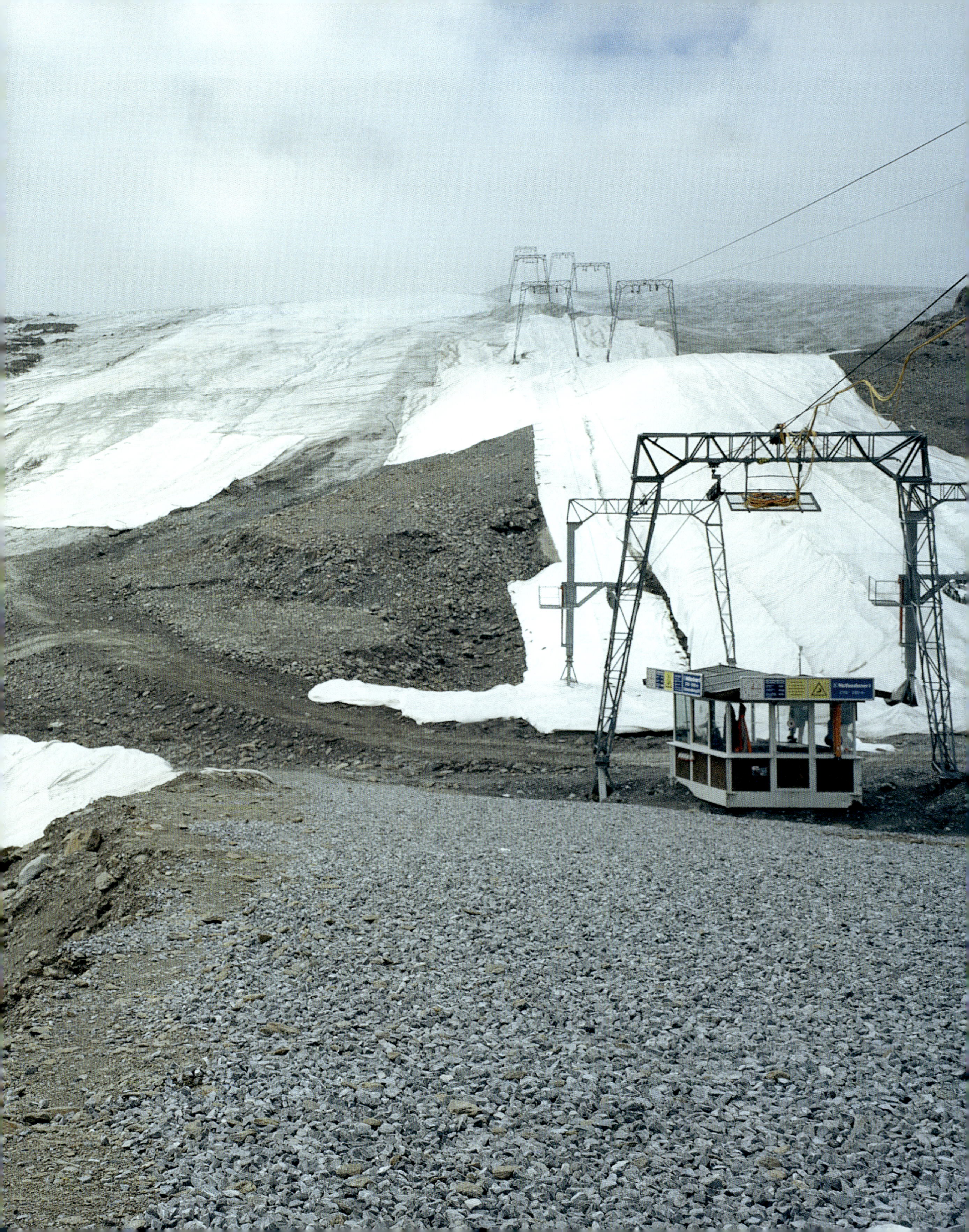

Ladiz

Diese Serie ist im alpinen Hochgebirge im österreichischen Bundesland Tirol entstanden, eine Gegend, die Gregor Sailer sehr vertraut ist, denn er ist nicht nur dort aufgewachsen, sondern lebt auch heute wieder dort. Er hat die Entwicklung des Massentourismus in den letzten Jahrzehnten selbst erlebt. Bereits 2006 beginnt er mit der Werkgruppe *LADIZ_alpen™*. Speziell das hochgestellte TM im Titel, das für „Trade Mark", also für eine unregistrierte Warenmarke steht, macht klar, dass es hier um die Kommerzialisierung von Natur und Landschaft geht. Um die Alpen als Ware.

Sailers Bilder zeigen die Ausbeutung und Verunstaltung der Alpenlandschaft. Die Natur wird unter enormem Aufwand angepasst und umgestaltet, um der Tourismuswirtschaft zweckdienlich zu sein.

This series came about in the high alpine mountains of Tyrol, the Austrian federal province all too familiar to Gregor Sailer. Indeed, not only did he grow up there, but he has now returned there to live. He himself has witnessed the development of mass tourism in recent decades. Back in 2006, he began with the group of works, *LADIZ_alpen™*. The title's TM (trademark) superscript in particular makes it clear that this is all about the commercialisation of nature and landscape and about the alps as a commodity.

Sailer's photographs depict the exploitation and defacement of the alpine landscape. Nature is being moulded and refashioned at enormous expense to indulge the whims of the tourism industry.

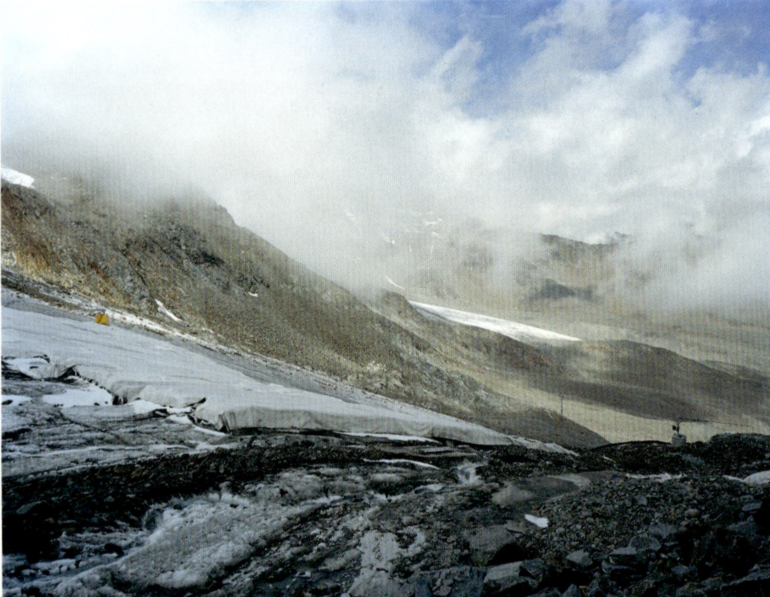
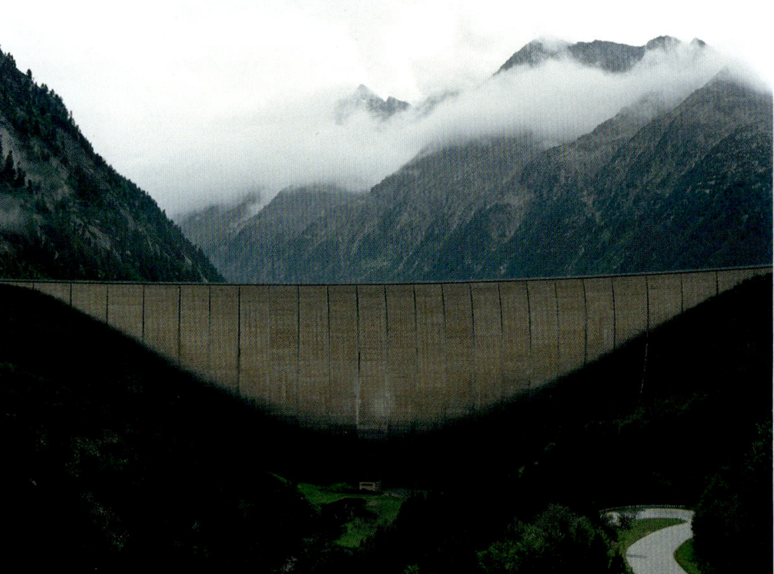

1
2

3

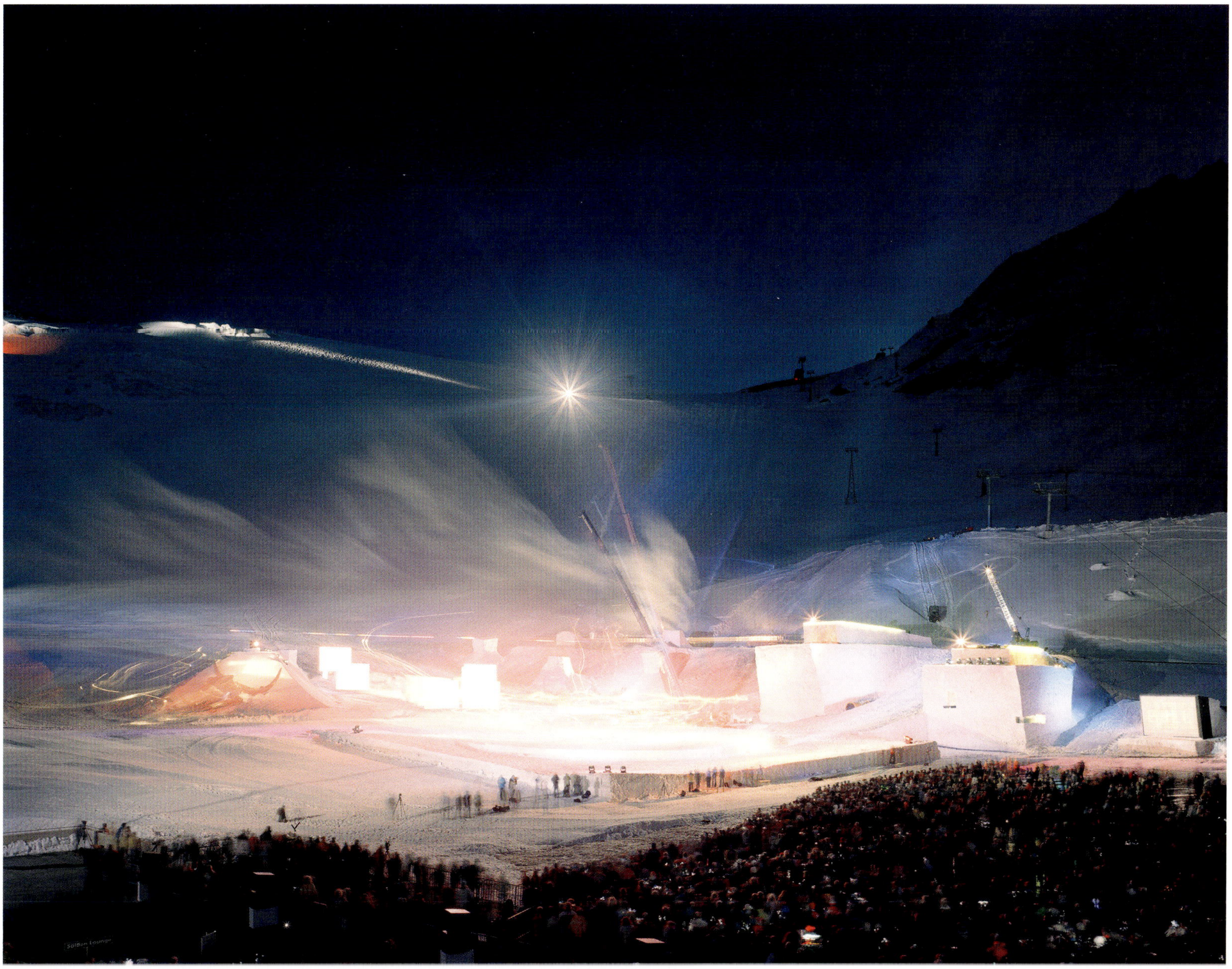

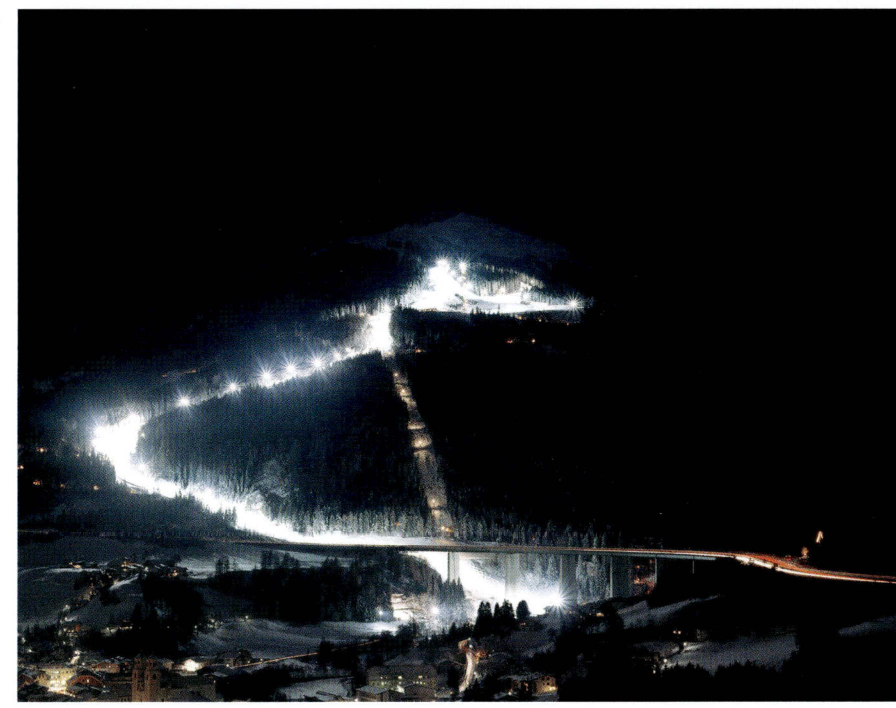

4

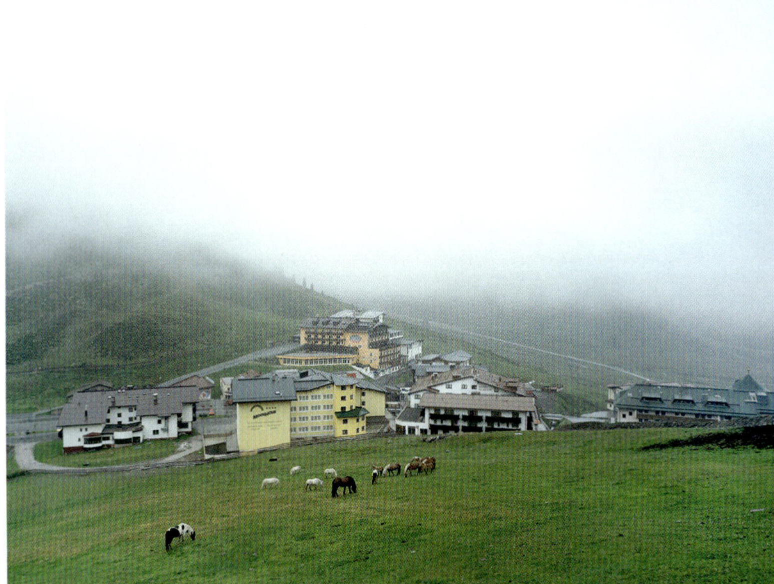 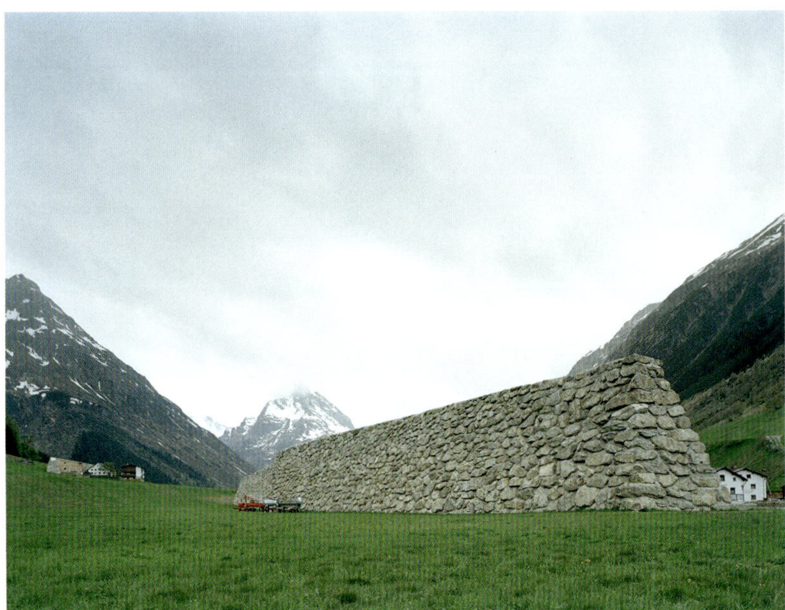

„Der Fotograf zeigt in seinen Bildern, was aus den in unserer Phantasie weit entrückten und doch so nahen Landschaften geworden ist. Sailer dokumentiert die oft Jahrzehnte, oft Jahre, oft erst Wochen und Monate zurückreichende Inbesitznahme der Berge in Bildern. Mit der Präzision der Großformatkamera zeichnet er alles auf, was sich im Bildfeld zeigt: Geröll, Schnee, Eis, und dazwischen immer wieder menschliche Spuren. Spuren des Lebens, der touristischen Nutzung, Spuren der Technik und der Architektur, die die alpine Landschaft oft buchstäblich bis zum letzten Gipfel kennzeichnen. Manche seiner Aufnahmen sind weniger Landschafts- als vielmehr Architekturbilder. Sie zeigen die Alpen als überdimensionales Bauwerk."

Anton Holzer, „Recherchen im Hochgebirge", in: *Gregor Sailer. Ladiz,* Salzburg 2008, S. 6.

"In his pictures, the photographer shows what has become of landscapes, which, in our imagination, are so far removed yet so near. Sailer captures and documents the appropriation of the mountains, a process that has often been ongoing for decades, years, or simply a matter of weeks and months. With the preciseness of his large-format camera, he records everything that appears in the viewfinder: the scree, the snow, the ice — and in between, time and time again, the traces left by humankind. Traces of life, of tourist exploitation; traces of technology and architecture that often literally define the alpine landscape, right up to the highest summit. Some of his photographs are not so much landscape pictures as architectural images, showcasing the alps as an oversized edifice."

Anton Holzer, "Recherchen im Hochgebirge," in *Gregor Sailer, Ladiz* (Salzburg 2008), 6.

7

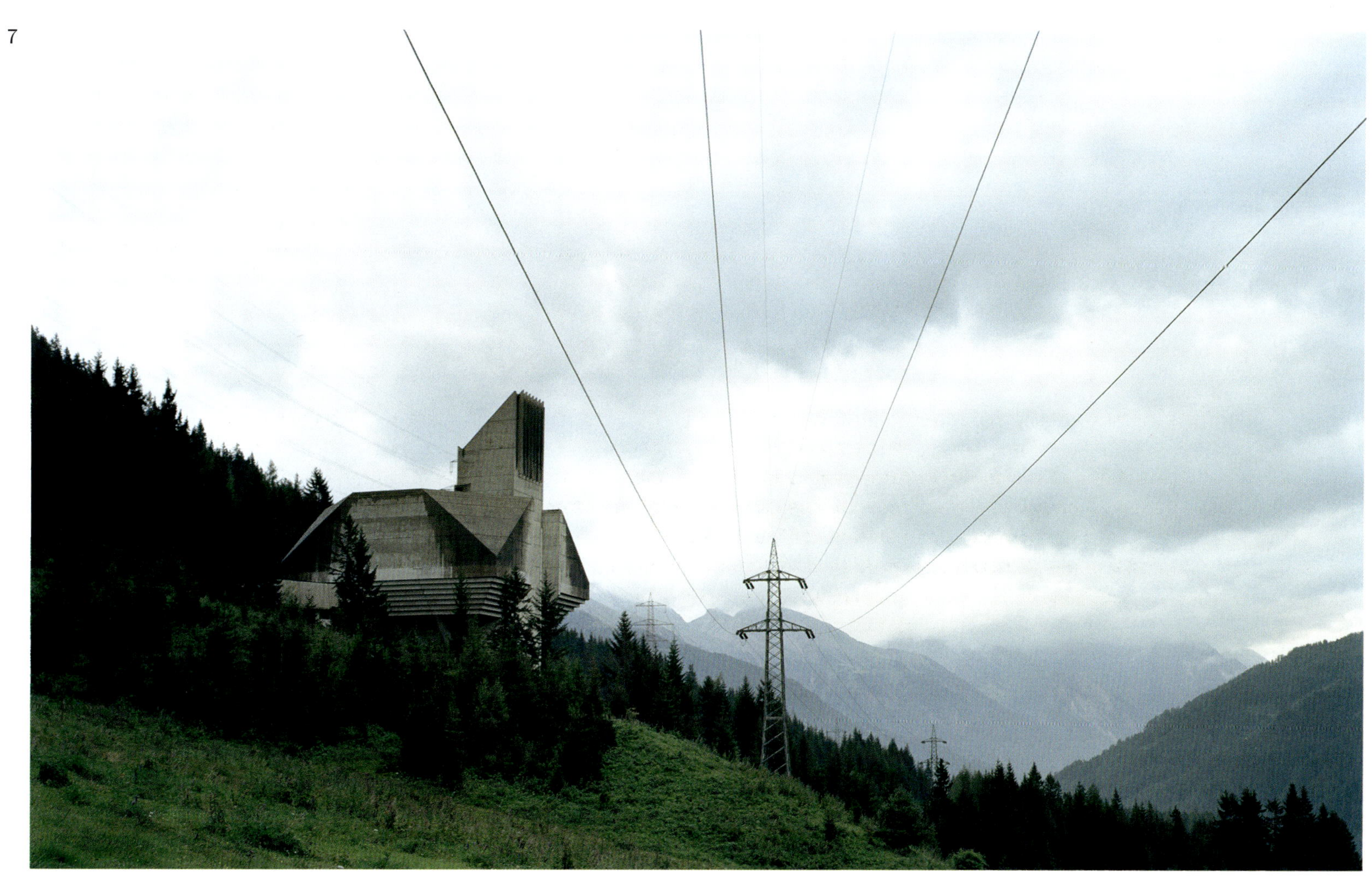

8

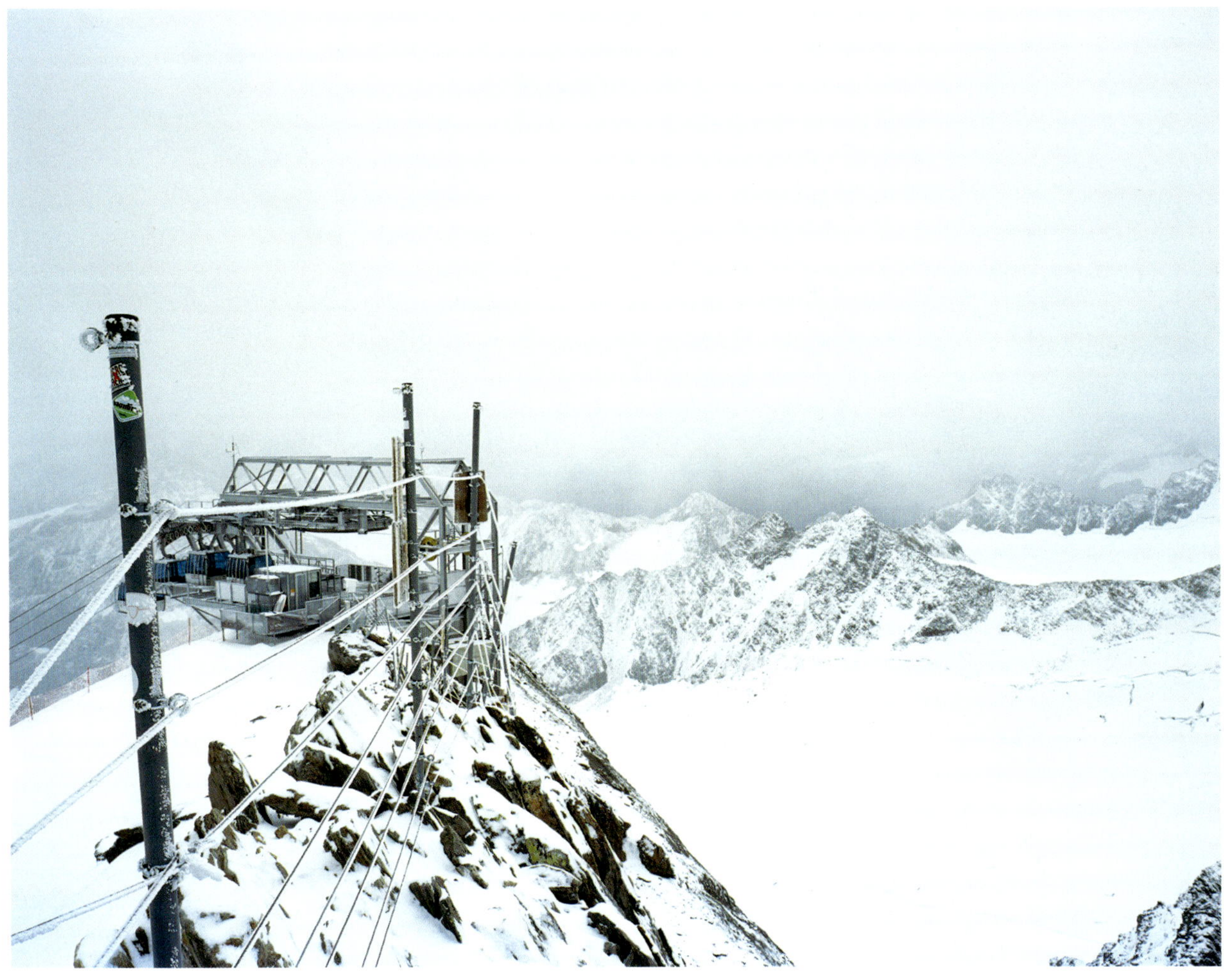

9

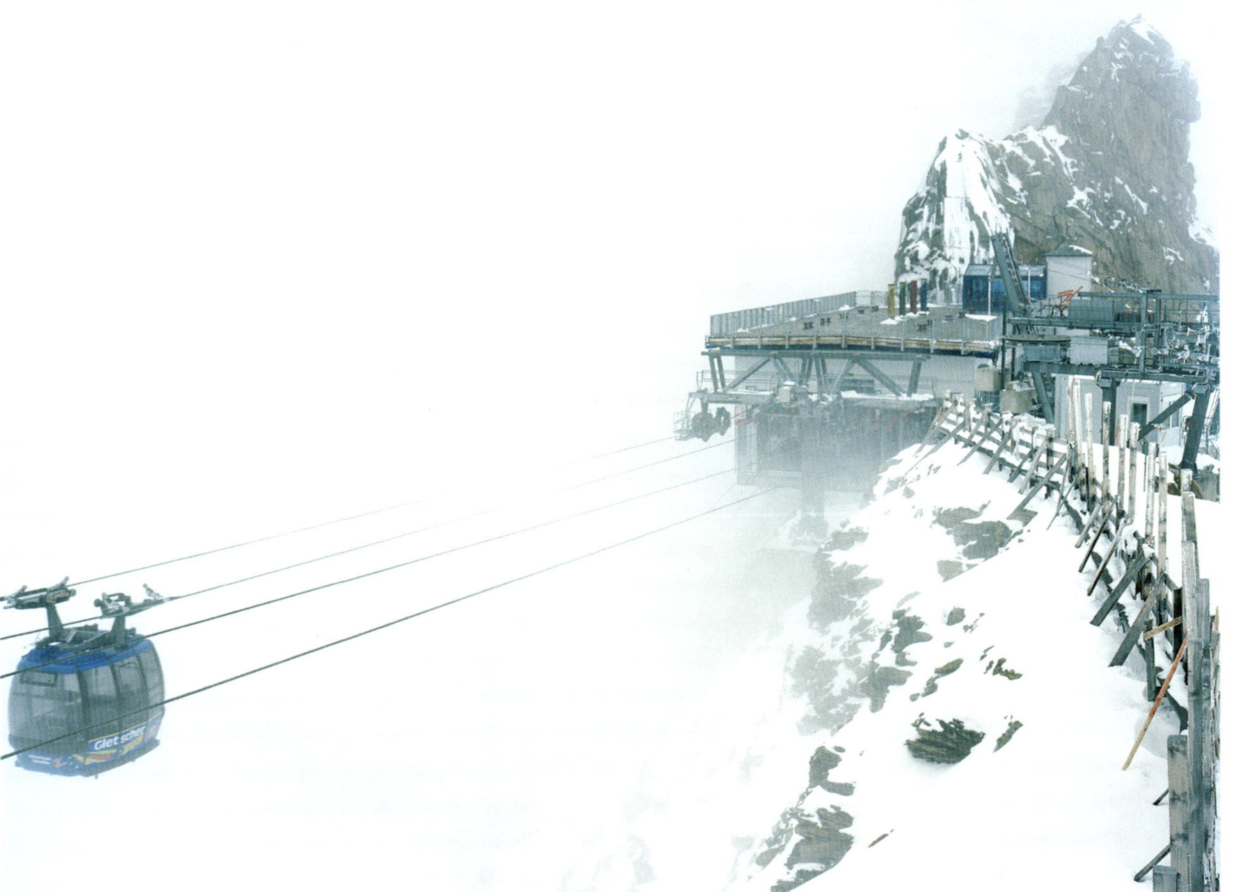

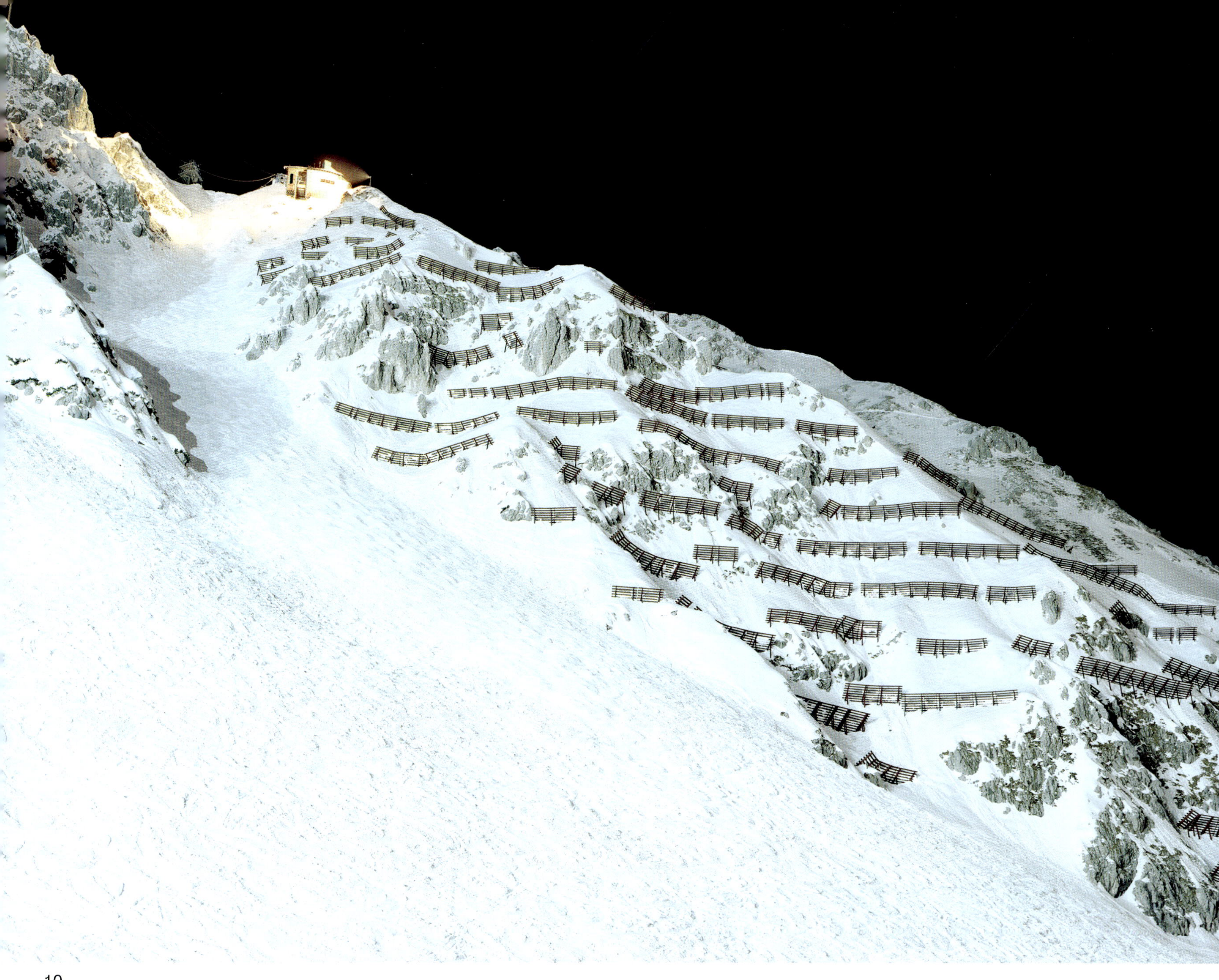

10

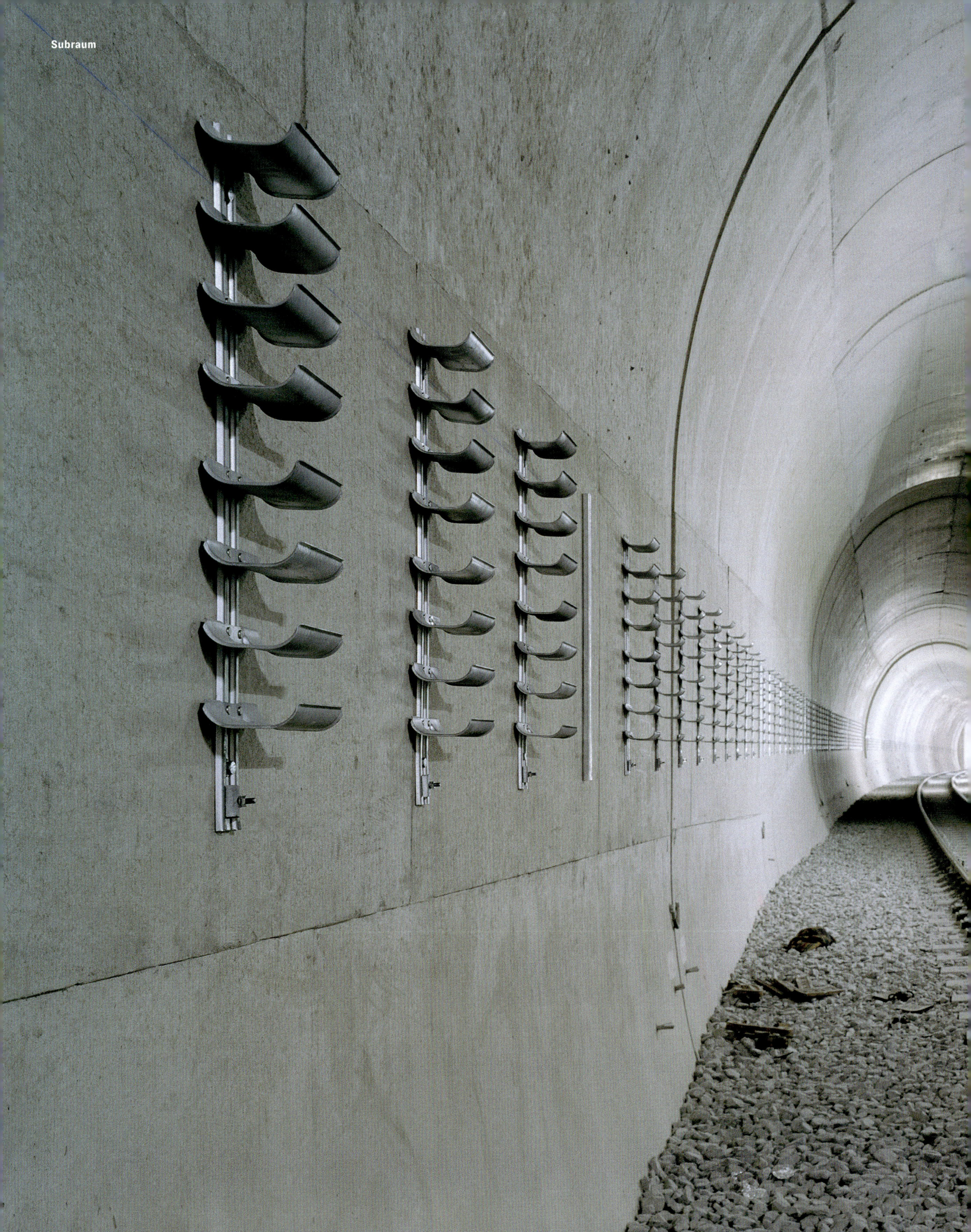
Subraum

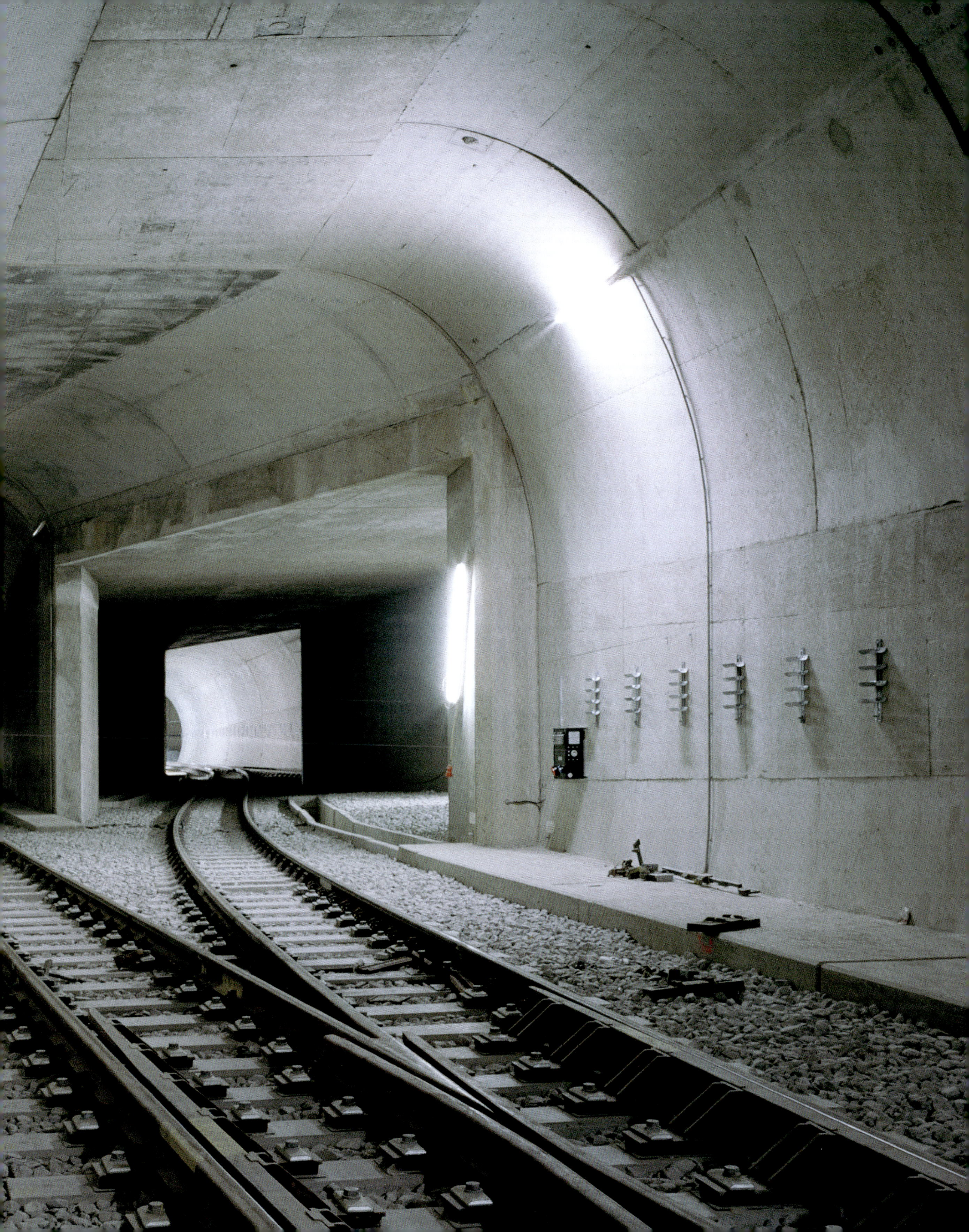

Subraum

Gregor Sailer studierte in Dortmund Kommunikationsdesign mit Schwerpunkt Fotografie. Dort im Ruhrgebiet ist in Zusammenarbeit mit seinen Kommilitonen Johannes Naumann und Stefan Tuschy die Serie *Subraum* entstanden. Die Kamera ist das Forschungsinstrument der jungen Fotografen, mit dem sie sich den weitgehend unbekannten unterirdischen Stadtlandschaften nähern. Ihre Stadtexpeditionen führen sie in das Landesarchiv NRW in Düsseldorf, in einen Zivilschutzbunker in Duisburg, in die Bochumer Untergrundbahn sowie auf den Flughafen und in die Stadt- und Landesbibliothek Dortmund.

Subraum zeigt repräsentative unterirdische Orte in diesem einstigen industriellen Zentrum Deutschlands. Die unter der Oberfläche der Städte liegenden Infrastrukturen sind einem Großteil der Bevölkerung nicht zugänglich und befinden sich außerhalb der allgemeinen Wahrnehmung. Durch die stark auf Formen und Farben fokussierenden Aufnahmen bleiben die Räume jedoch abstrakt und vage. Die Bilder zielen nicht auf die Dokumentation und Nachvollziehbarkeit der Orte, sondern setzen den fotografischen Rahmen entsprechend dem ästhetischen Potenzial der architektonischen Formen und Farben, unabhängig vom Nutzungszweck der Infrastruktur.

Gregor Sailer studied communication design in Dortmund, with a focus on photography. And it was there, in the Ruhr area, that the *Subraum* series came about in a collaboration with his fellow students, Johannes Naumann and Stefan Tuschy. The camera became the young photographers' research instrument of choice as they set about taking a closer look at these largely unexplored subterranean urban landscapes. Their urban expeditions took them to the NRW State Archive in Düsseldorf, a civil defence bunker in Duisburg, the Bochum underground railway, the airport, and the Dortmund City and State Library.

Subraum features representative locations below ground in what was once Germany's industrial heartland. The vast majority of the resident population has no access to the infrastructure that lies beneath the surface of these towns and cities; indeed, most of it does not even impinge on their general awareness. Yet, as a result of the strong emphasis on shapes and colours, these spaces remain abstract and vague. The photographs are not intended to document and retrace these sites; rather, they provide the photographic framework, in keeping with the aesthetic potential of the architectural shapes and colours, regardless of the infrastructure's intended use.

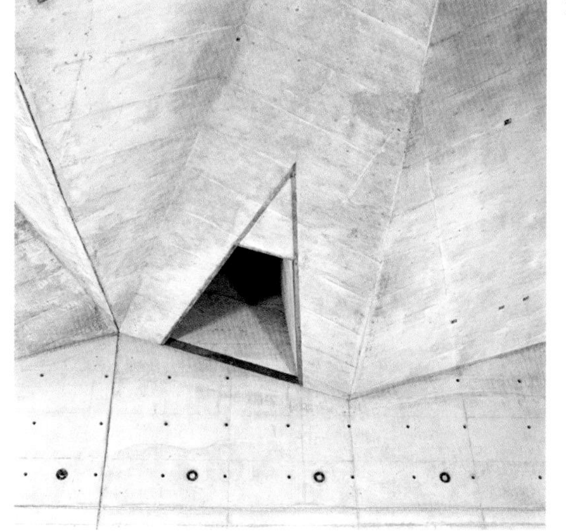

1 →

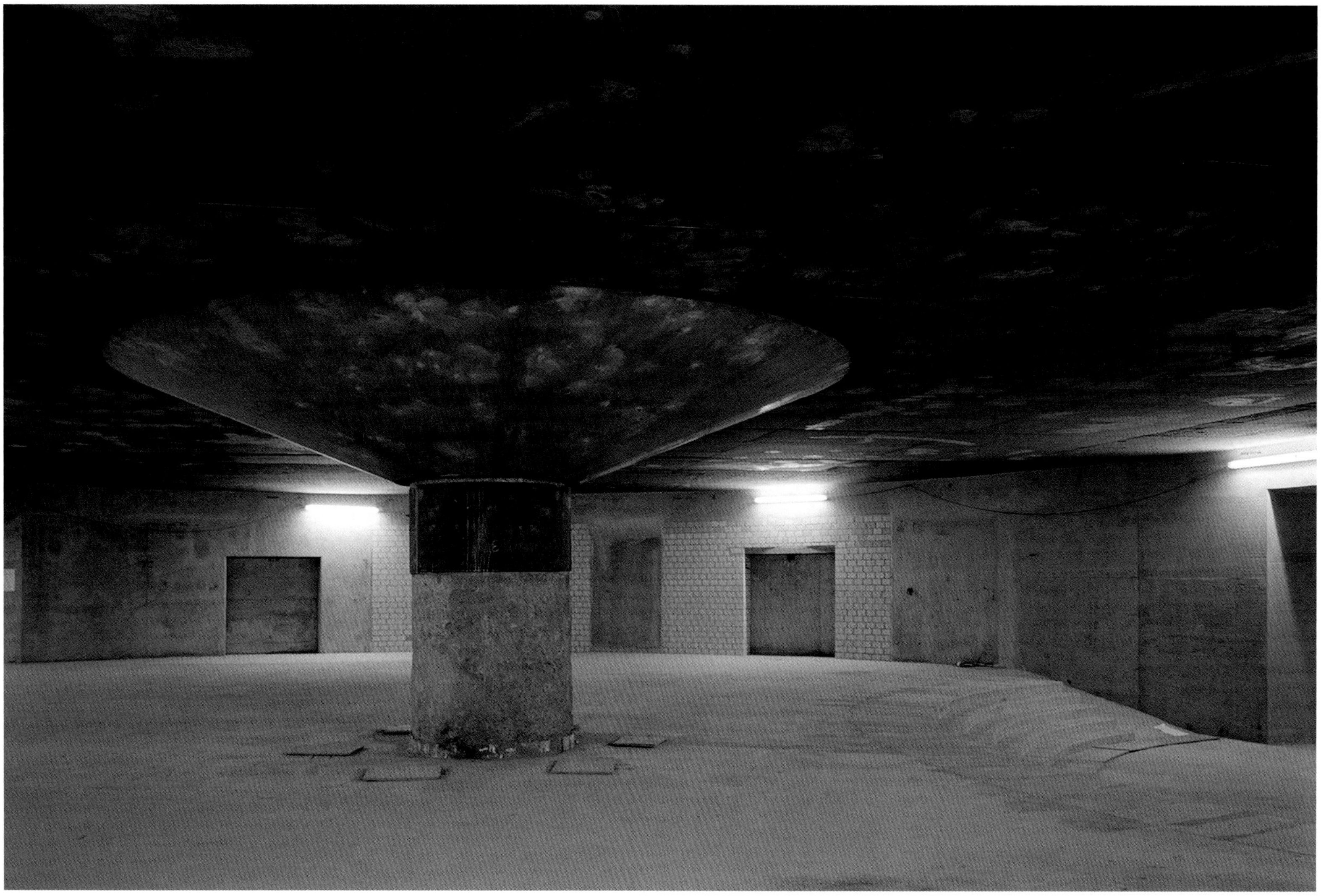

2

3 →

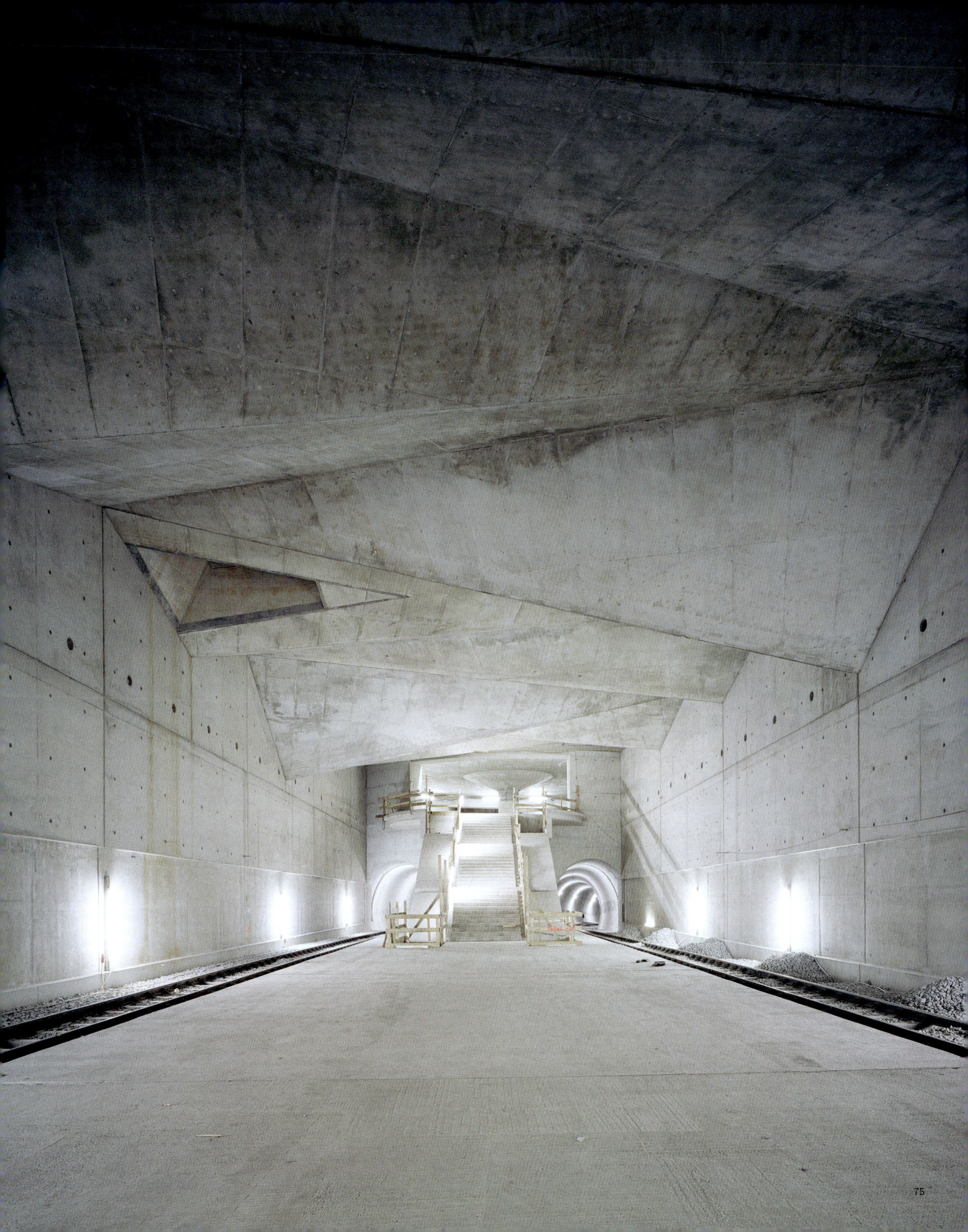

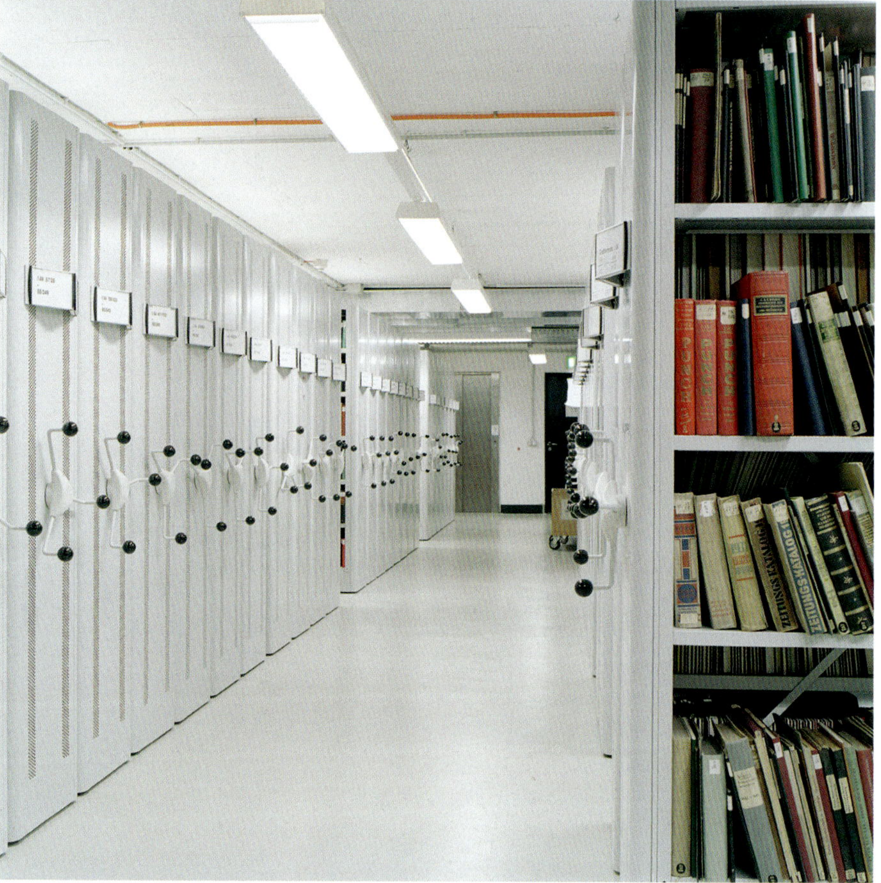

5

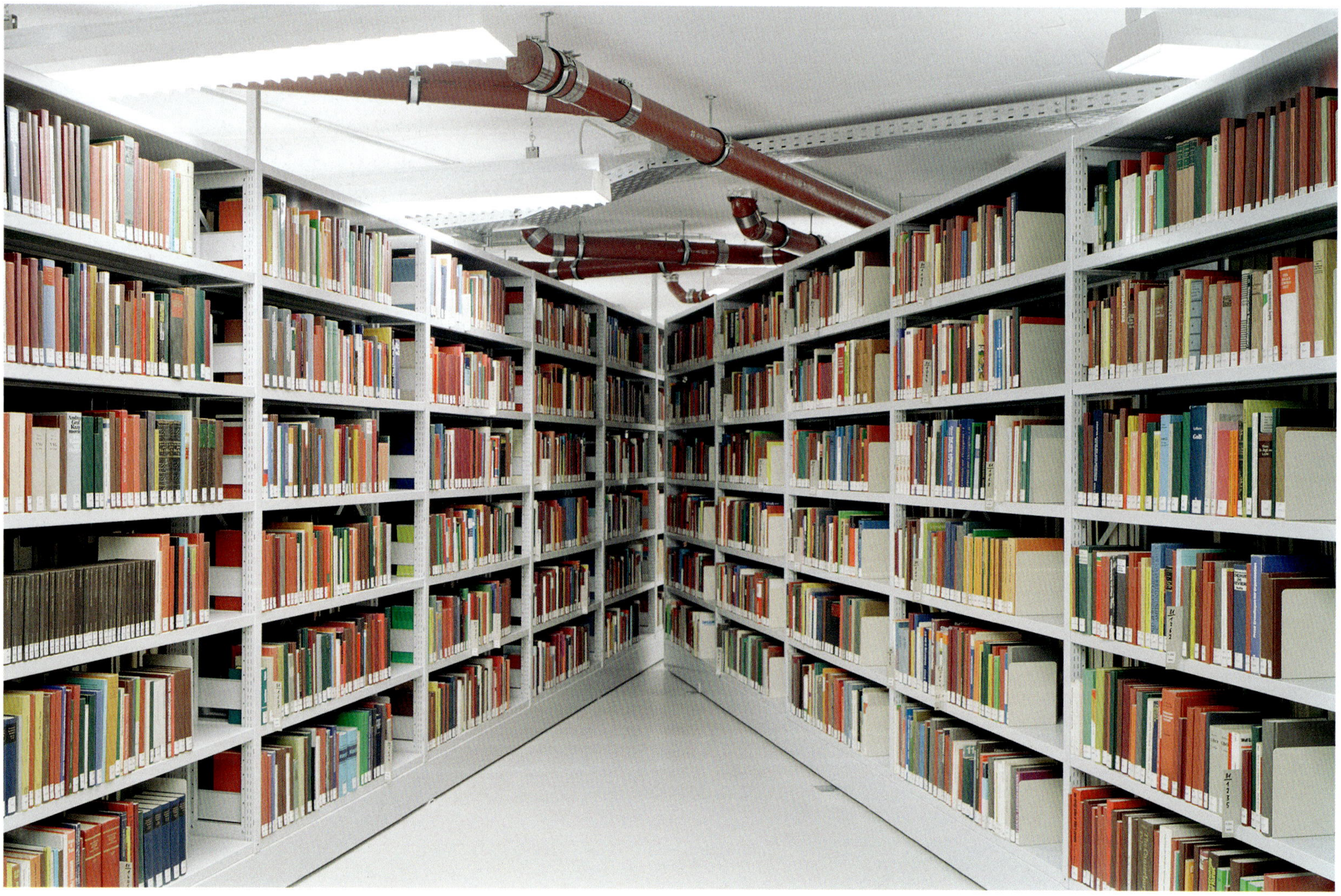

6

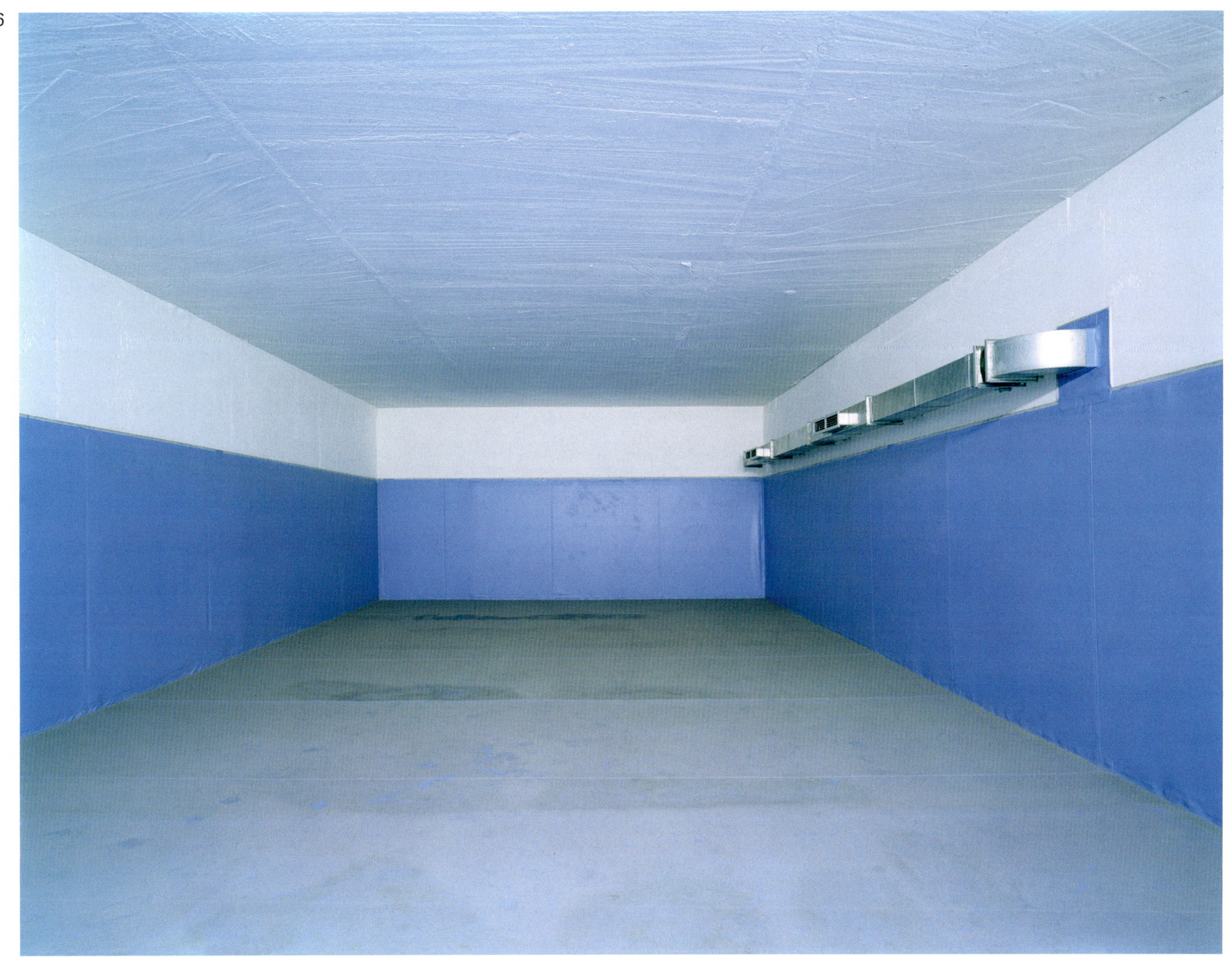

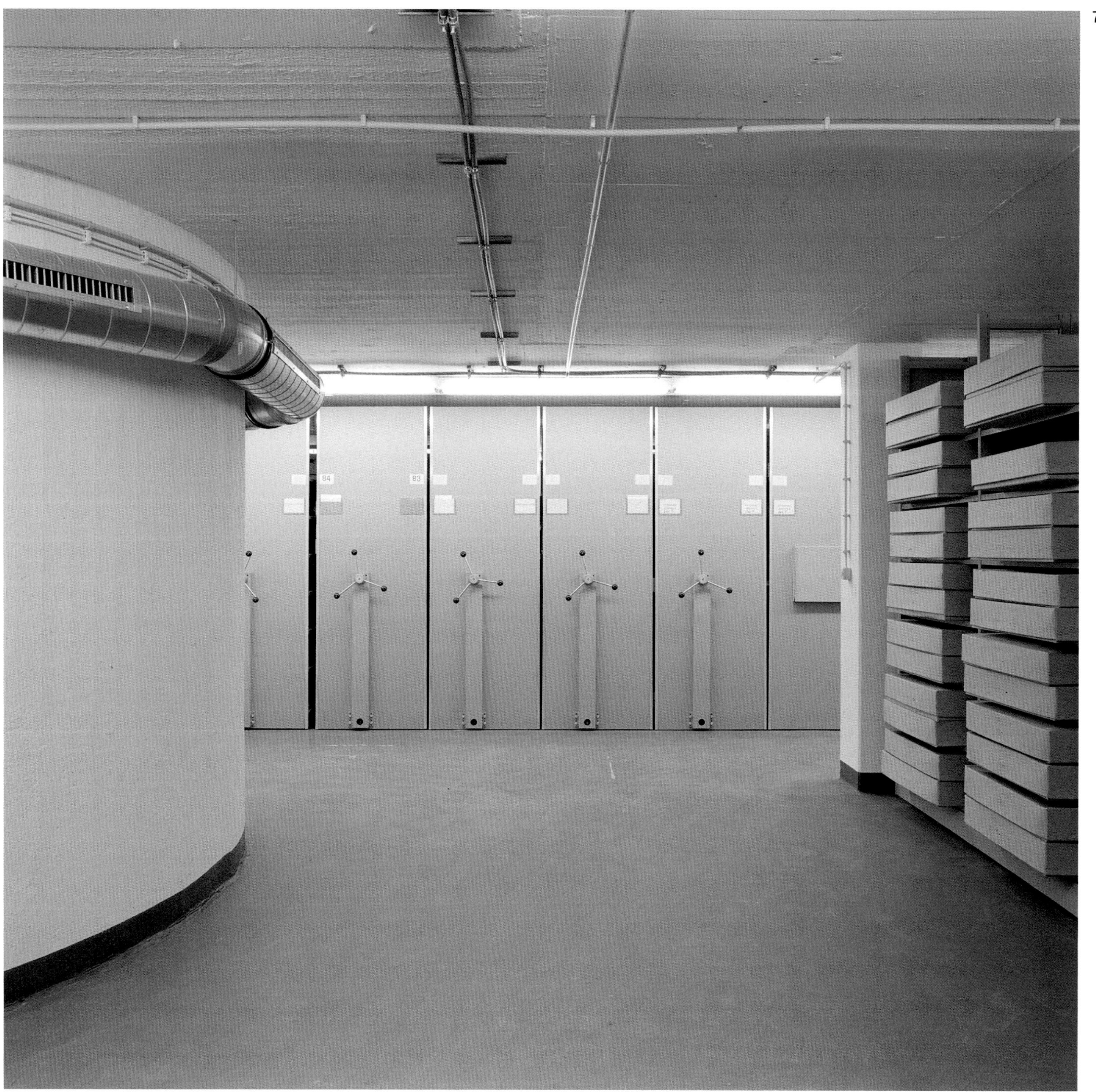

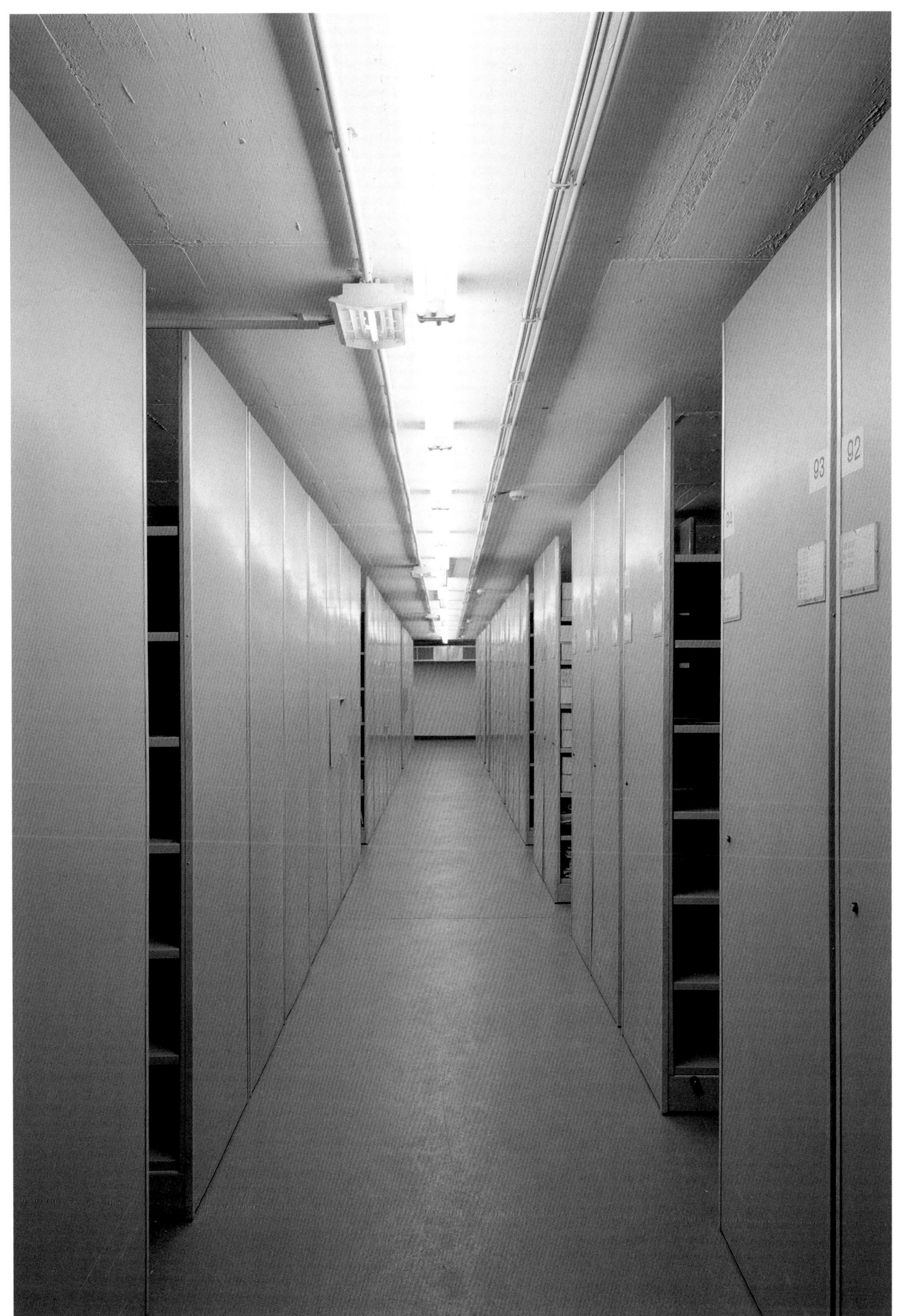

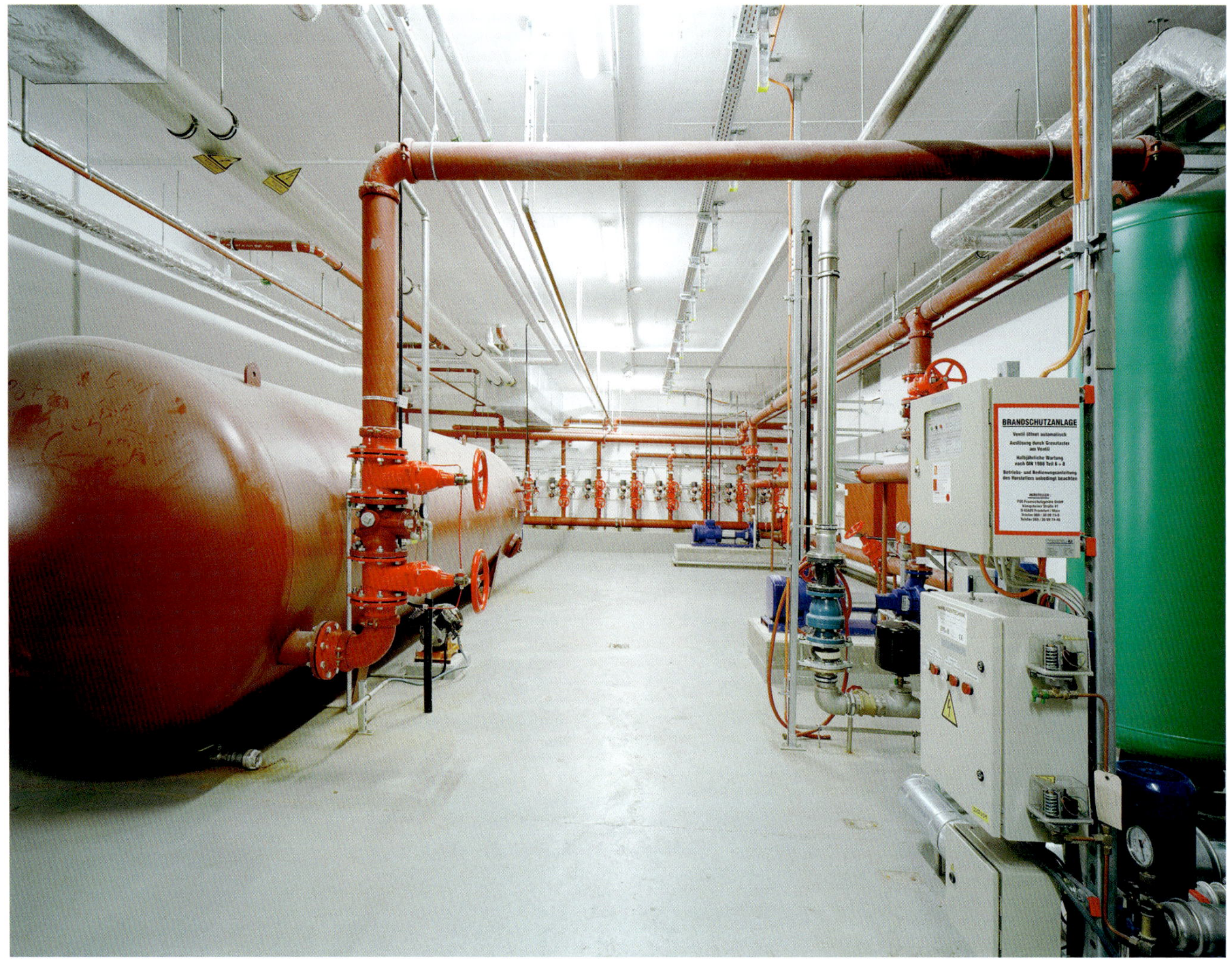

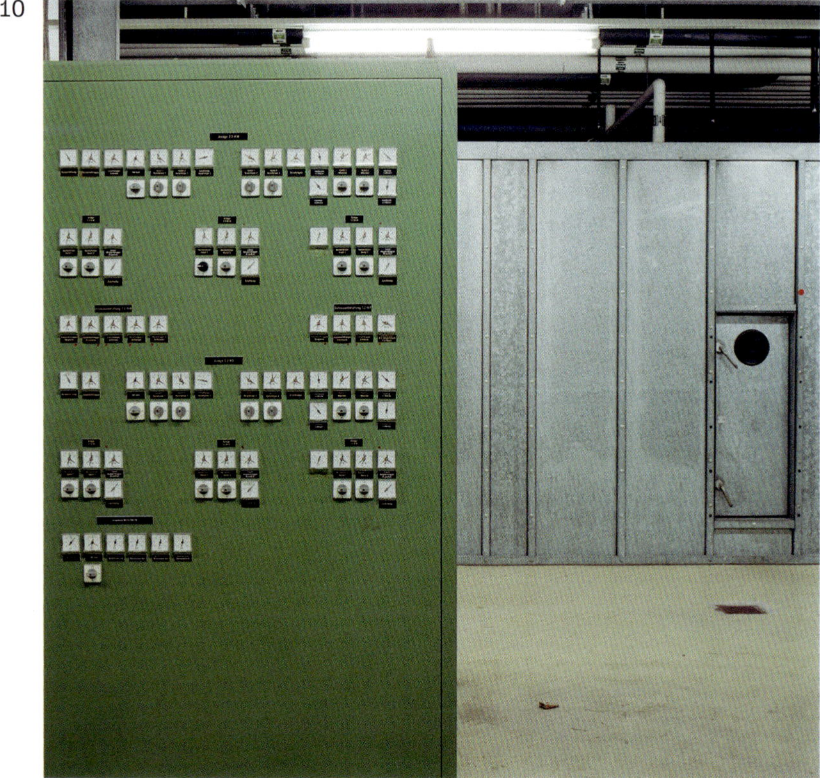

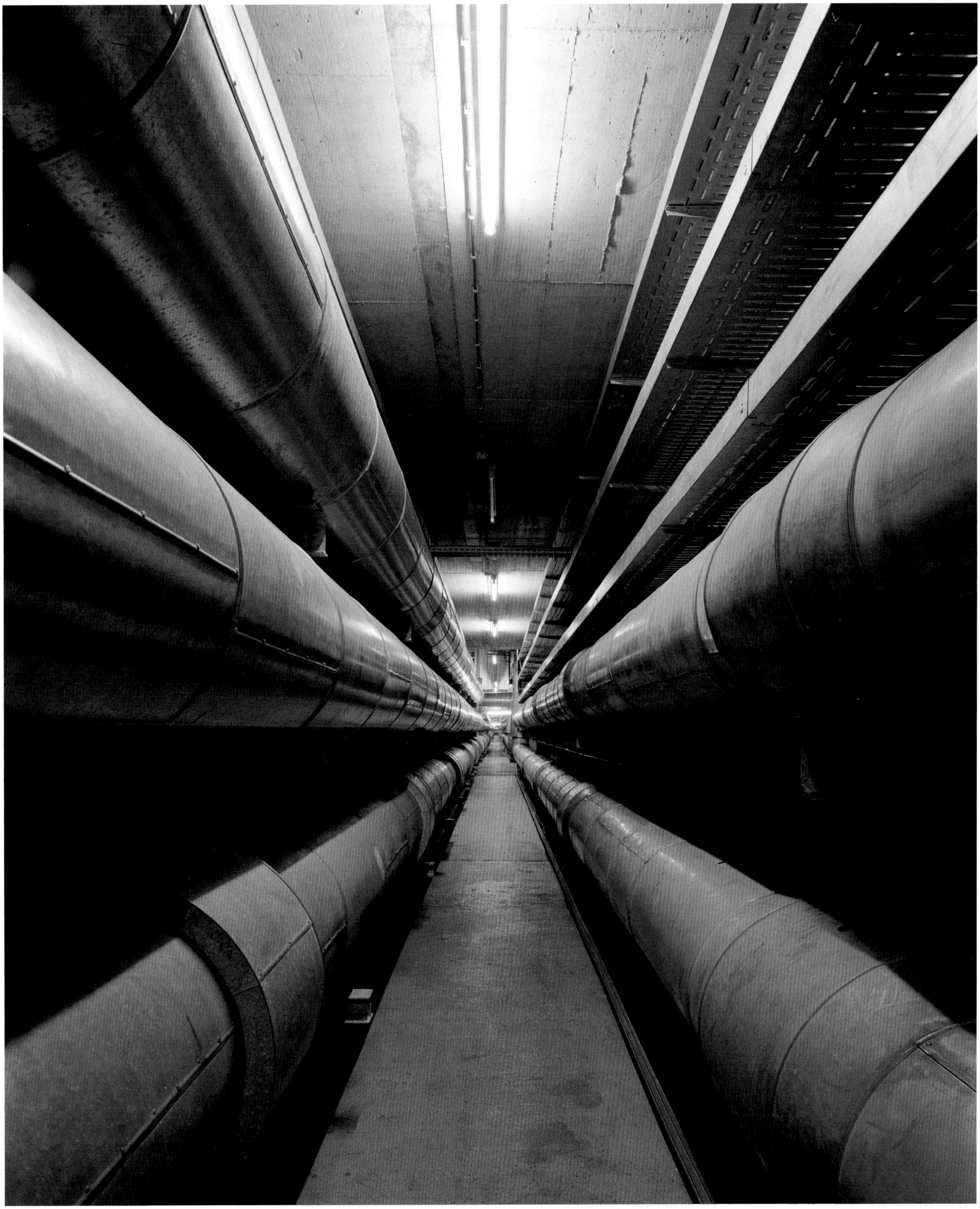

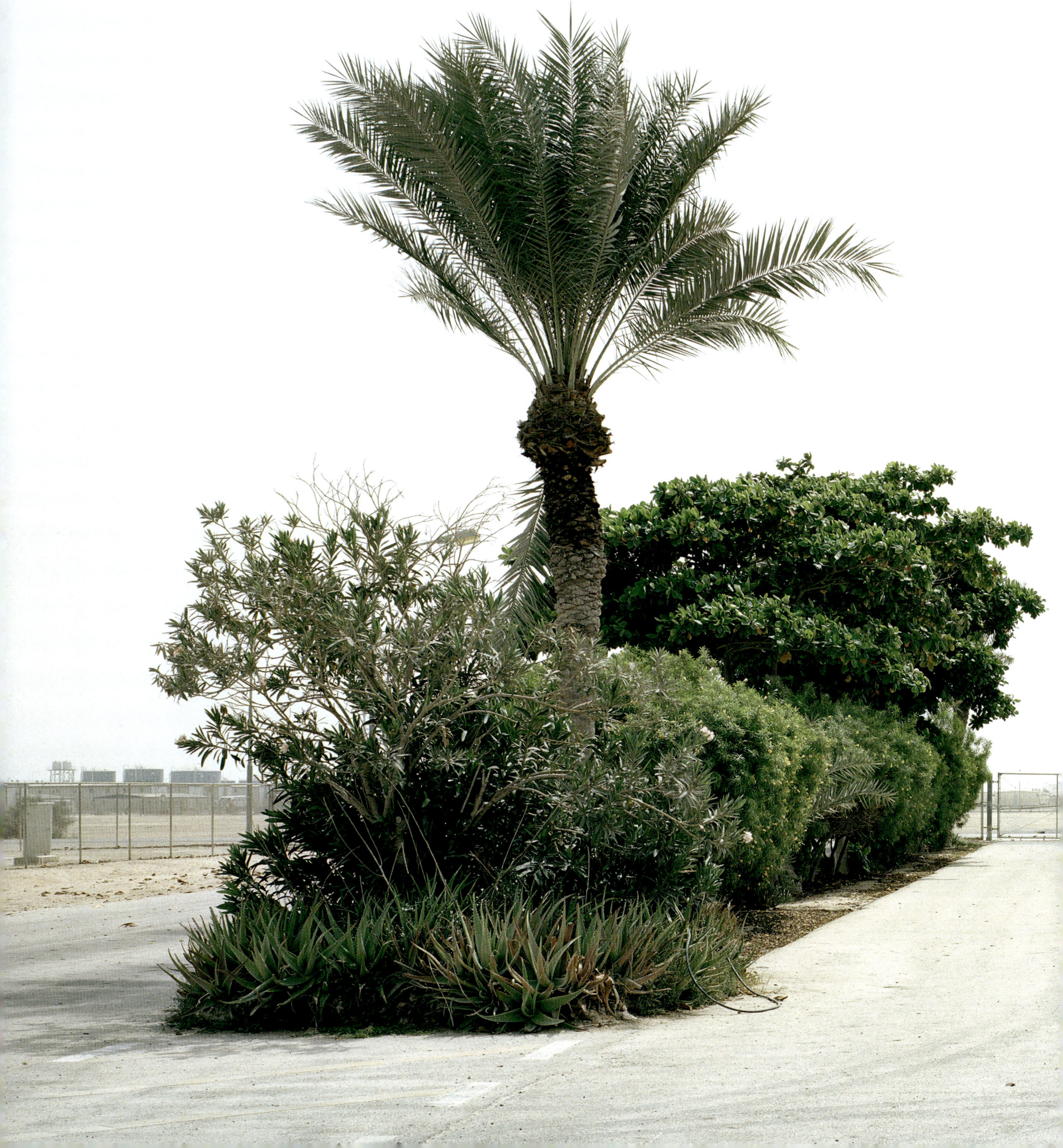

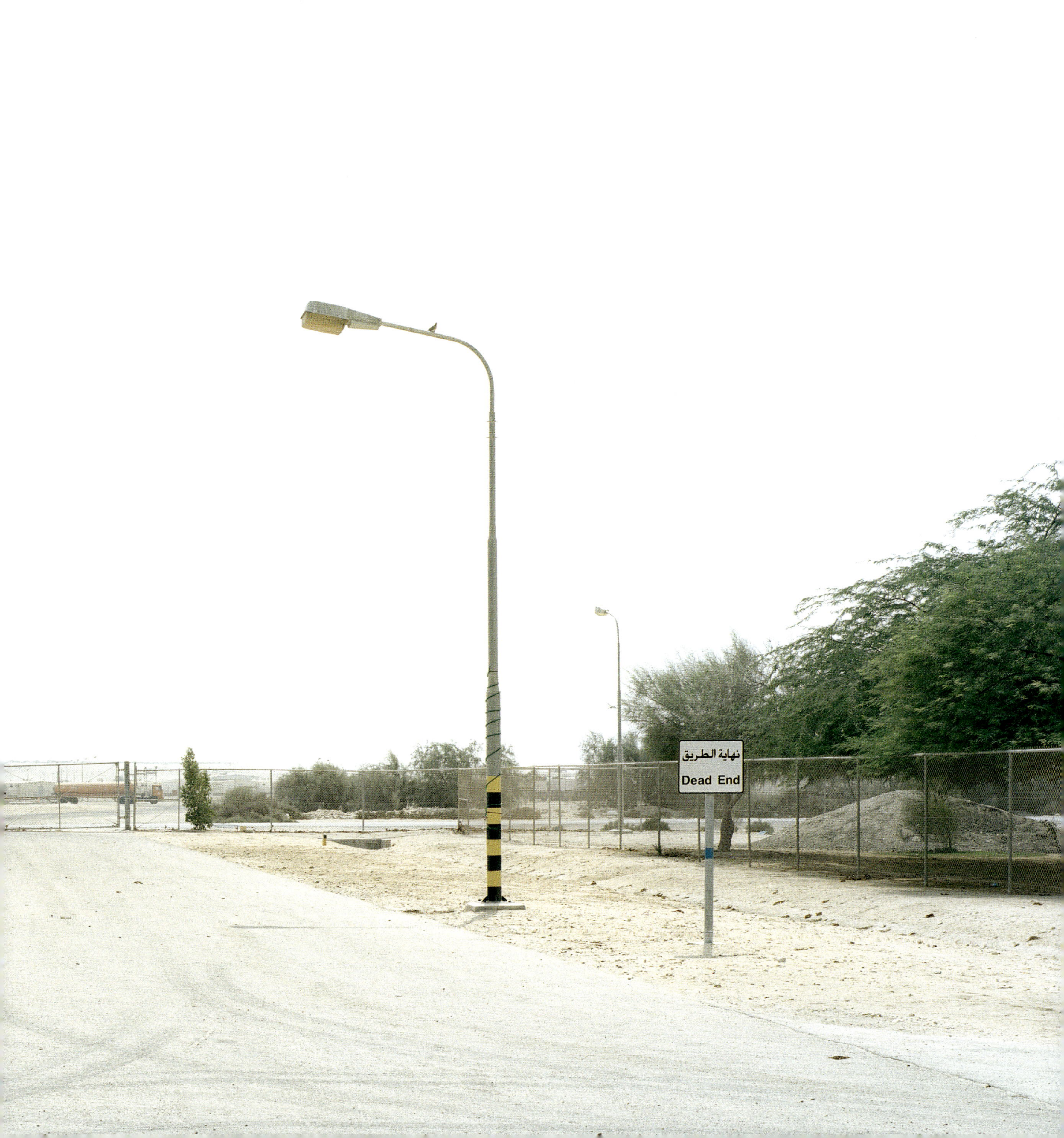
نهاية الطريق
Dead End

Closed Cities

Gregor Sailers Werk ist geprägt von dem Wunsch, ungewöhnli-che und komplexe, vom Menschen geprägte Gegenden visuell und inhaltlich zu untersuchen, zu verstehen und zu vermitteln. Um solche Orte ausfindig zu machen, dorthin zu reisen und vor Ort zu fotografieren, nimmt er eine lange und intensive Vorbe-reitungszeit in Kauf.

Mit *Closed Cities* erkundet Sailer Orte, denen die Abschottung nach außen gemein ist. Die bewusste Abgrenzung lässt erahnen, wie aufwendig und schwierig es ist, dort hineinzukommen, noch dazu mit einer Kamera. Sailers Engagement, sein diplomati-sches Geschick und seine Ausdauer helfen ihm dabei, Sonder-genehmigungen, Leumundszeugnisse und Referenzen zu bekom-men und so den Verdacht der Sensationsgier oder gar Spionage auszuräumen. Sein großer Werkzyklus von abgeriegelten Städ-ten in verschiedenen Weltgegenden umfasst Bilder von einer Diamanten-, einer Kupfer-, einer Öl- und einer Flüchtlingsstadt sowie einer Gated Town.

Gregor Sailer's work is characterised by a desire to explore, understand, and convey visually and contextually unusual and complex places that have been shaped by human be-ings. It takes a long and intense phase of preparations for Gregor Sailer to locate such places, travel there, and photo-graph on site.

In *Closed Cities,* Sailer explores places that have one trait in common: they are all closed off from the outside world. Their intentional isolation gives some idea of how elaborate and difficult it is to reach these locations, even more so with a camera. Sailer's commitment, diplomatic skills, and perseverance have enabled him to obtain the necessary special permits, certificates of good conduct, and references, thereby dispelling any suspicions of sensationalism, let alone espionage. His major series of works, featuring sealed-off towns and cities in various parts of the world, include pho-tographs of a diamond town, copper town, oil town, refugee town, and gated town.

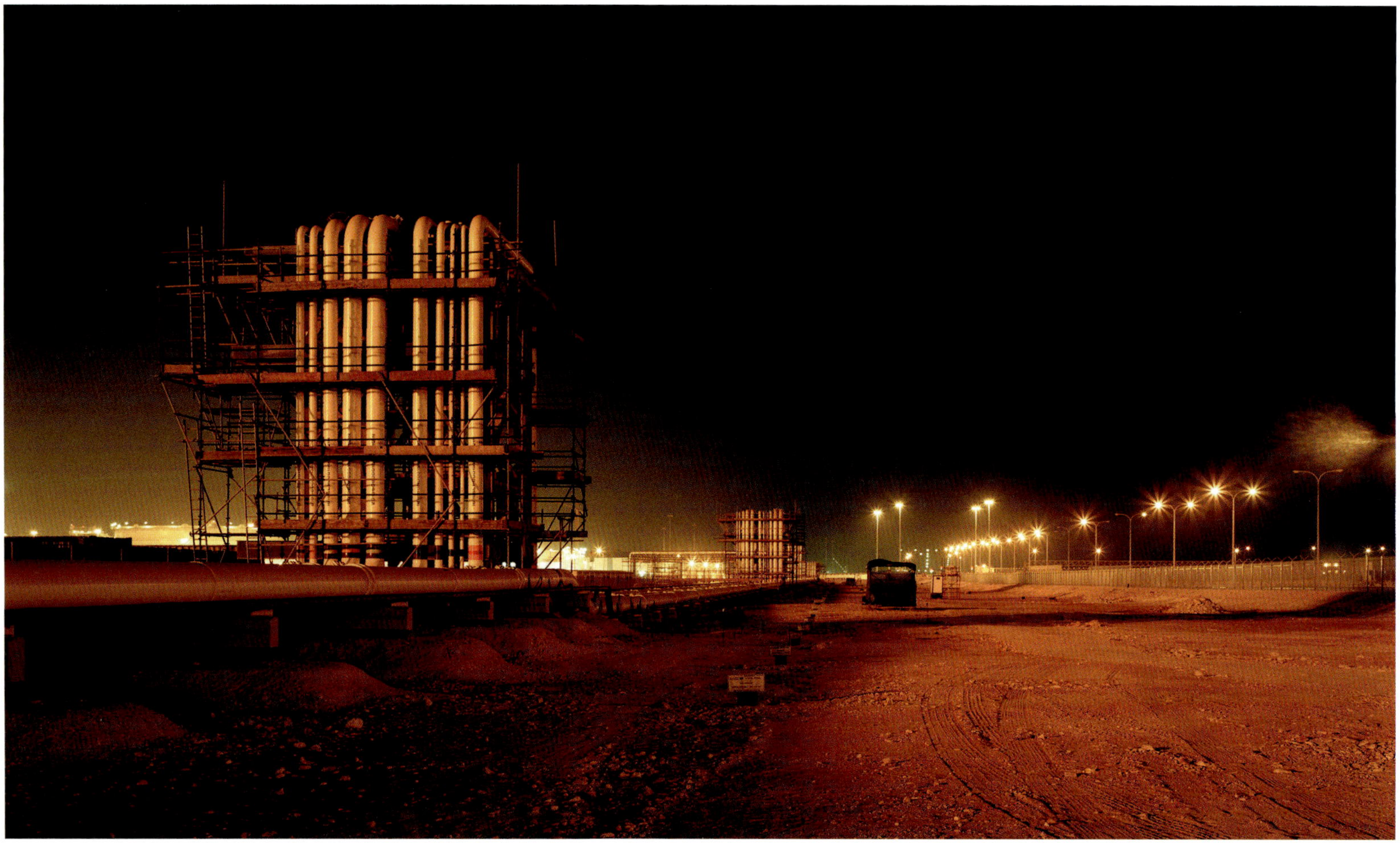

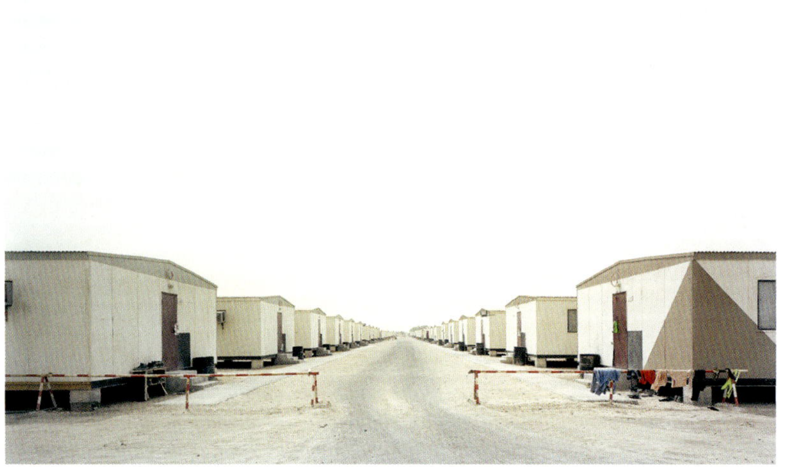

1

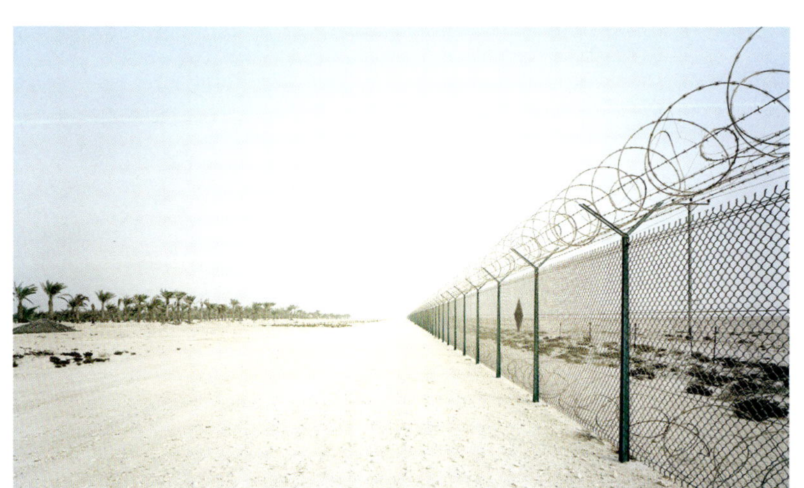

2
3

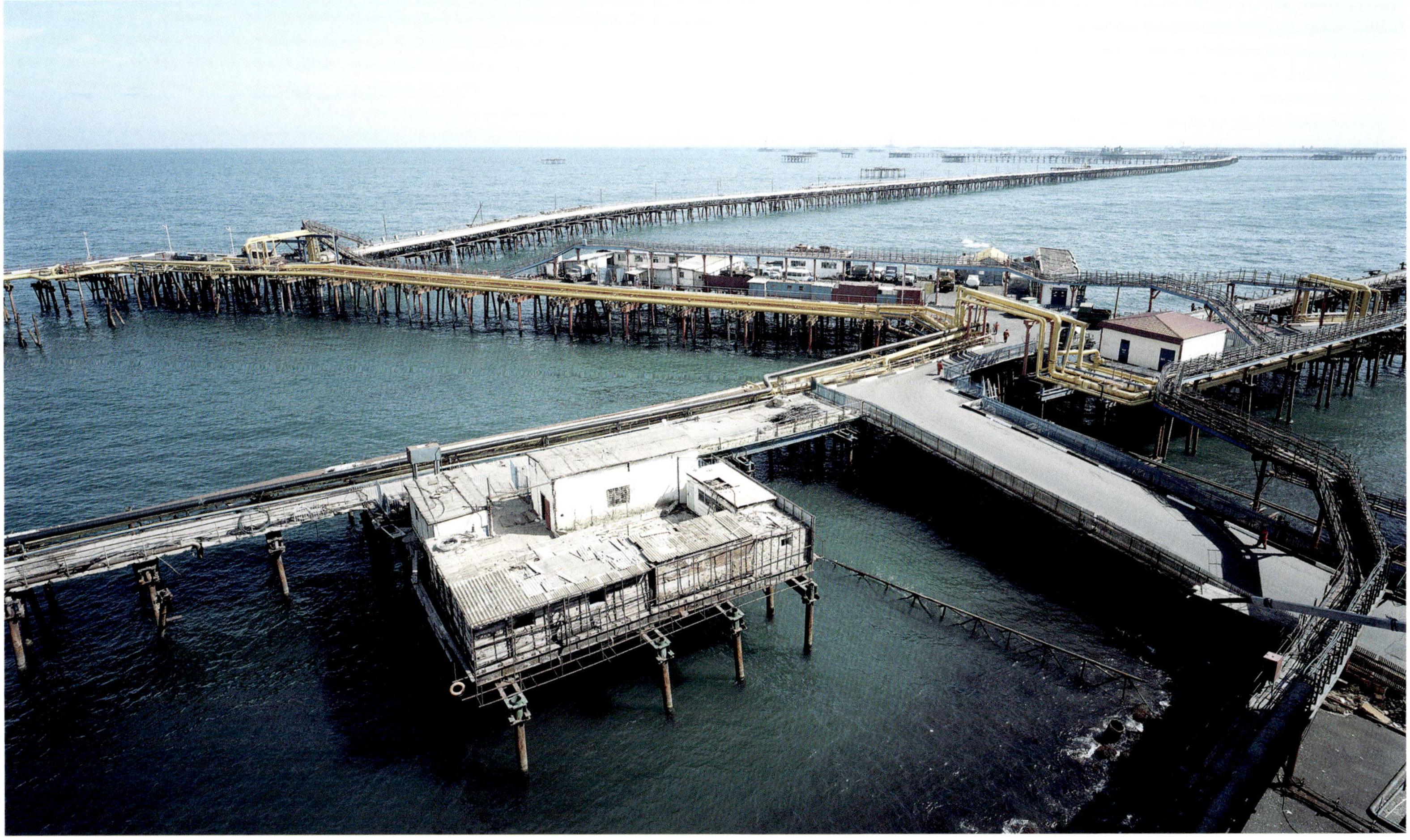

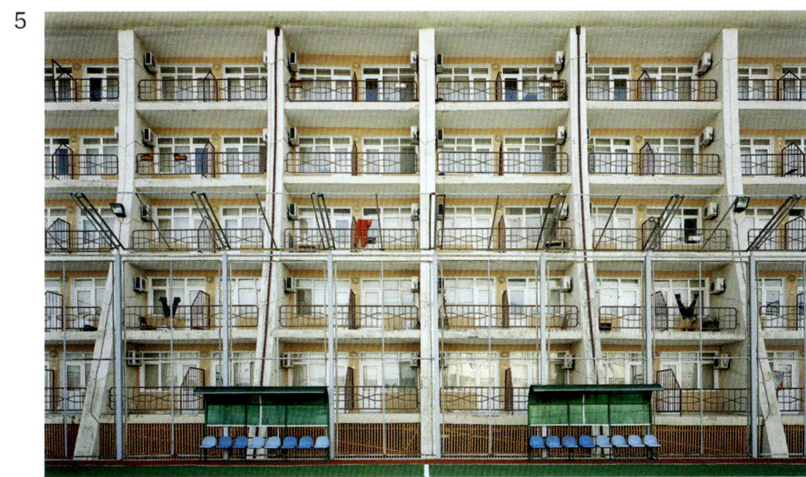

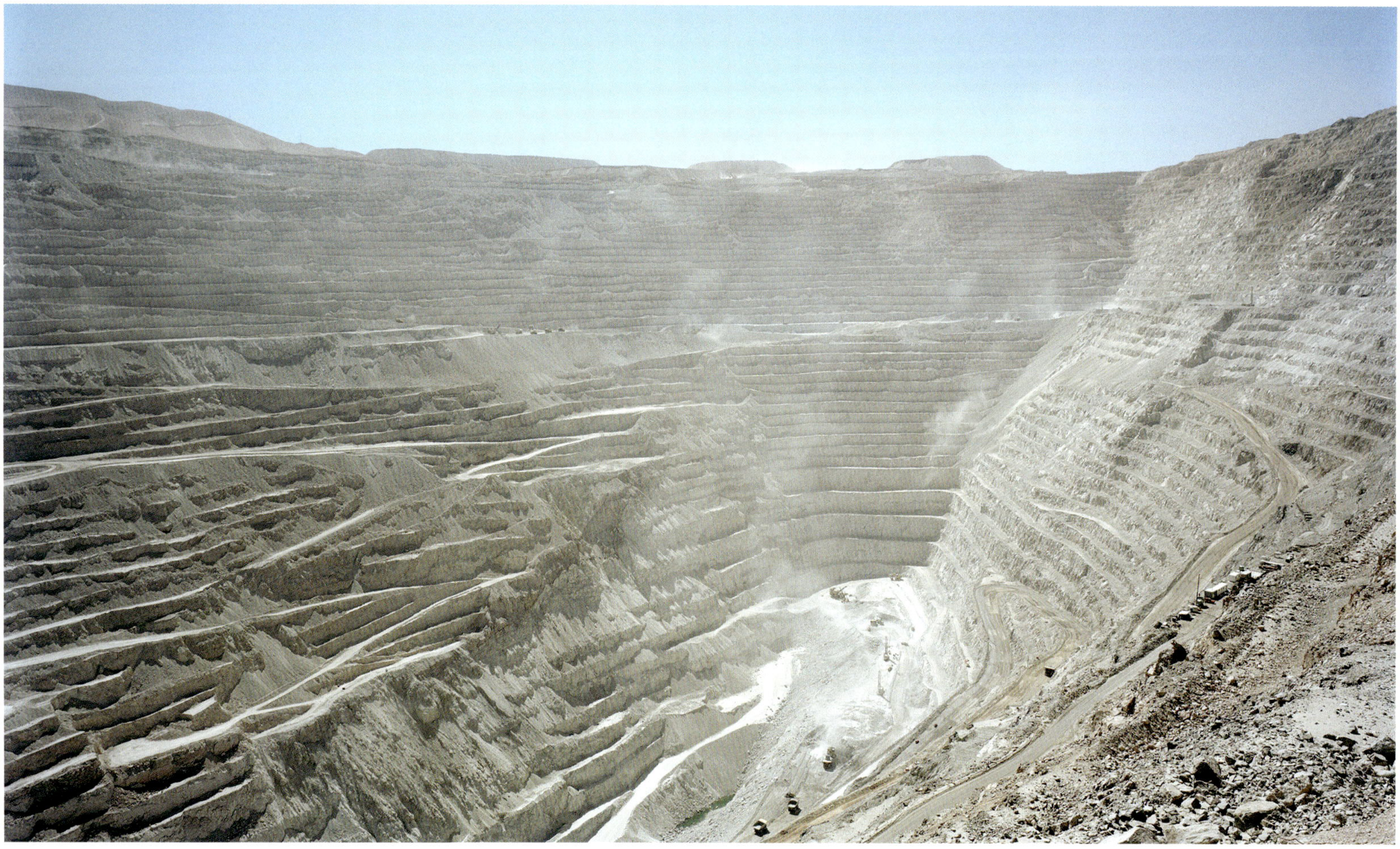

6

7
8

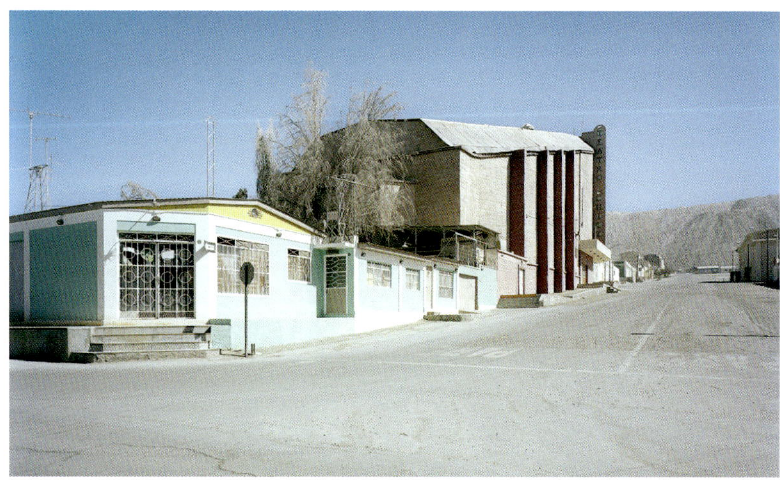

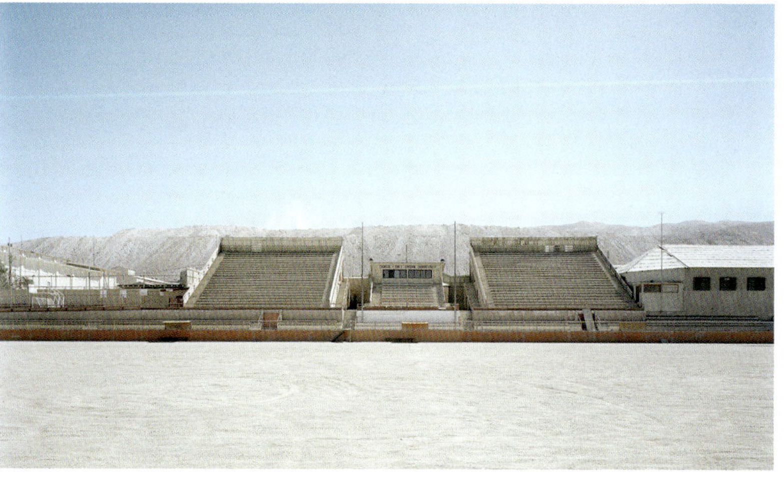

9

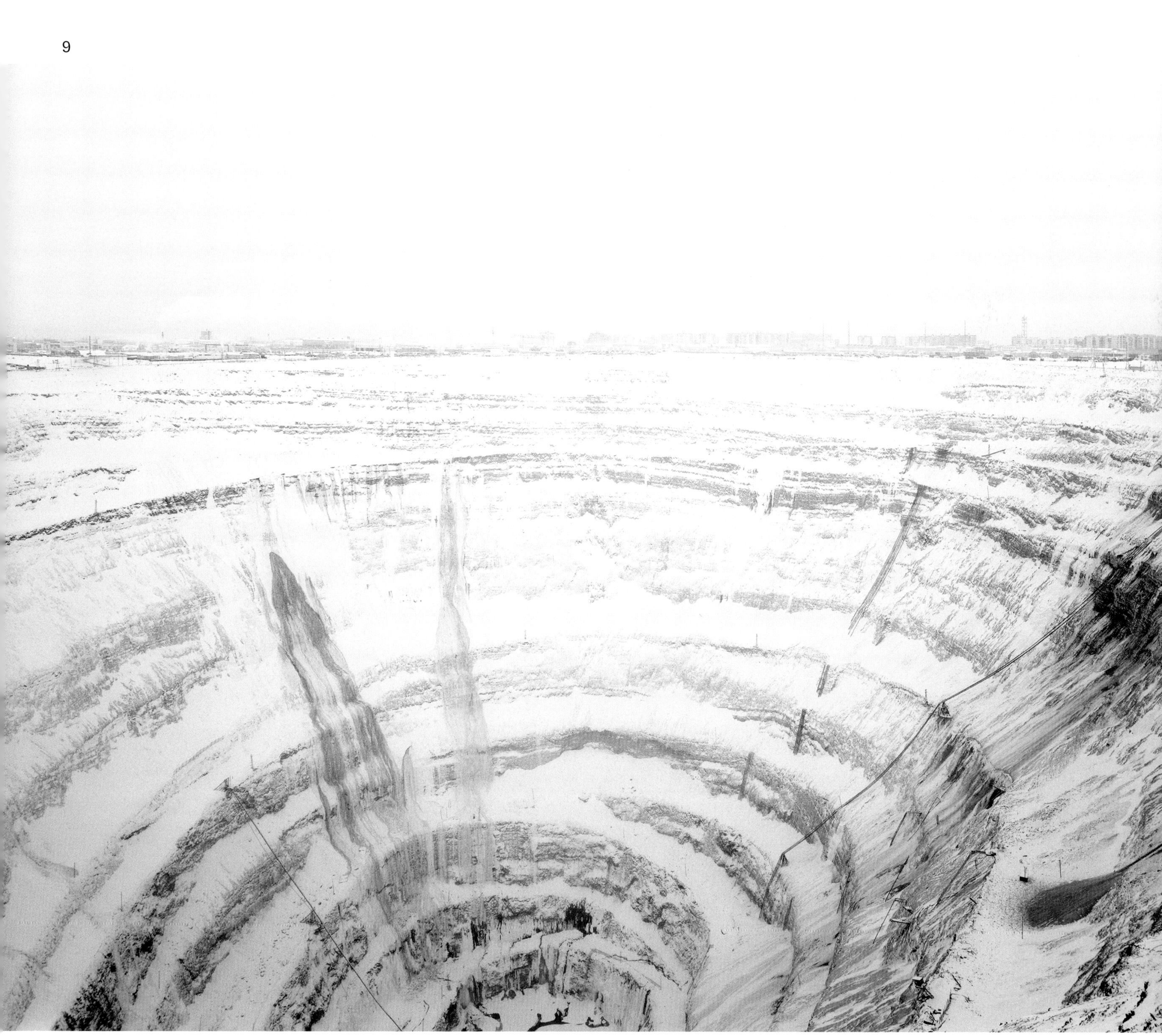

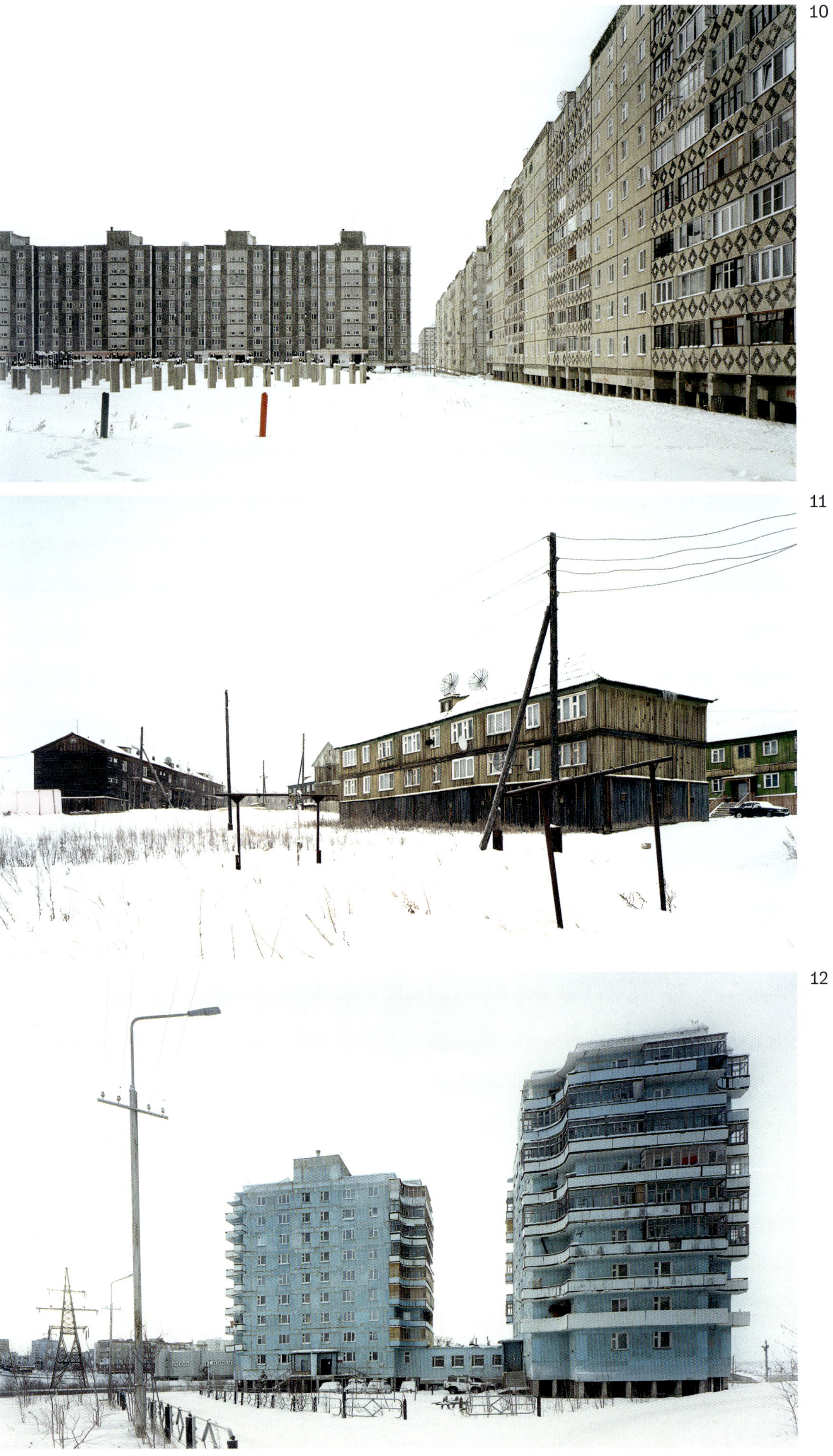

10

11

12

13

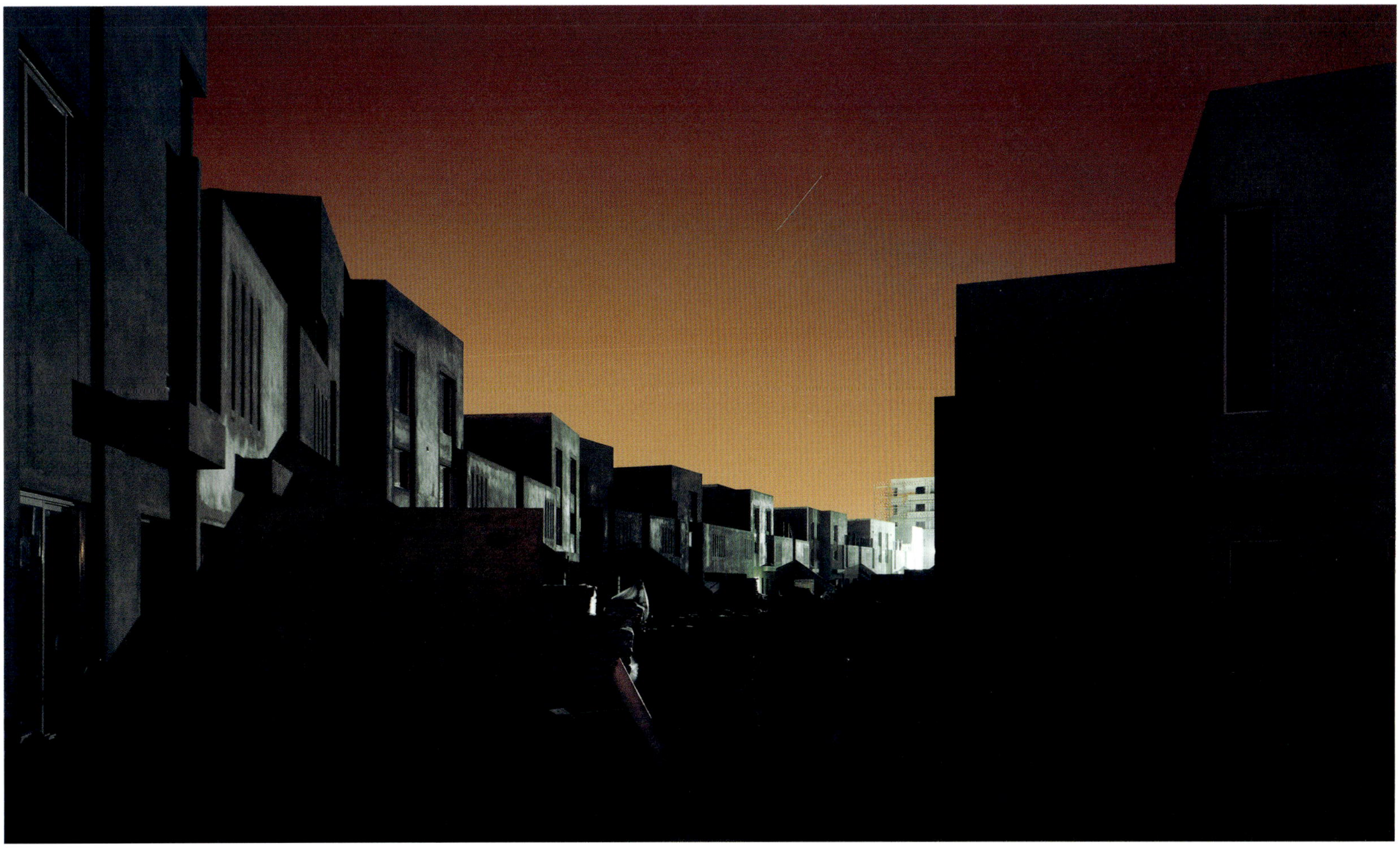

14

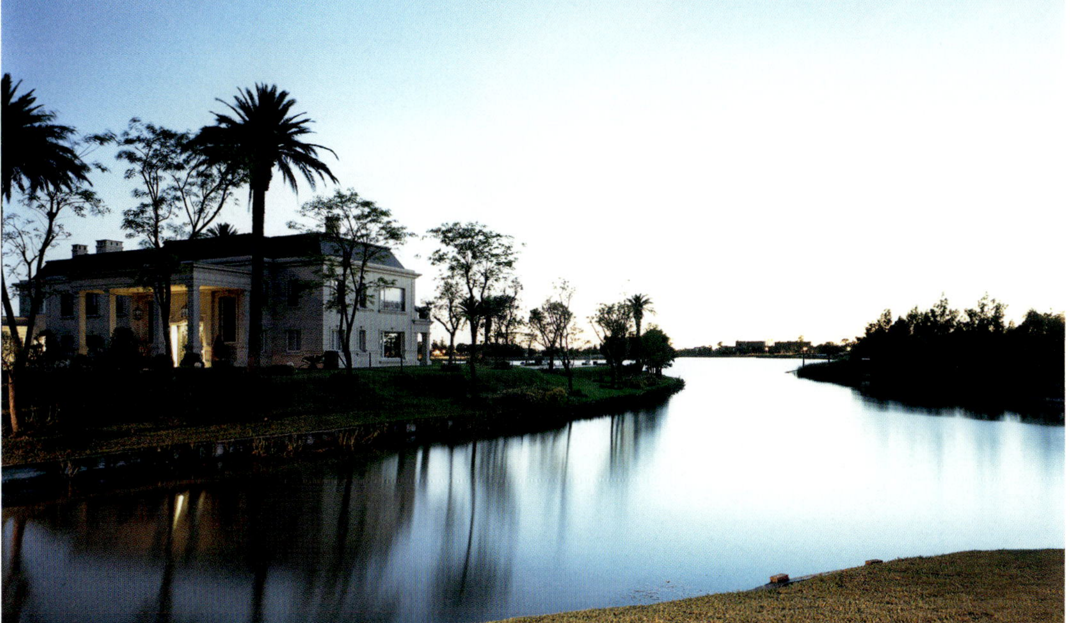

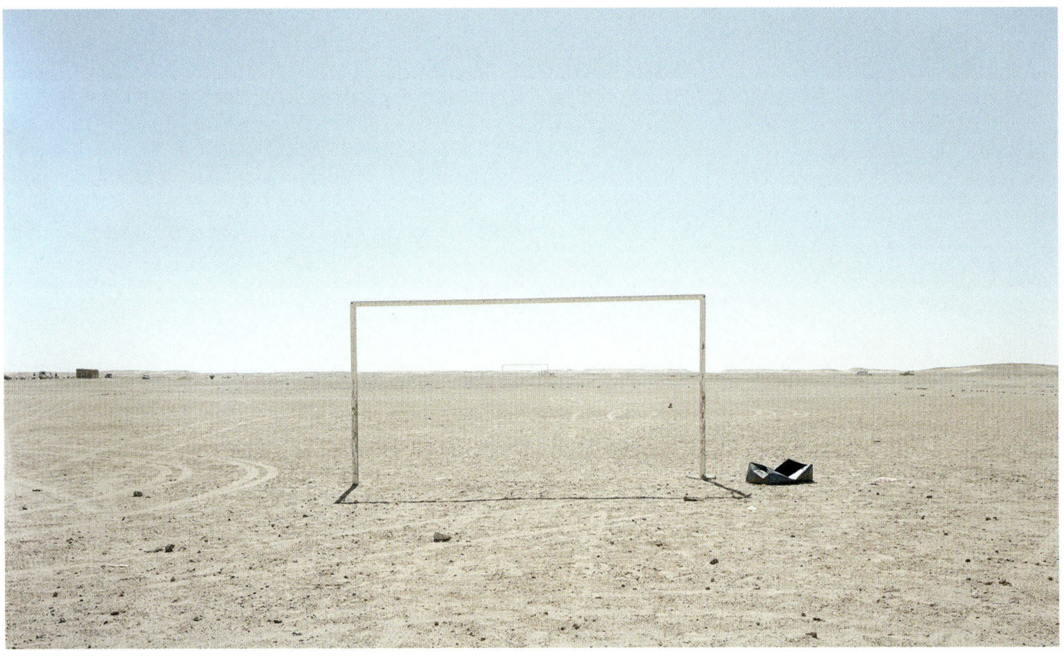

15

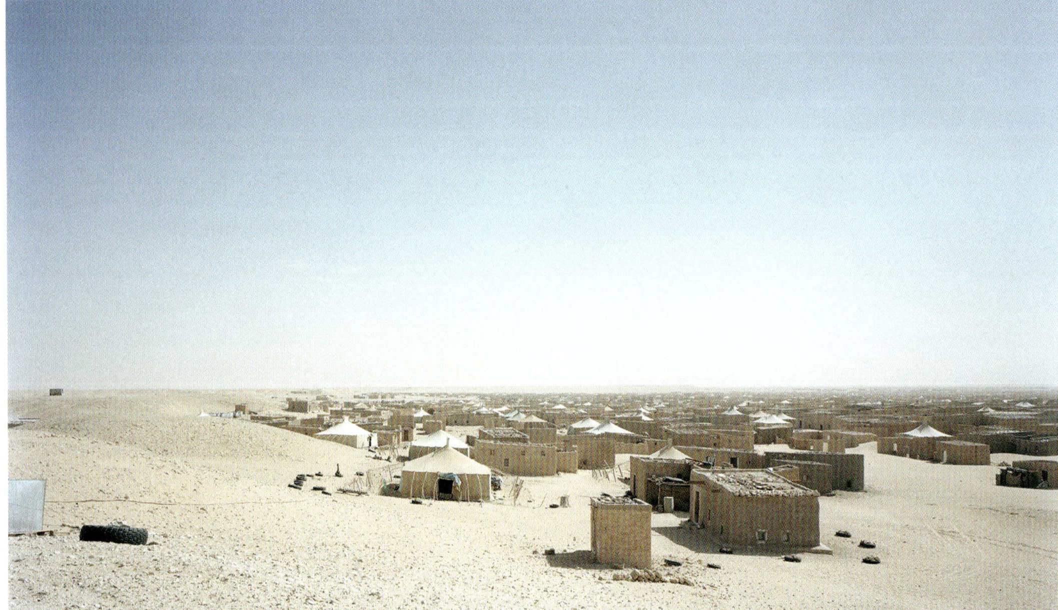

16

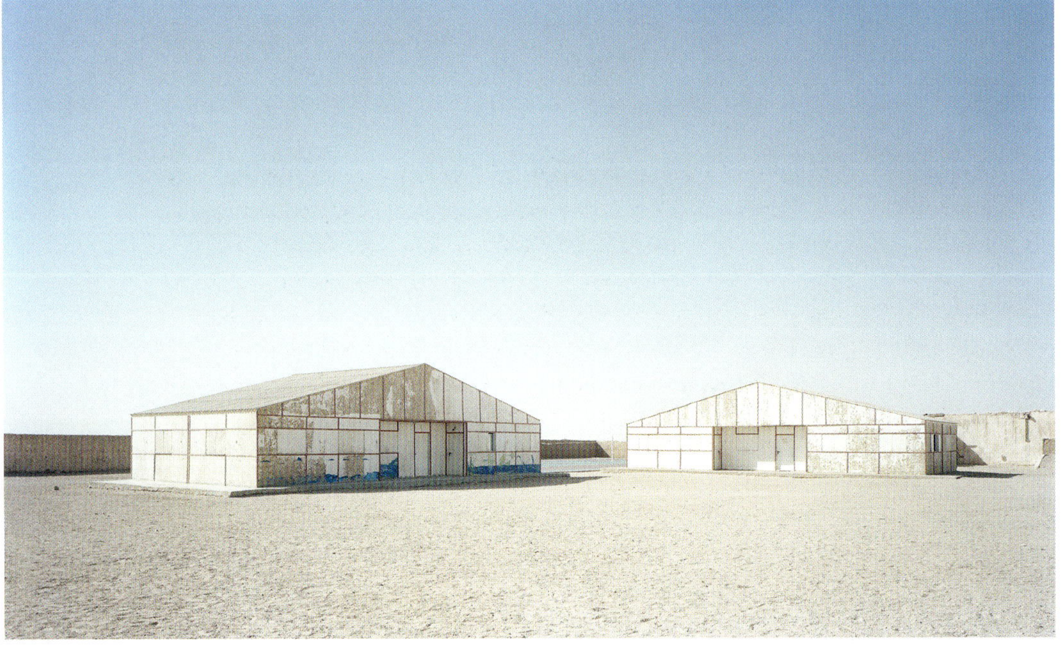

17

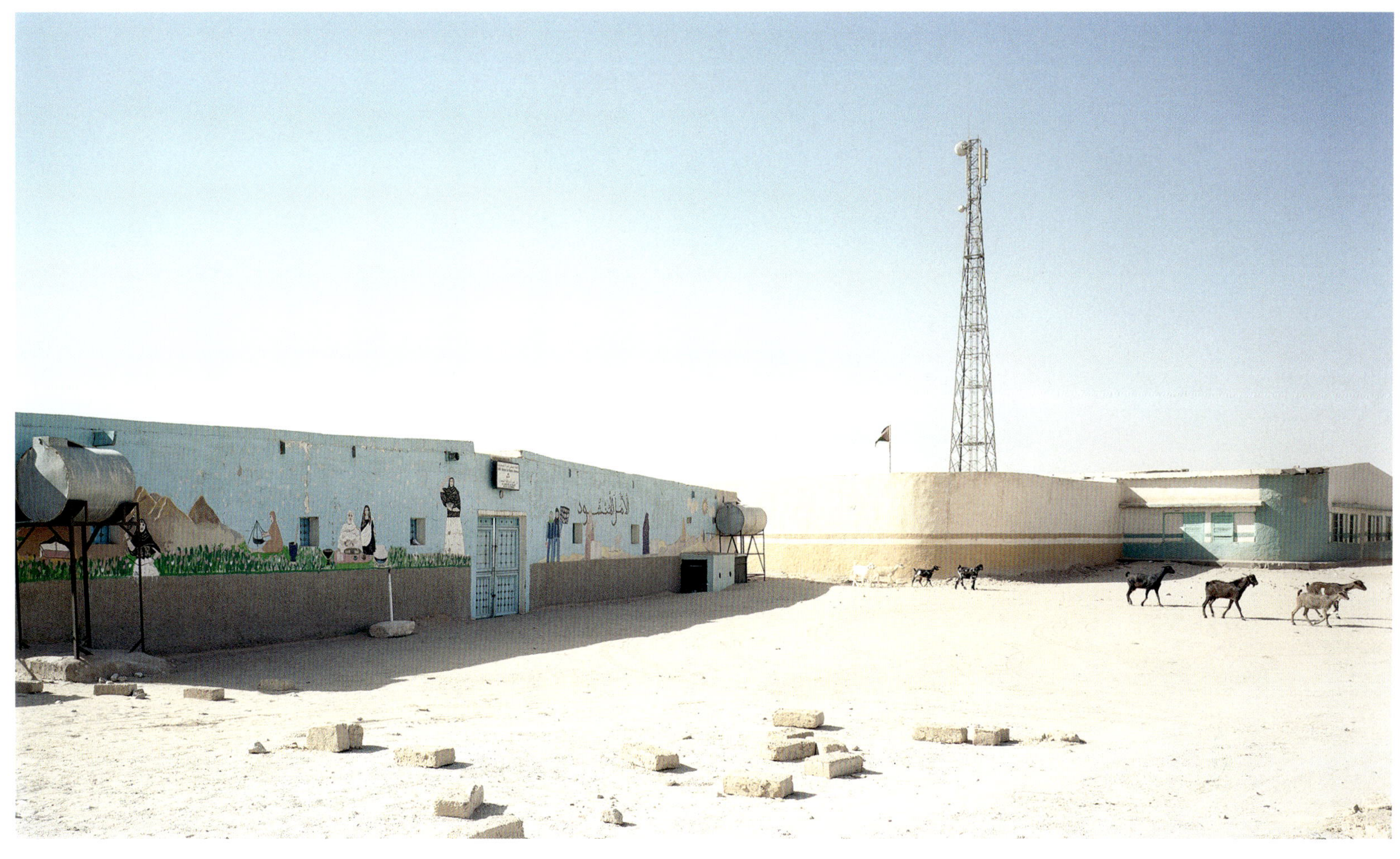

18

„Mittels aufwendiger Architektur- und Landschaftsfotografie bewege ich mich in diesem künstlich geschaffenen, durch Mauern oder die ihn umgebende lebensfeindliche Landschaft hermetisch abgeriegelten urbanen Raum, um seine verborgene Existenz sichtbar zu machen. Es sind Orte der Rohstoffförderung, Militäranlagen, Flüchtlingslager oder aber Gated Communities für Wohlhabende. Diese zeitlich begrenzten urbanen Siedlungsformen repräsentieren auf prägnante Weise die Herausforderungen, denen die Menschheit Anfang des 21. Jahrhunderts ausgesetzt ist: schwindenden Ressourcen, Klimawandel, politischen Konflikten oder dem Bedürfnis nach uneingeschränkter Sicherheit."

Gregor Sailer, „Closed Cites, 2009–2012", www.gregorsailer.com/Projects/Closed-Cities [20. Juli 2022].

"By means of refined architectural and landscape photography, I visualize these otherwise effectively invisible, artificially created urban agglomerations that are hermetically sealed off from the eyes of the world either by walls or by their hostile surroundings. The subjects are raw-material mines, military bases, and refugee camps, as well as gated communities for the wealthy. These temporally circumscribed forms of urban settlement succinctly reflect and reveal a historical turning point that the world is now experiencing at the turn of the 21st century: dwindling resources, climate changes, political conflicts, and the wish for absolute security."

Gregor Sailer, "Closed Cites, 2009–2012," www.gregorsailer.com/Projects/Closed-Cities [July 20, 2022].

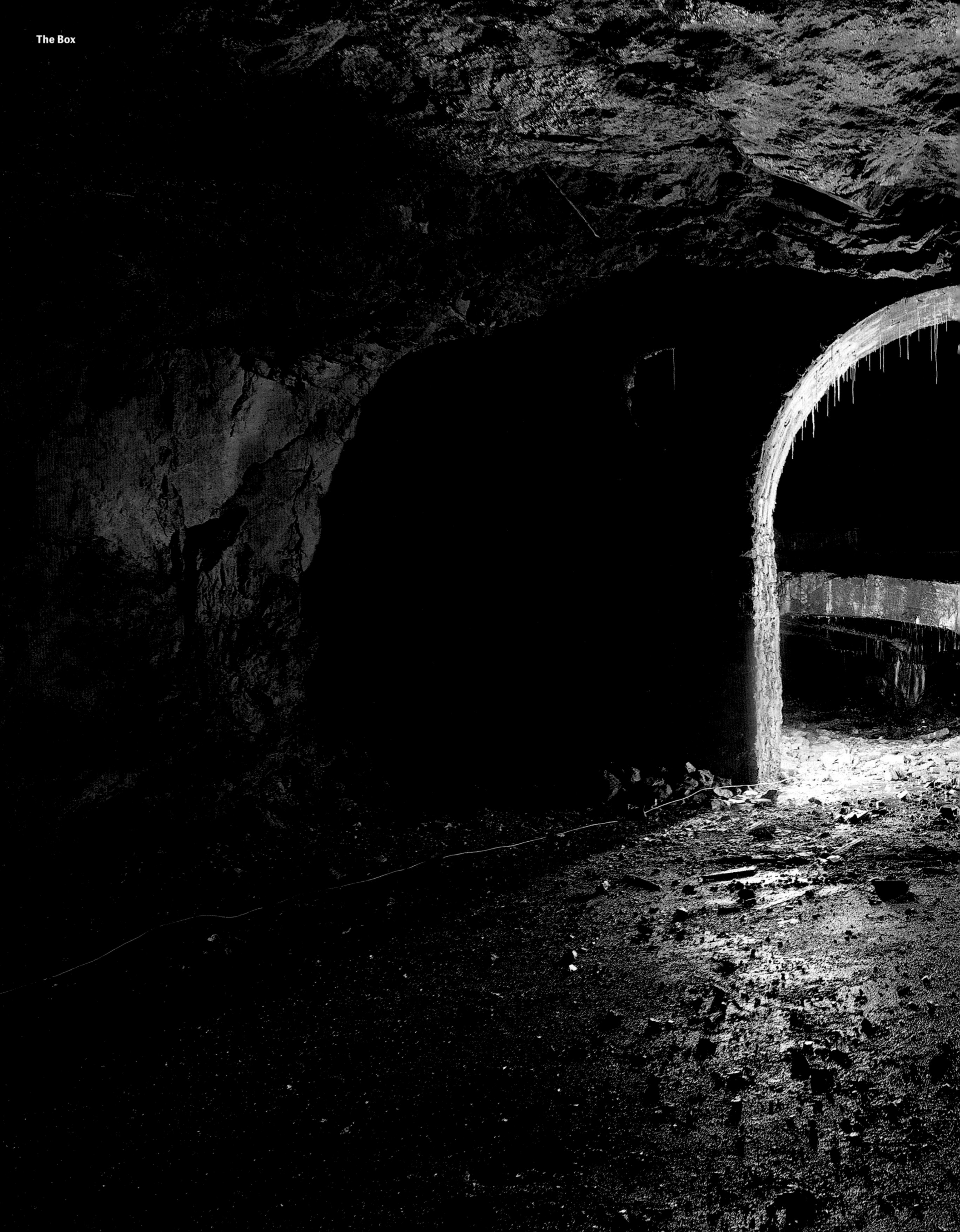

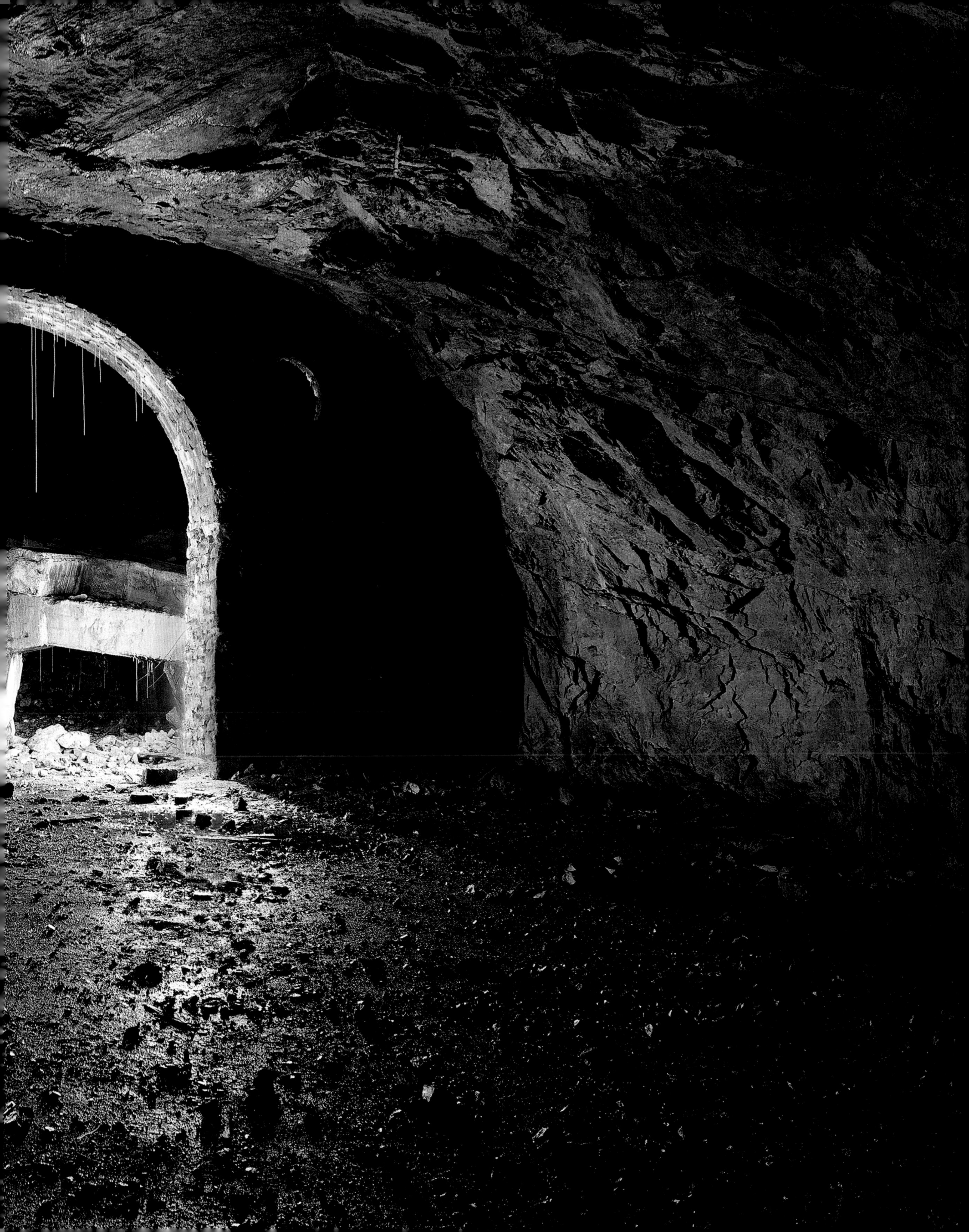

2014–2015

The Box

Diese großformatigen, in hartem Schwarz-Weiß-Kontrast aufgenommenen Bilder zeigen einen seit vielen Jahrzehnten für die Öffentlichkeit unzugänglichen Produktionsort des weltweit ersten Kampfflugzeugs mit Strahltriebwerktechnologie. Dieses wurde im Zweiten Weltkrieg unter unmenschlichen Bedingungen von Zwangsarbeiter:innen in einem Stollen des ehemaligen Schwazer Bergwerks produziert. Die sogenannte „Messerschmitthalle" liegt heute ohne jegliche Infrastruktur in absoluter Dunkelheit in einem Tiroler Bergwerk. Mit einem eigens konzipierten und aufwendig installierten Beleuchtungskonzept bringt Sailer diesen Unort in all seiner Brutalität und Härte zum Vorschein und liefert ein fotografisches Dokument einer sonst unsichtbaren Realität.

These large-format photographs, shot in harshly contrasting black and white, feature a production facility for the world's first fighter aircraft with jet engine propulsion that has remained inaccessible to the general public for many decades. The aircraft were manufactured in an underground gallery of the former Schwaz mine during World War II, but under inhumane conditions using forced labourers. Today, what was once the Messerschmitthalle lies in absolute darkness inside a Tyrolean mine devoid of any infrastructure. Using a purpose-built and elaborately staged lighting concept, Sailer brings to light this inhospitable place in all its brutality and harshness, providing a photographic document of a reality otherwise invisible.

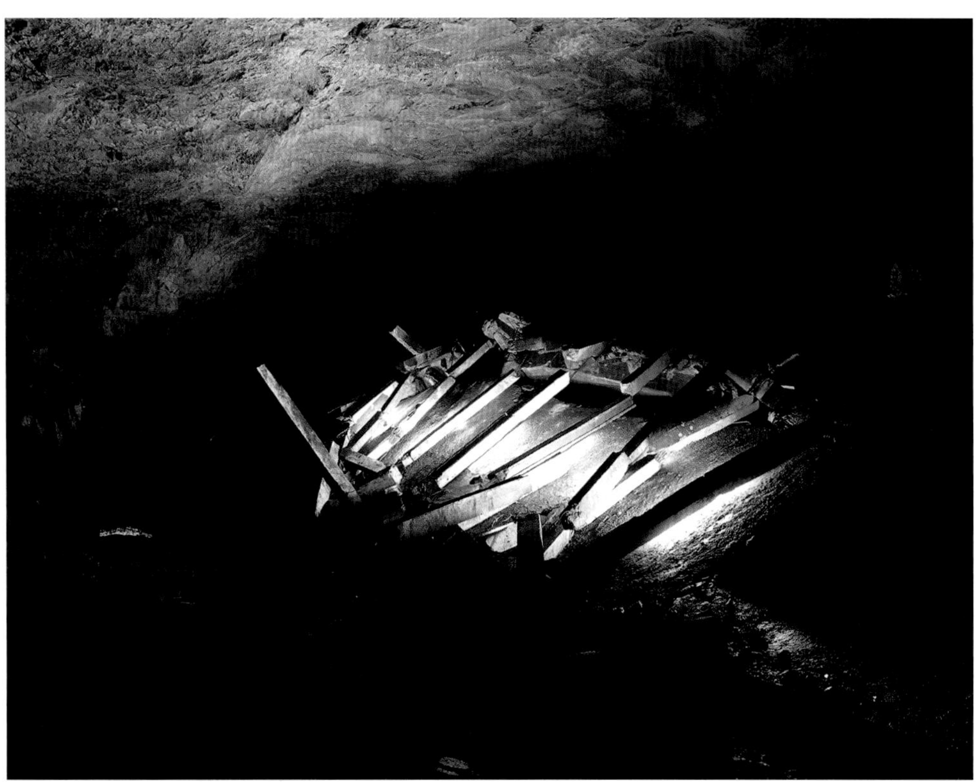

1

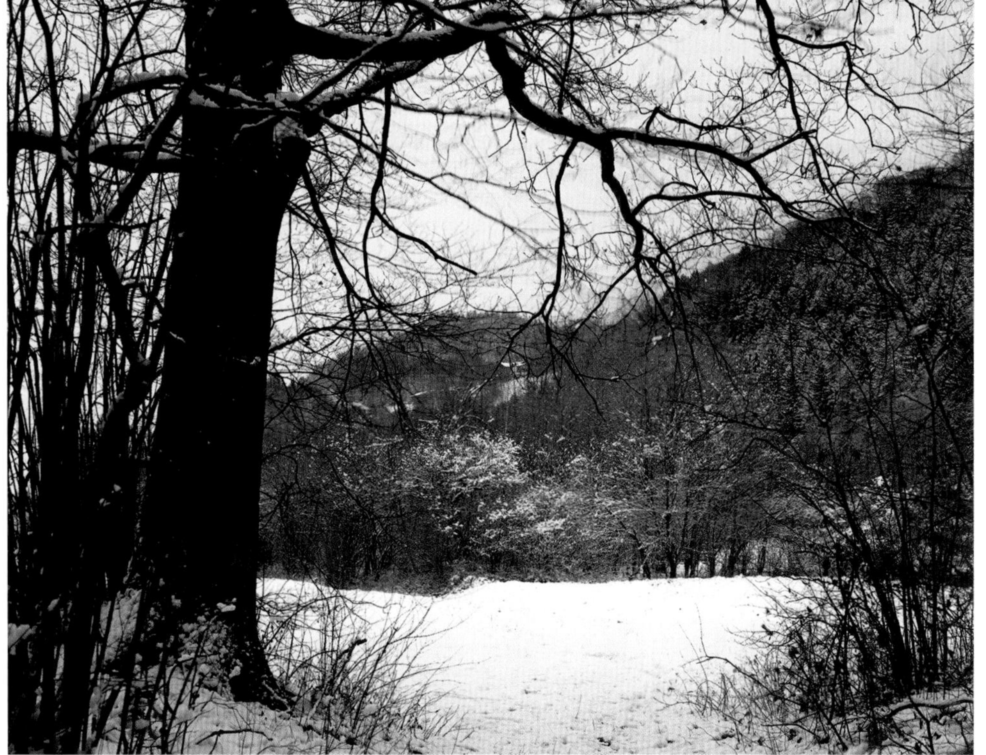

2

3

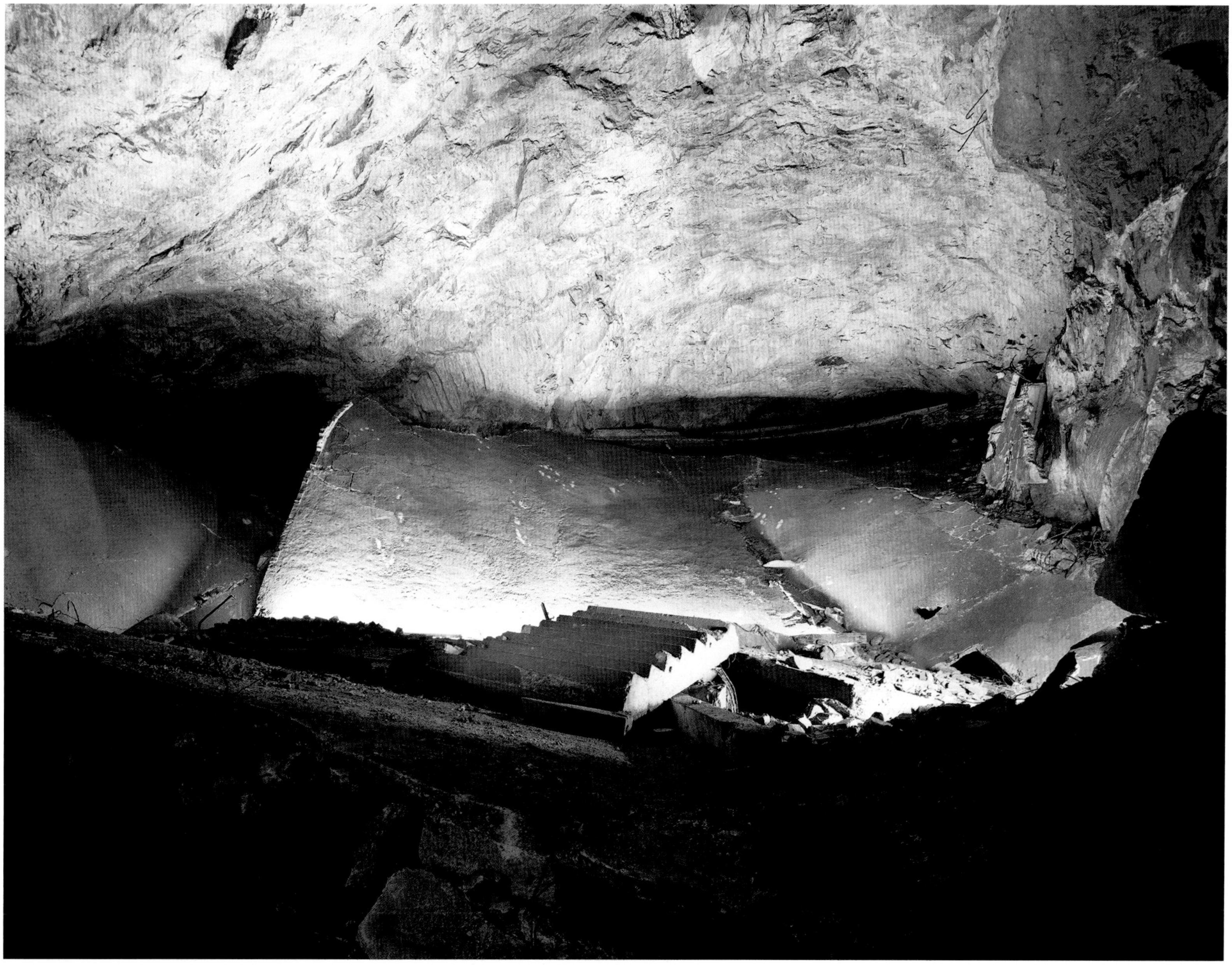

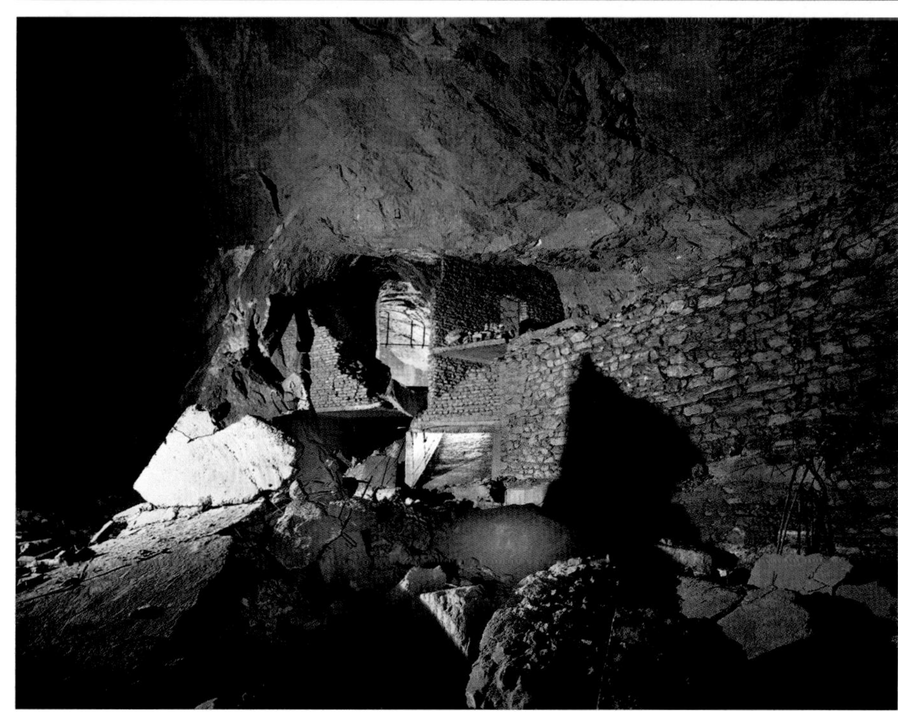

4

5

6

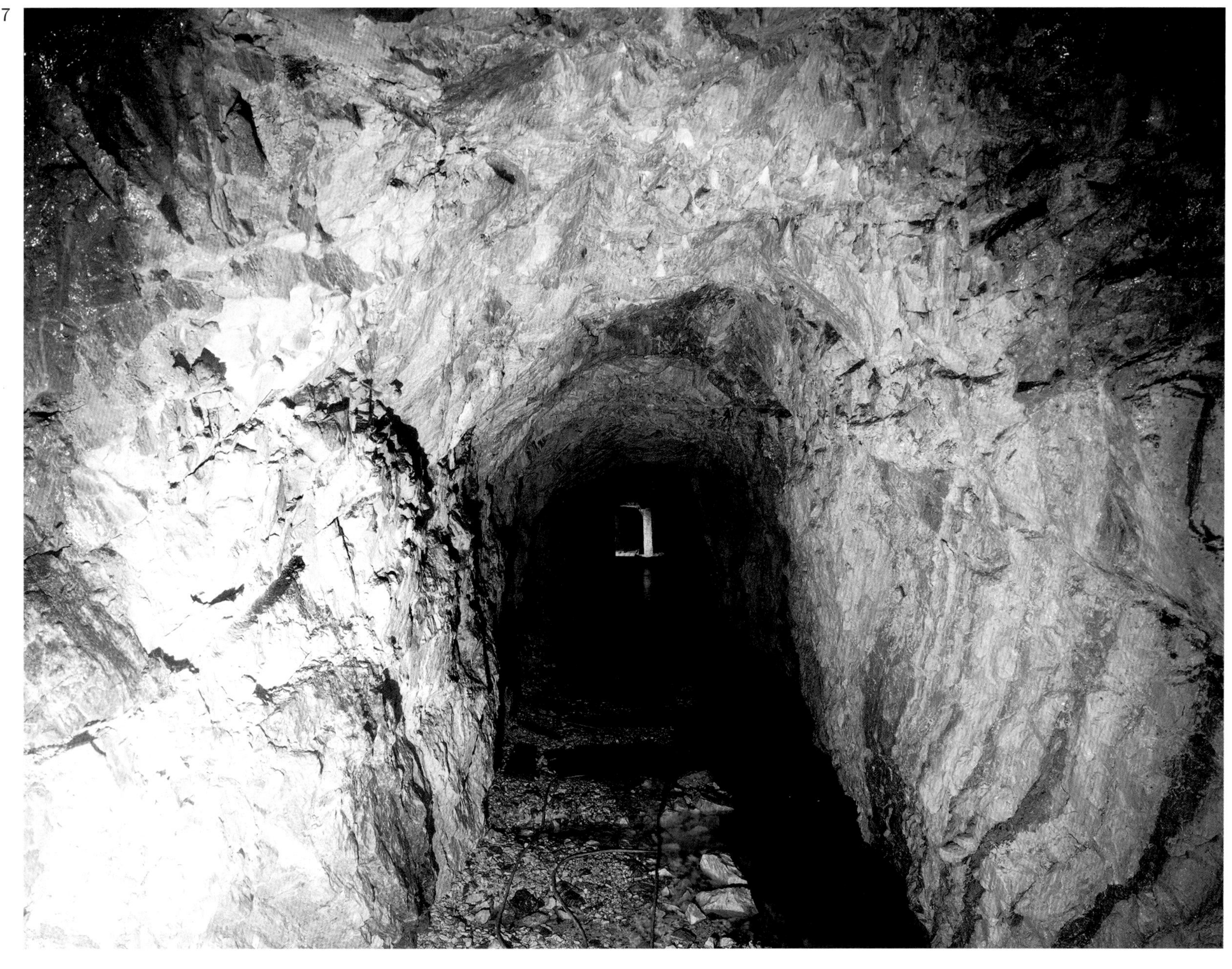

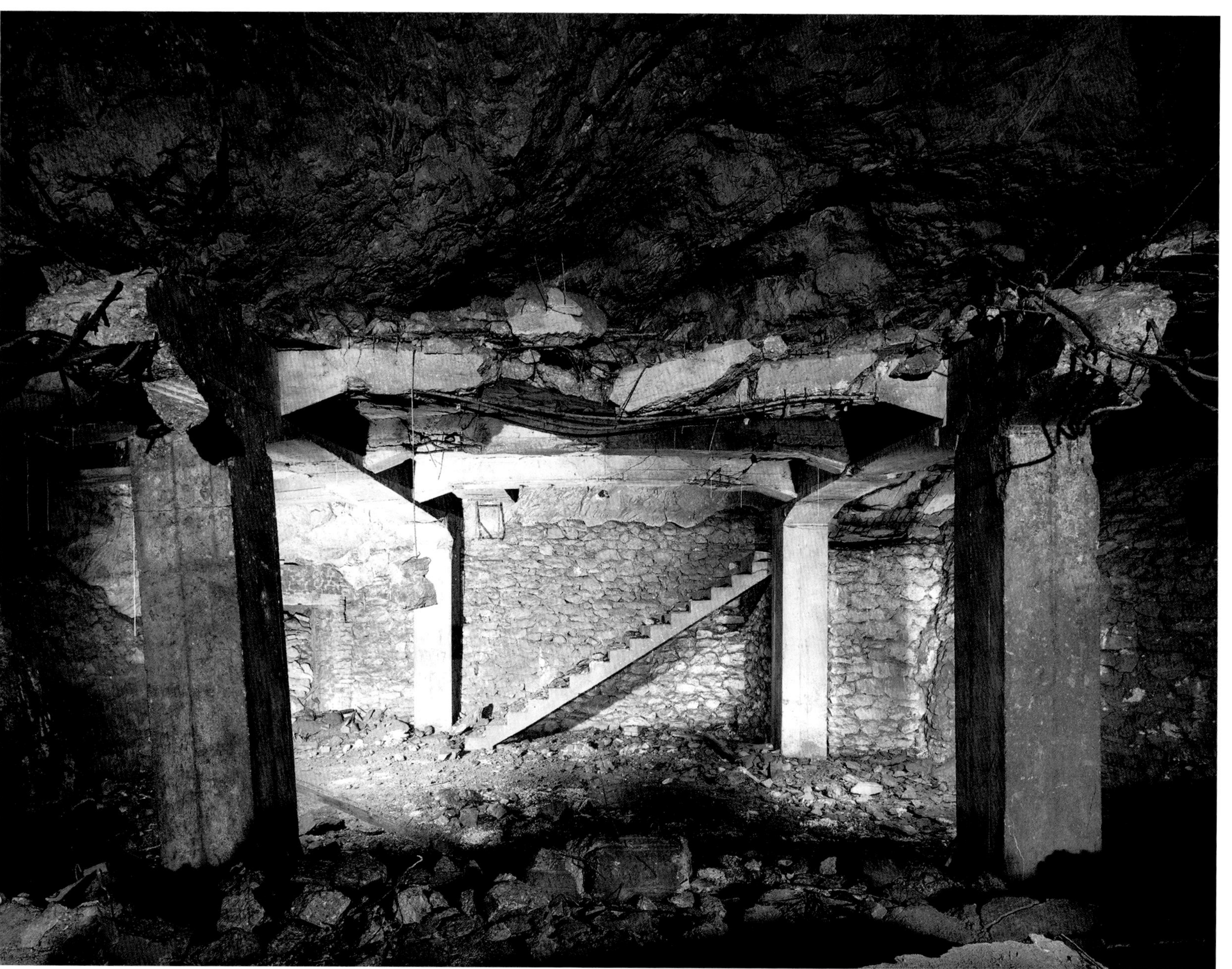

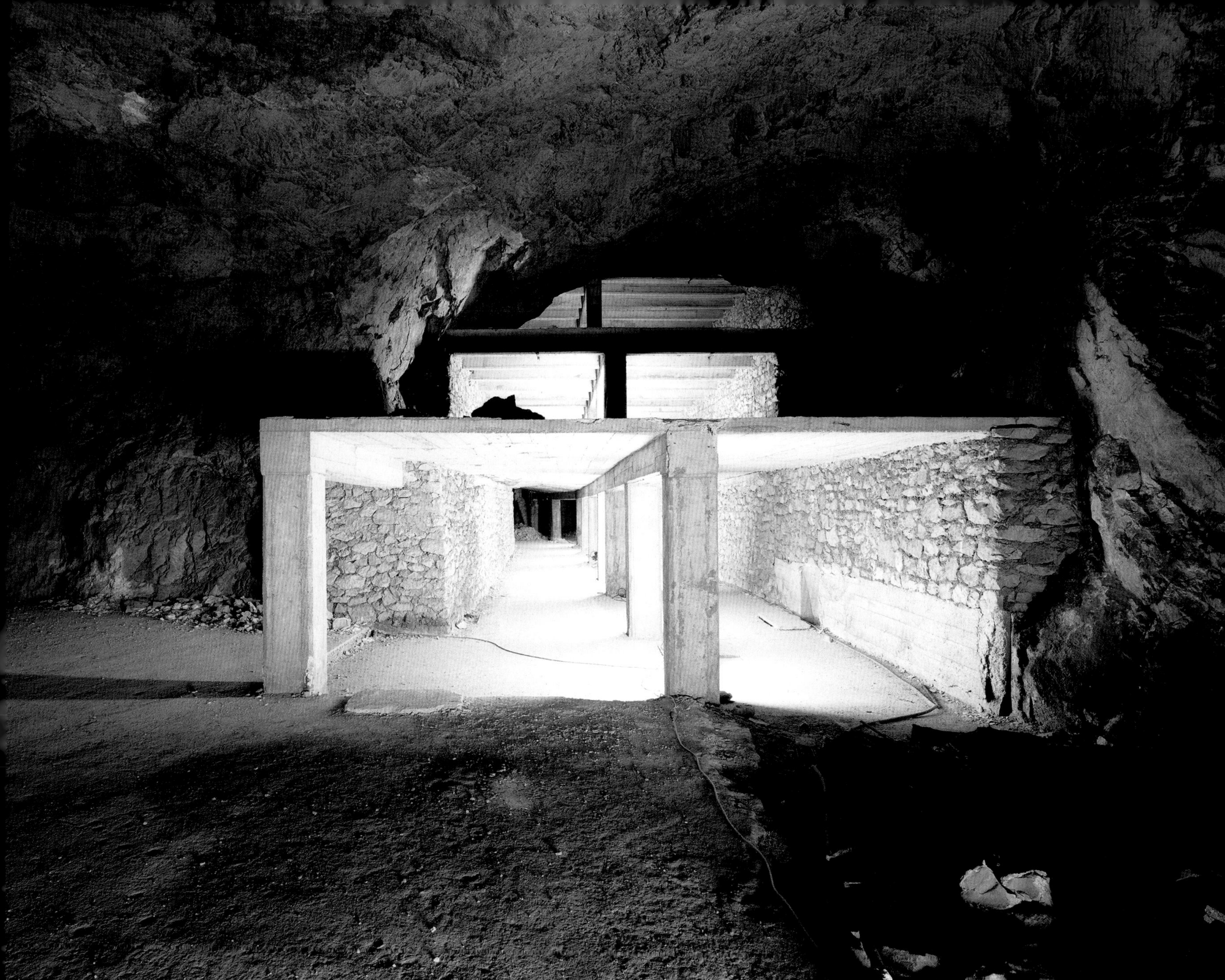

9

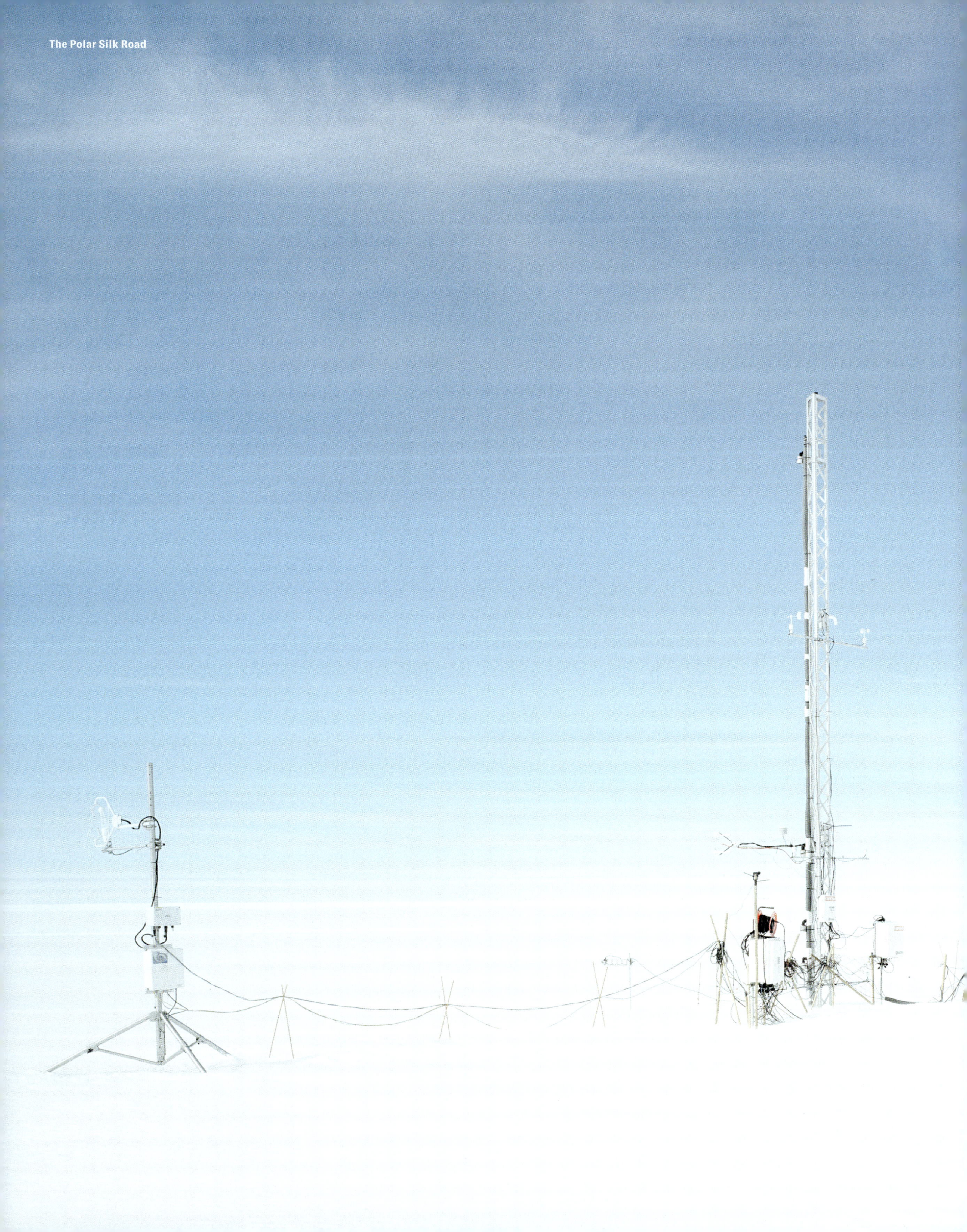

7

The Polar Silk Road

An das Nordpolarmeer grenzen fünf Staaten: Dänemark (durch Grönland), Kanada, Norwegen, Russland und die USA. Über territoriale Bereiche verfügen überdies Finnland, Island und Schweden. Zudem leben in der Region indigene Volksgruppen, allerdings ist diese Gegend aufgrund der lebensfeindlichen Bedingungen sehr dünn besiedelt. Es gibt drei Seerouten die, je nach Jahreszeit und Ausdehnung der Eisfläche, eine Durchquerung des Nordpolarmeers zulassen. Durch das Abschmelzen des Meereises wird zukünftig eine kürzere Handelsroute – die sogenannte polare Seidenstraße – entstehen und der Zugang zu neuen Rohstoffvorkommen (Erdgas und Erdöl) ermöglicht. Staaten inner- und außerhalb der Arktis machen Ansprüche geltend.

Gregor Sailer recherchierte in einer langen Vorbereitungszeit nicht nur jene Orte, die thematisch, geografisch und visuell besonders spannend sind, sondern nahm auch die mühevolle und oft langwierige Aufgabe in Kauf, die erforderlichen Zutrittsberechtigungen zu erhalten. Er begab sich wiederholt auf mehrtägige fotografische Expeditionen zu Militärstützpunkten, Forschungseinrichtungen, Häfen, Öl- und Gasförderstätten. Utopie und Dystopie liegen in Sailers Bildern nah beieinander. Die ruhigen, konzentrierten Bilder sind trotz ihrer Nüchternheit inhaltlich stark aufgeladen, dennoch erscheinen viele dieser Orte wie Rampen ins Nichts.

Die Erforschung der Arktis ist eng verbunden mit den Anfängen der Fotografie. Als sich in der zweiten Hälfte des 19. Jahrhunderts Forscher:innen aufmachten, die unbekannte Weltgegend zu erkunden, waren Fotograf:innen stets Teil der Expedition. Sailer folgt somit einer langen fotografischen Tradition. Mit *The Polar Silk Road* legt er eine fotografische Großleistung vor, die uns einen tiefen Einblick in diese sowohl wirtschaftlich und militärisch als auch wissenschaftlich äußerst wichtige Region ermöglicht.

Five countries border the Arctic Ocean: Denmark (through Greenland), Canada, Norway, Russia, and the United States. Finland, Iceland, and Sweden also have territorial areas. The region is populated by Indigenous peoples, albeit very sparsely due to the severely adverse living conditions. Three maritime routes allow a crossing of the Arctic Ocean, depending on the season and the extent of the ice cover. But the melting of the sea ice is set to create a shorter trade route in the future, the so-called Polar Silk Road, providing access to new raw material deposits (natural gas and oil). Countries inside and outside the Arctic are already asserting their claims.

During a long preparatory phase Gregor Sailer not only researched those locations that were particularly exciting thematically, geographically, and visually, but he also took on the laborious and often tedious task of obtaining the necessary access authorisations. Gregor Sailer repeatedly set out on photographic expeditions of several days to military bases, research facilities, ports, and oil and gas production sites. In Sailer's photographs, utopia and dystopia are never far apart. For all their sobriety, these calm and concentrated photographs are nonetheless highly charged with content, yet many of these places seem like launching ramps to nowhere.

There are close ties between Arctic exploration and the early days of photography. When explorers set out to reconnoitre this unknown region of the world during the second half of the 19th century, photographers were always part of the expedition. Gregor Sailer is therefore following a long photographic tradition. With *The Polar Silk Road,* Sailer has pulled off a major photographic achievement, which gives us a deep insight into this region, one that is extremely important both economically and militarily as well as scientifically.

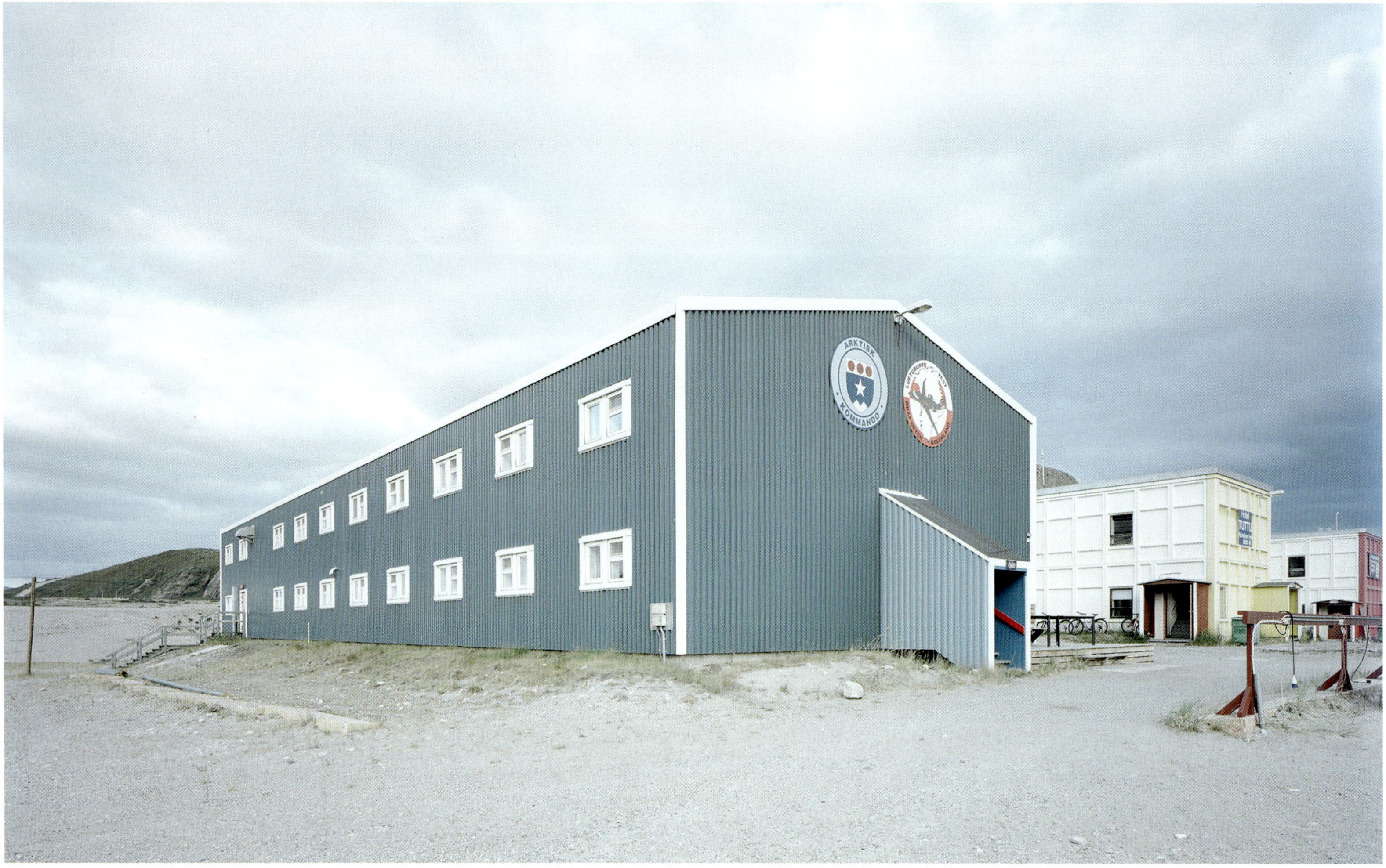

1

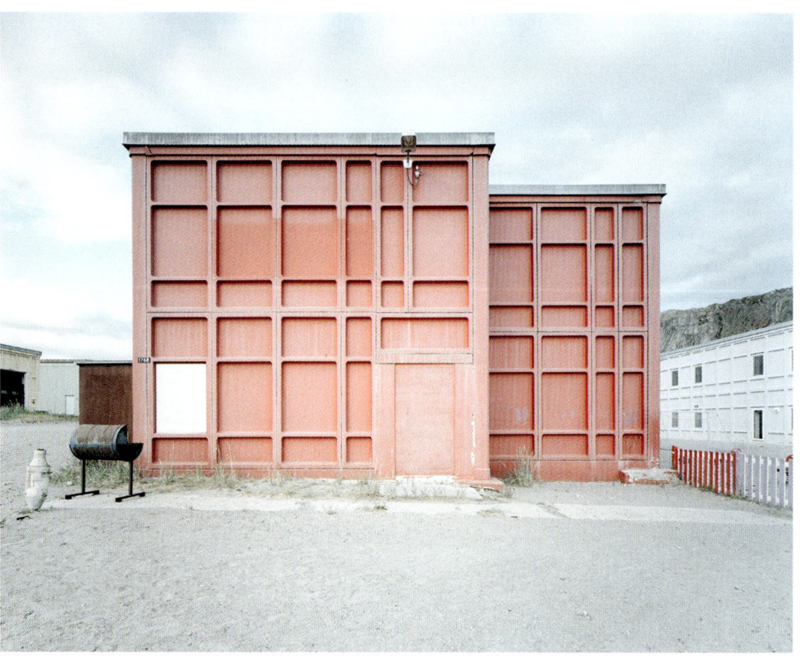

2

3

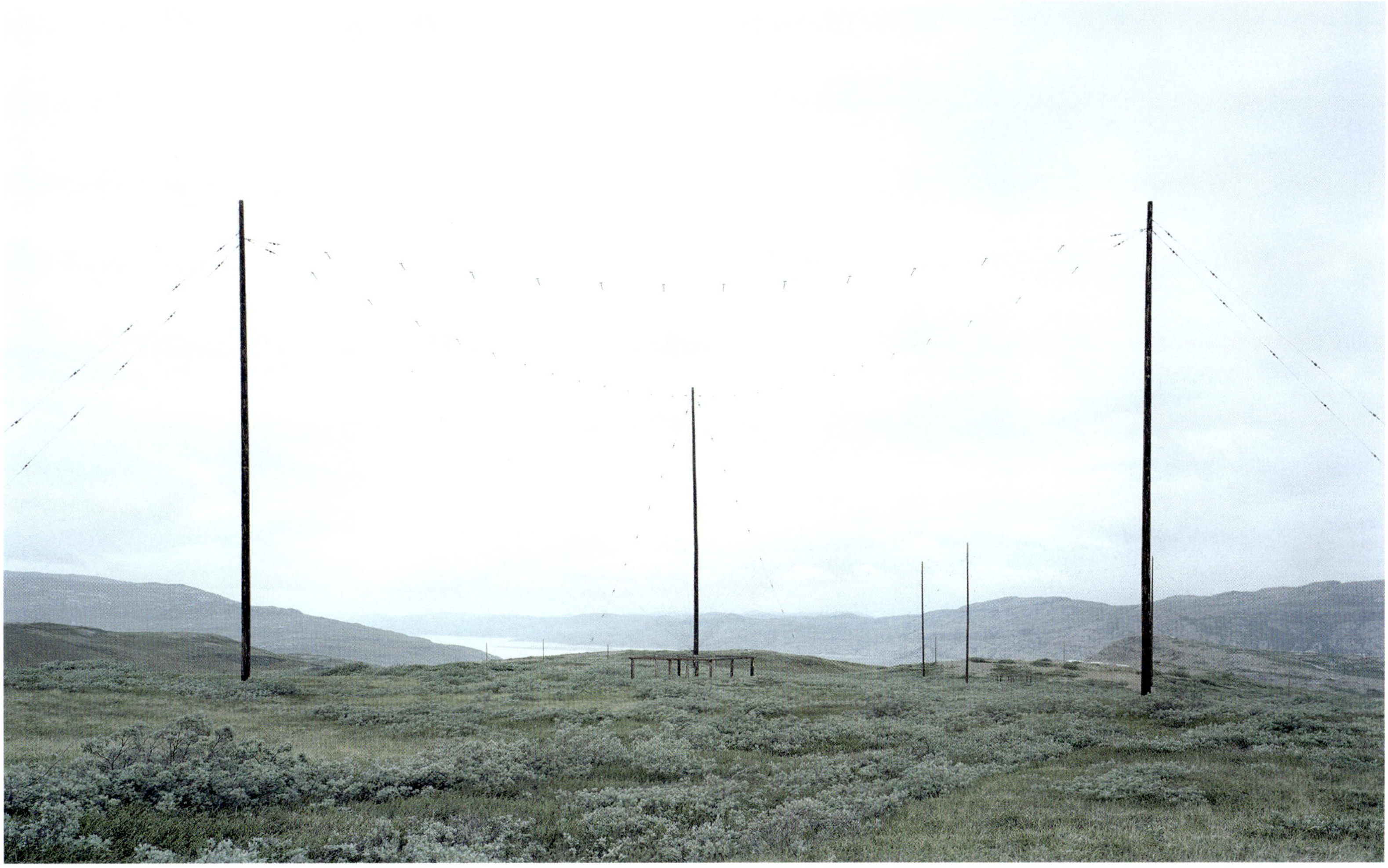

4
5
6

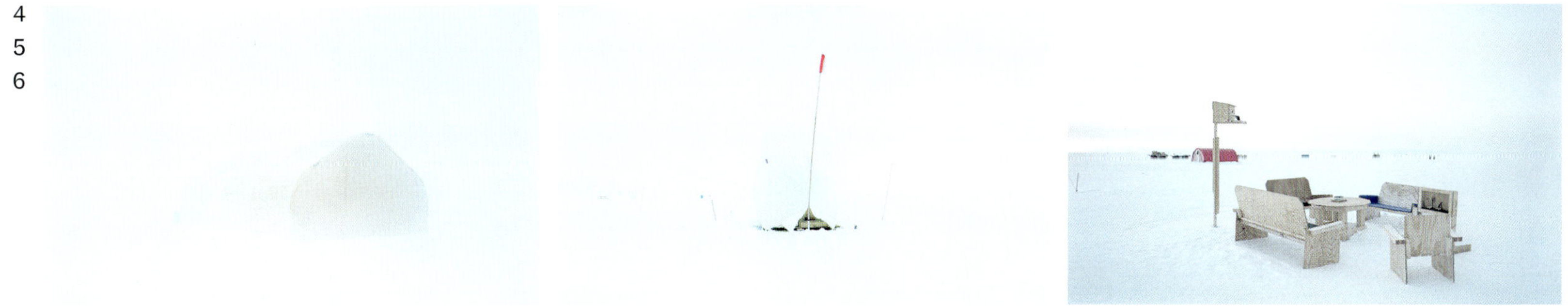

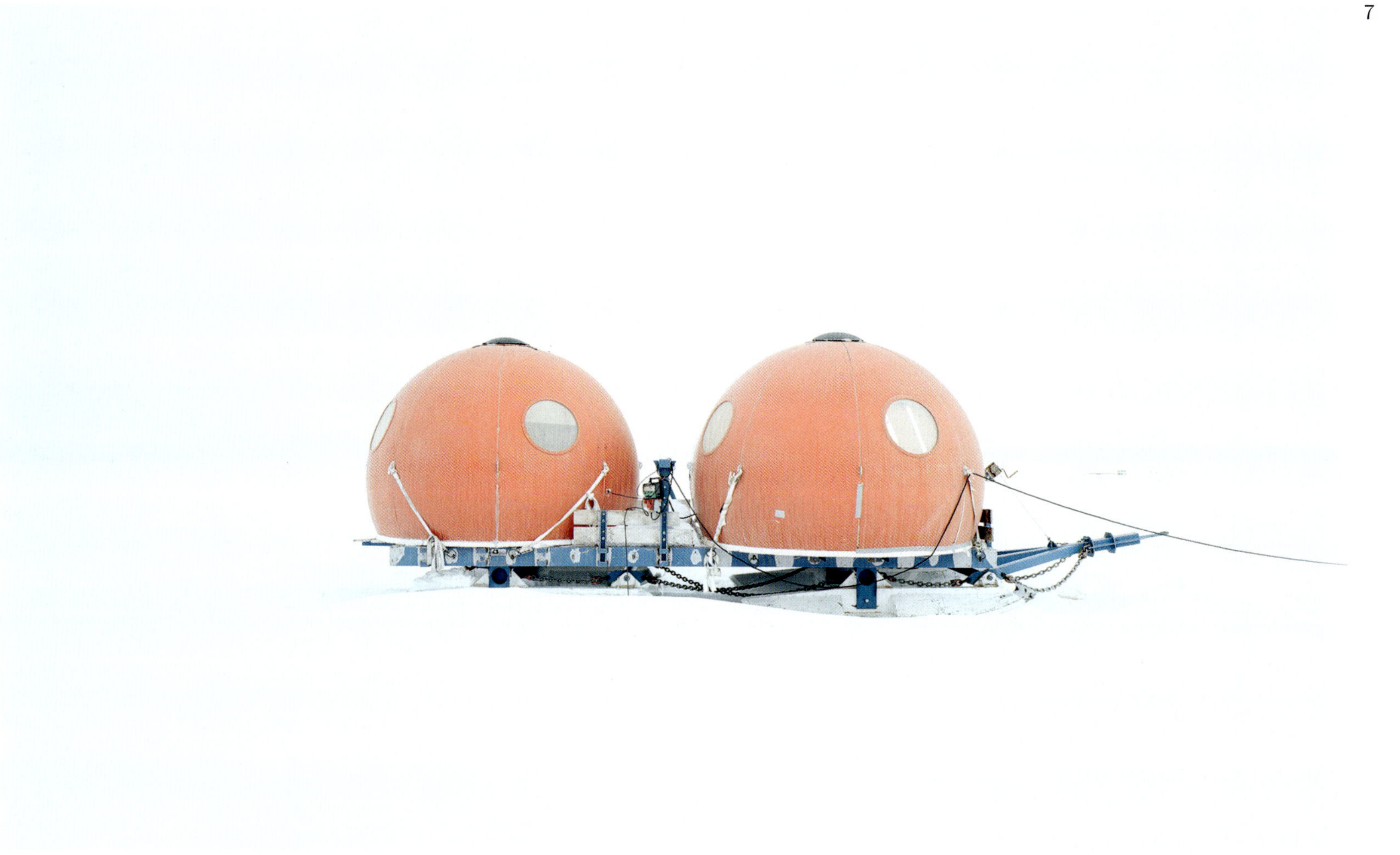

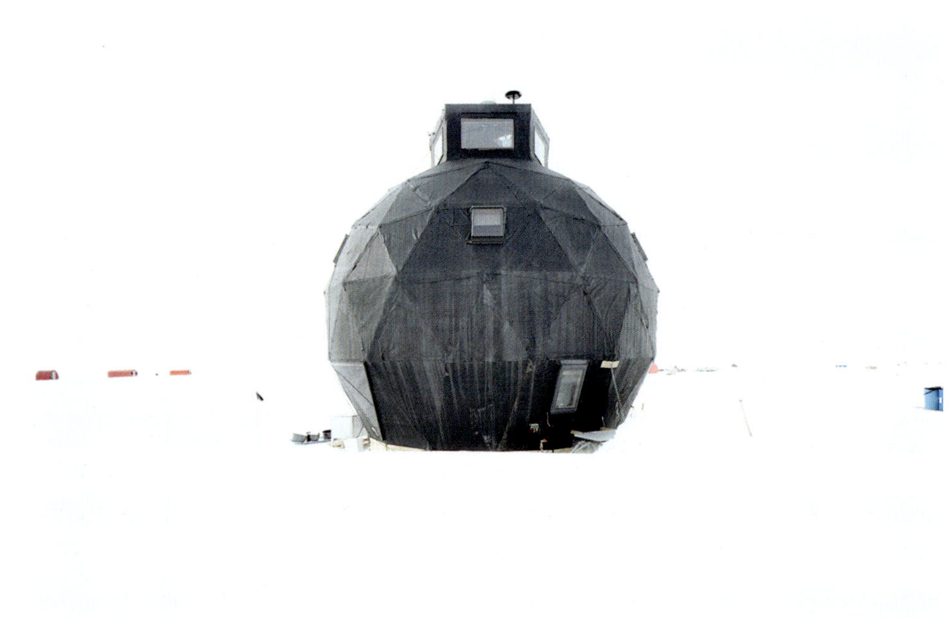

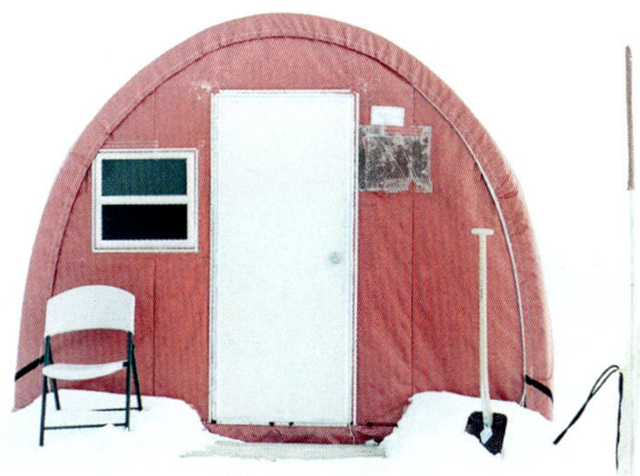

„Auch wenn er sich nicht direkt darauf bezieht, schließt Gregor Sailers [...] Projekt *The Polar Silk Road* an diese Tradition der historischen Arktisfotos an. Die Parallelen sind faszinierend: Auch Sailers Aufnahmen schwanken zwischen sachlicher Dokumentation und ästhetischer Gestaltung, gleichzeitig thematisieren sie die jahrhundertealten machtpolitischen Bestrebungen in der Arktis – hier jedoch unter dem zeitgenössischen Vorzeichen des Klimawandels, der die Polkappen schmelzen lässt und den Wettlauf um den nun leichteren Zugang zu Ressourcen und Seewegen neu anheizt."

Walter Moser, „Neue Perspektiven auf eine traditionsreiche Fotografie",
in: Gregor Sailer, *The Polar Silk Road,* Heidelberg 2021, S. 250.

"Even if he does not reference it directly, Gregor Sailer's [...] project *The Polar Silk Road* picks up on the tradition of historical photographs of the Arctic. The parallels are fascinating: Sailer's photographs, too, oscillate between factual documentation and aesthetic design; by the same token, they address the centuries-old power-political endeavours in the Arctic. But in this instance, it is under the contemporary aspect of climate change, which is causing the polar ice caps to melt and rekindling the race for access to resources and to sea routes, now made all the easier."

Walter Moser, "Neue Perspektiven auf eine traditionsreiche Fotografie,"
in Gregor Sailer, *The Polar Silk Road* (Heidelberg 2021), 250.

10

11
12

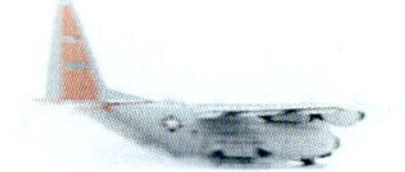

13
14
15

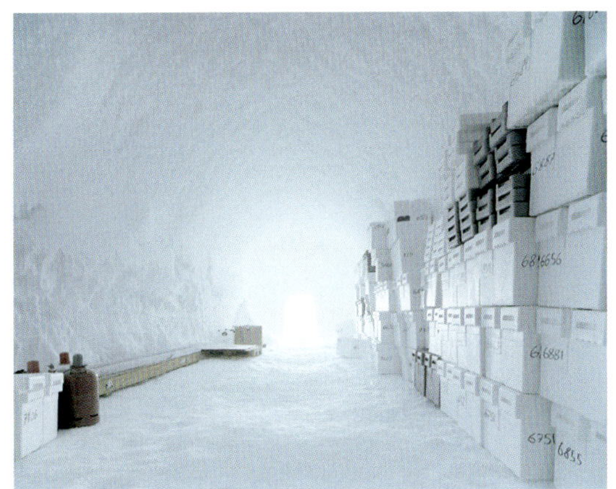
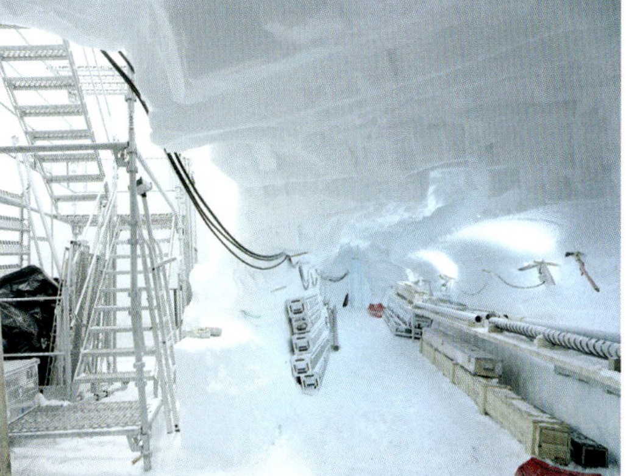
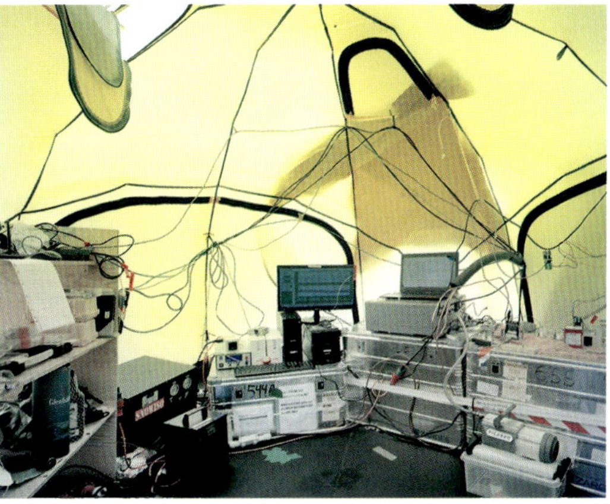

16

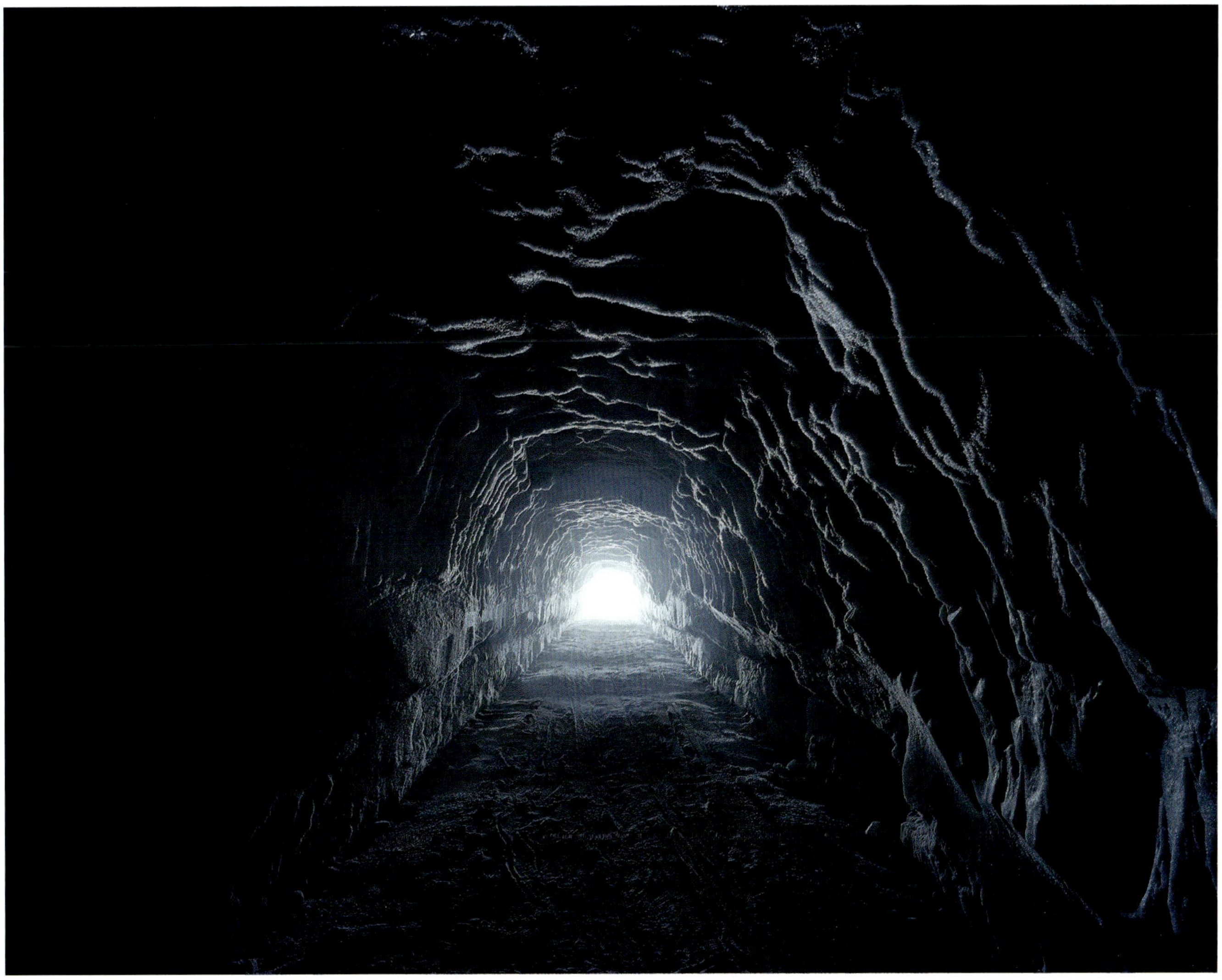

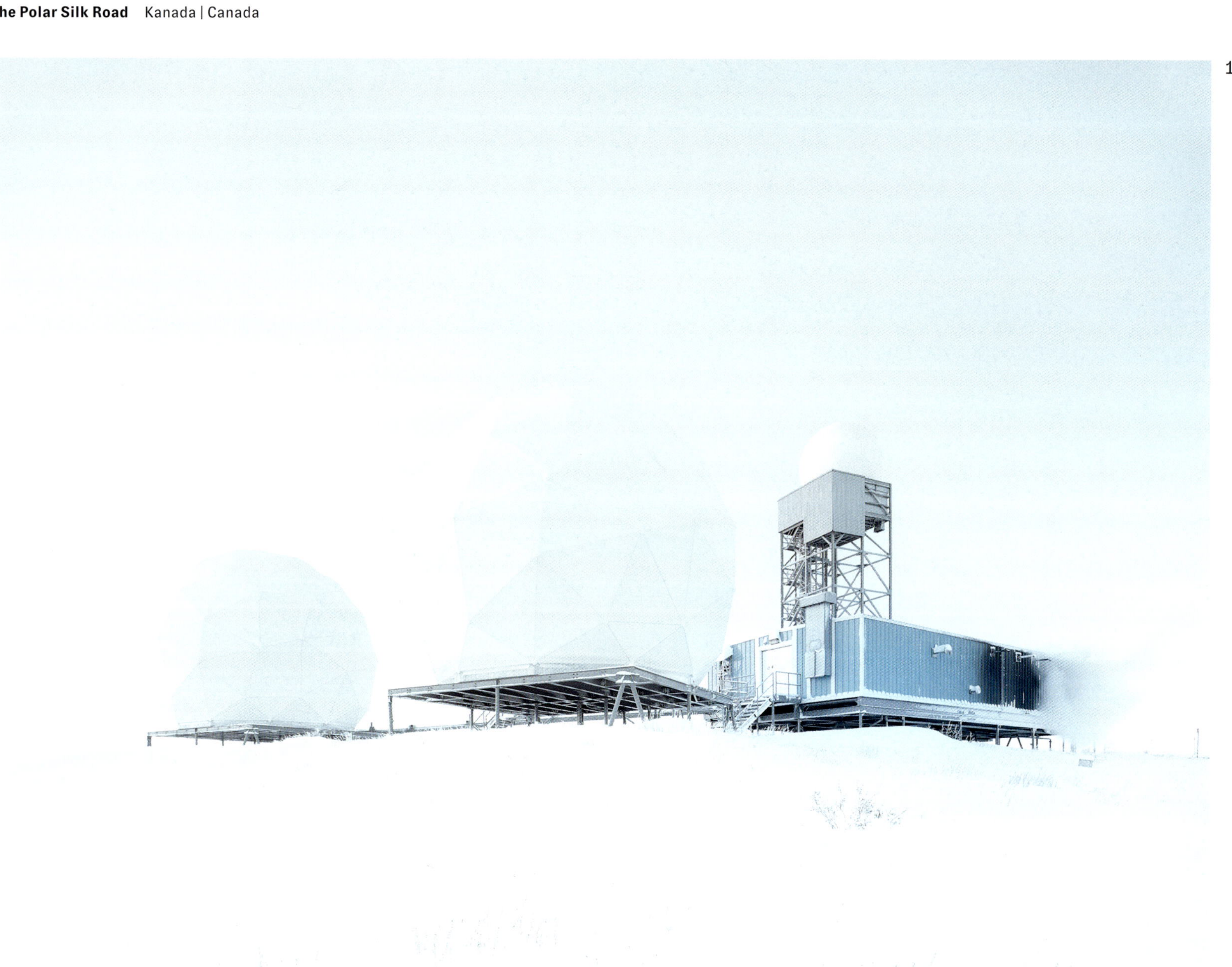

18

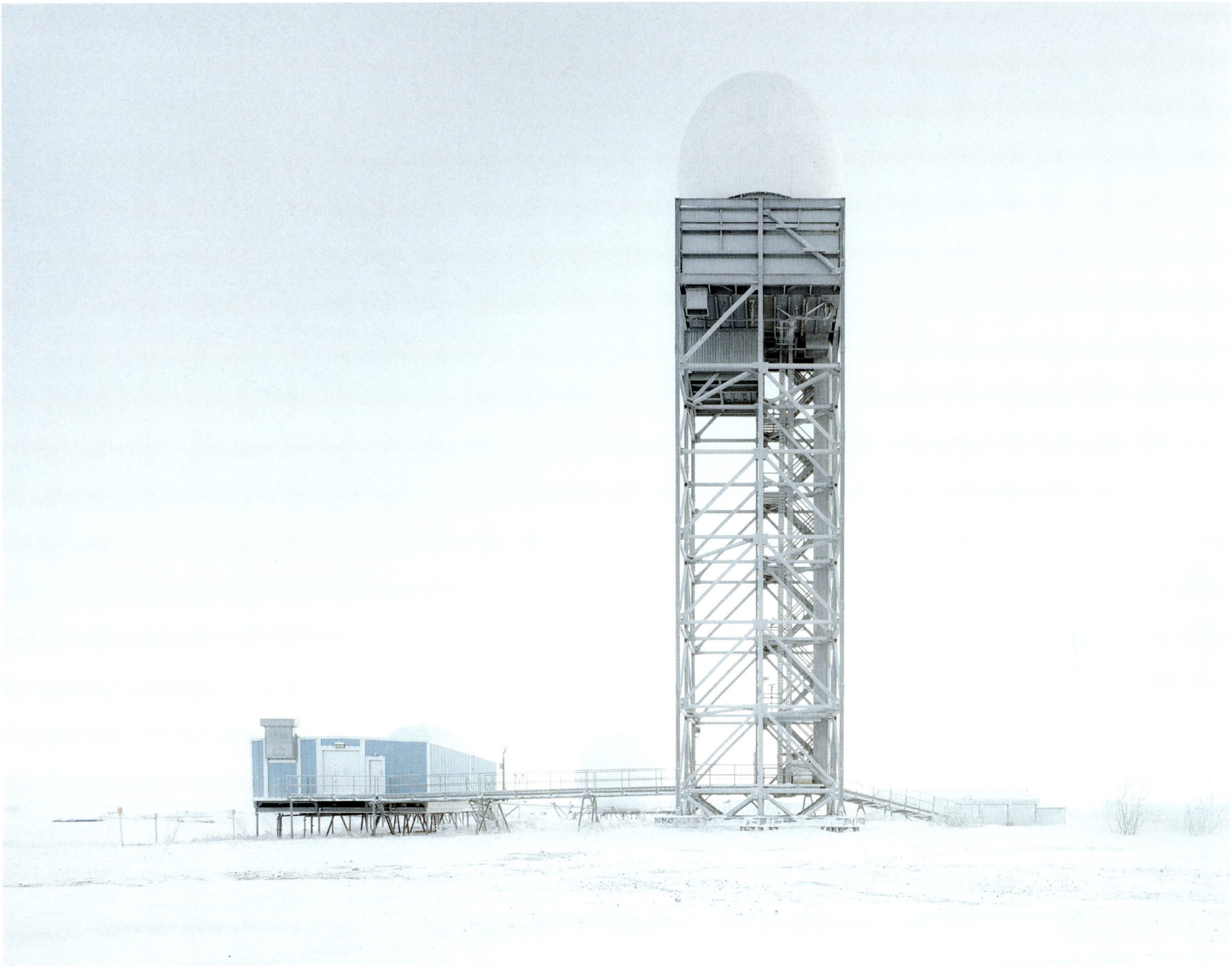

19

20

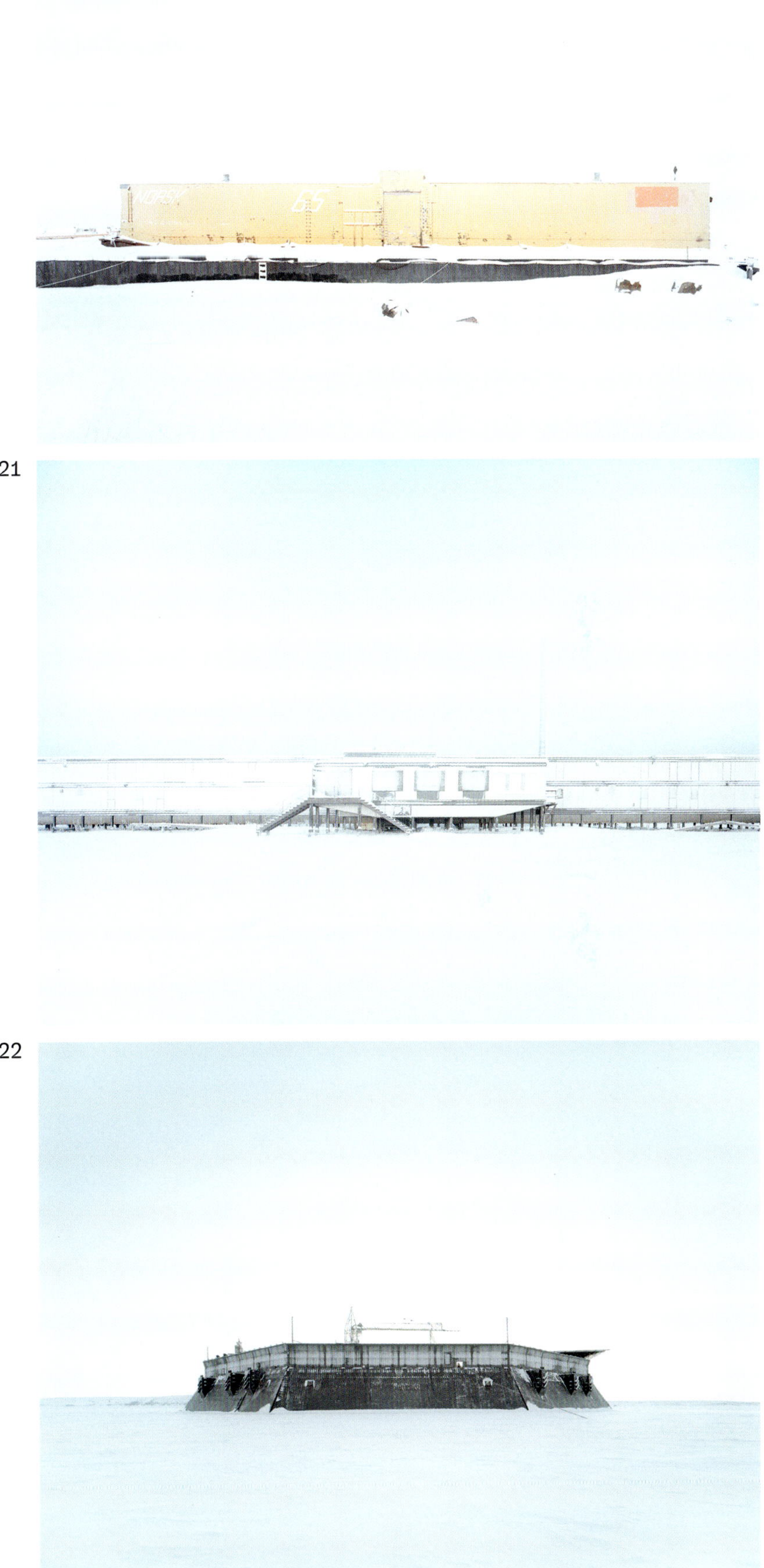

21

22

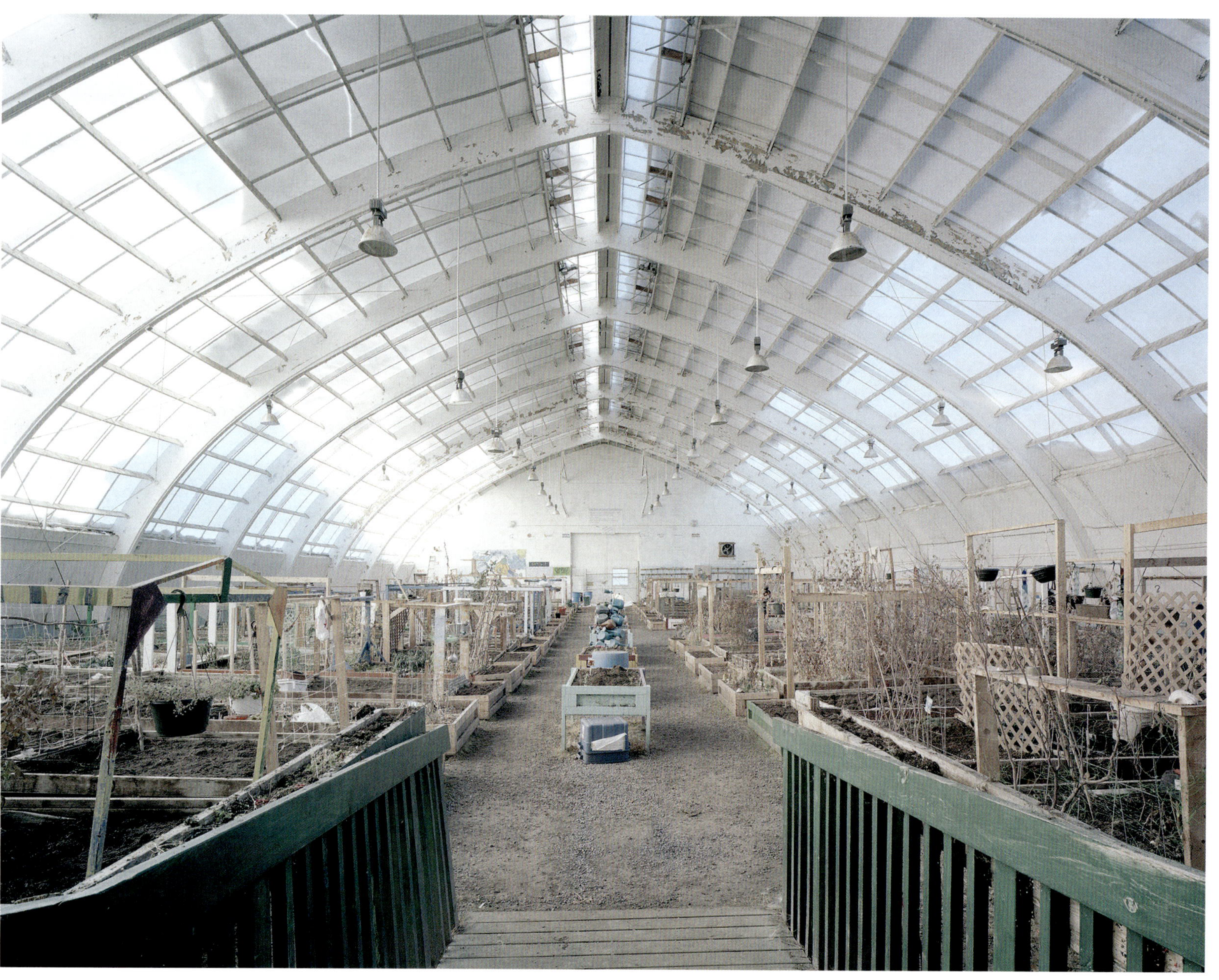

24

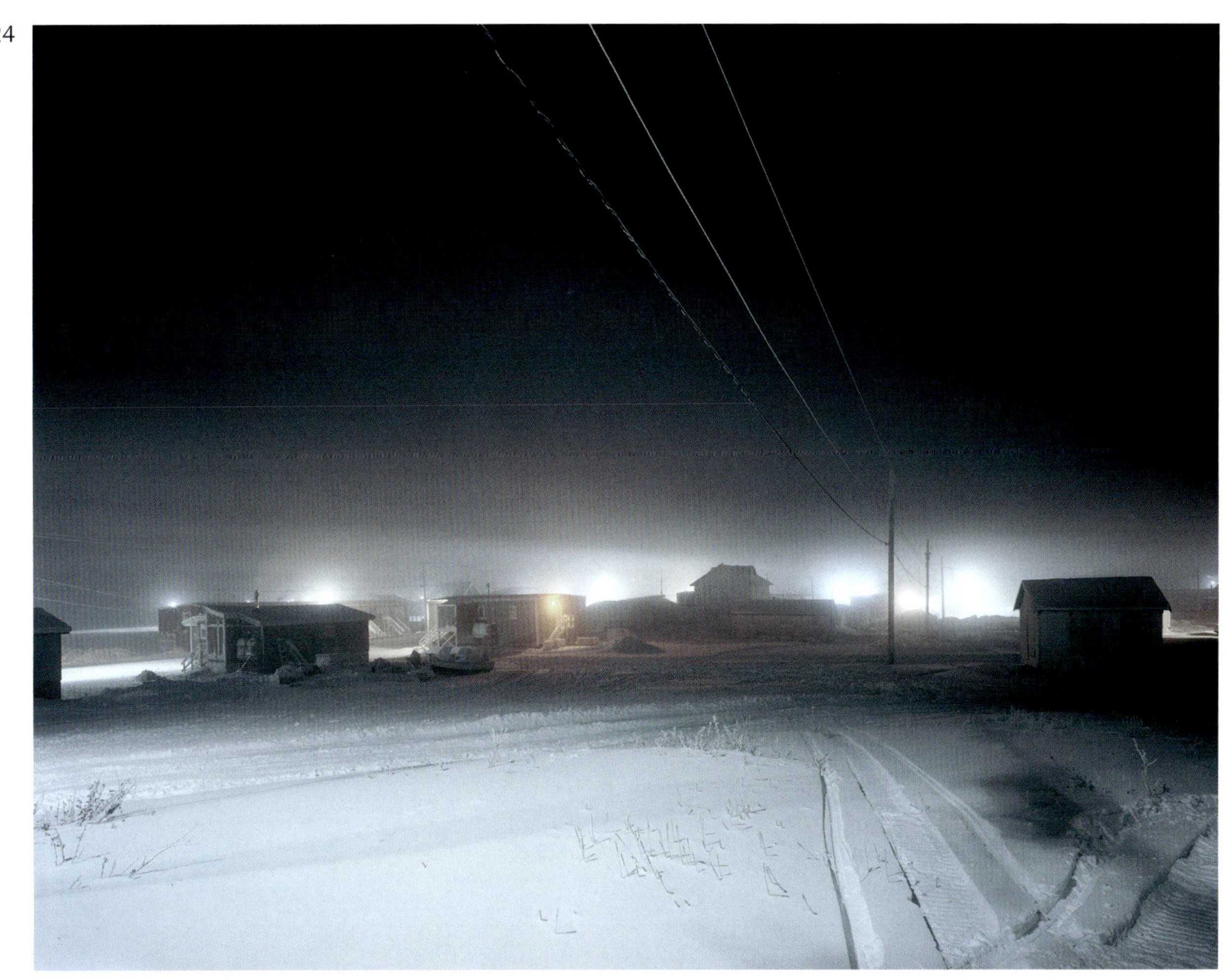

25

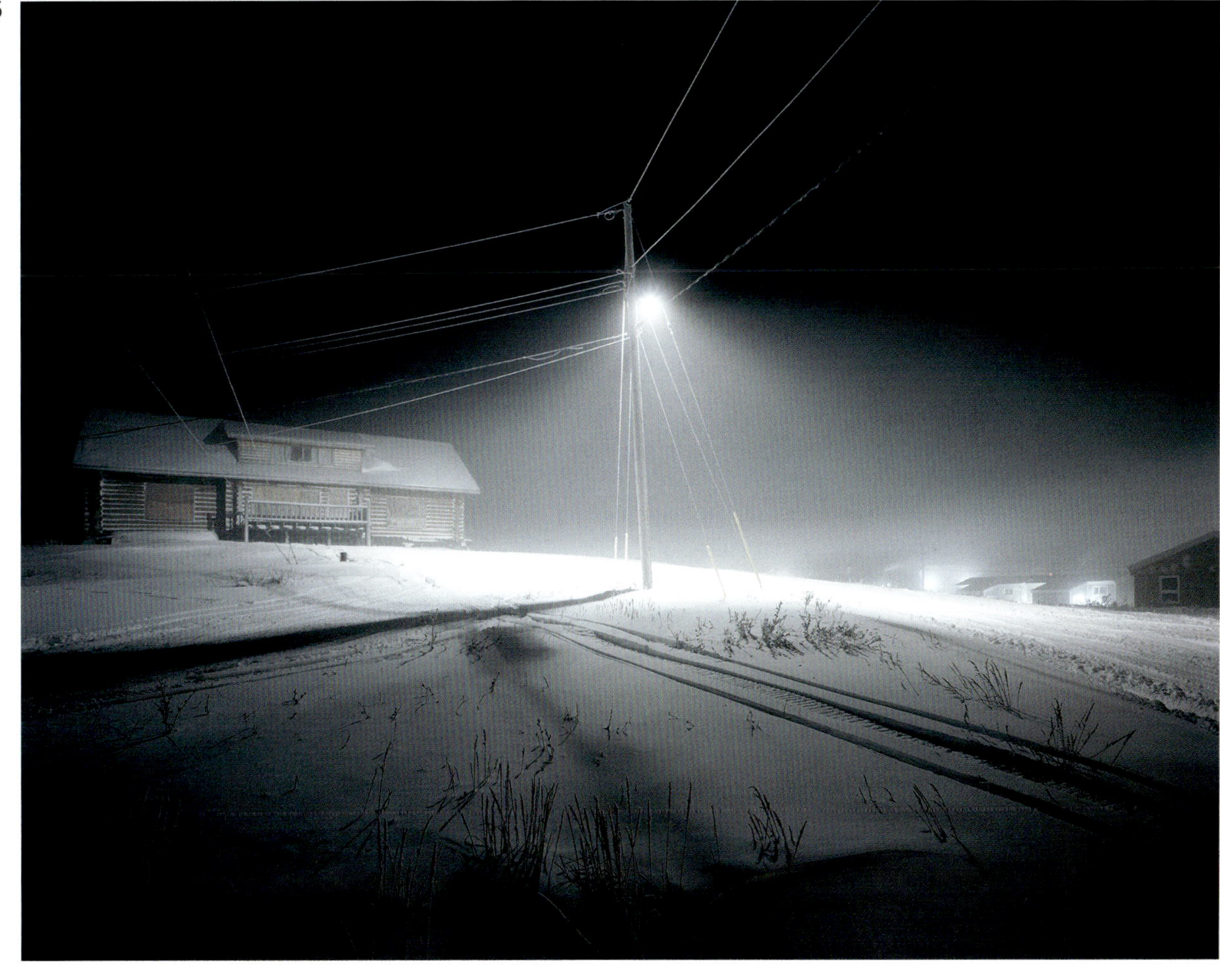

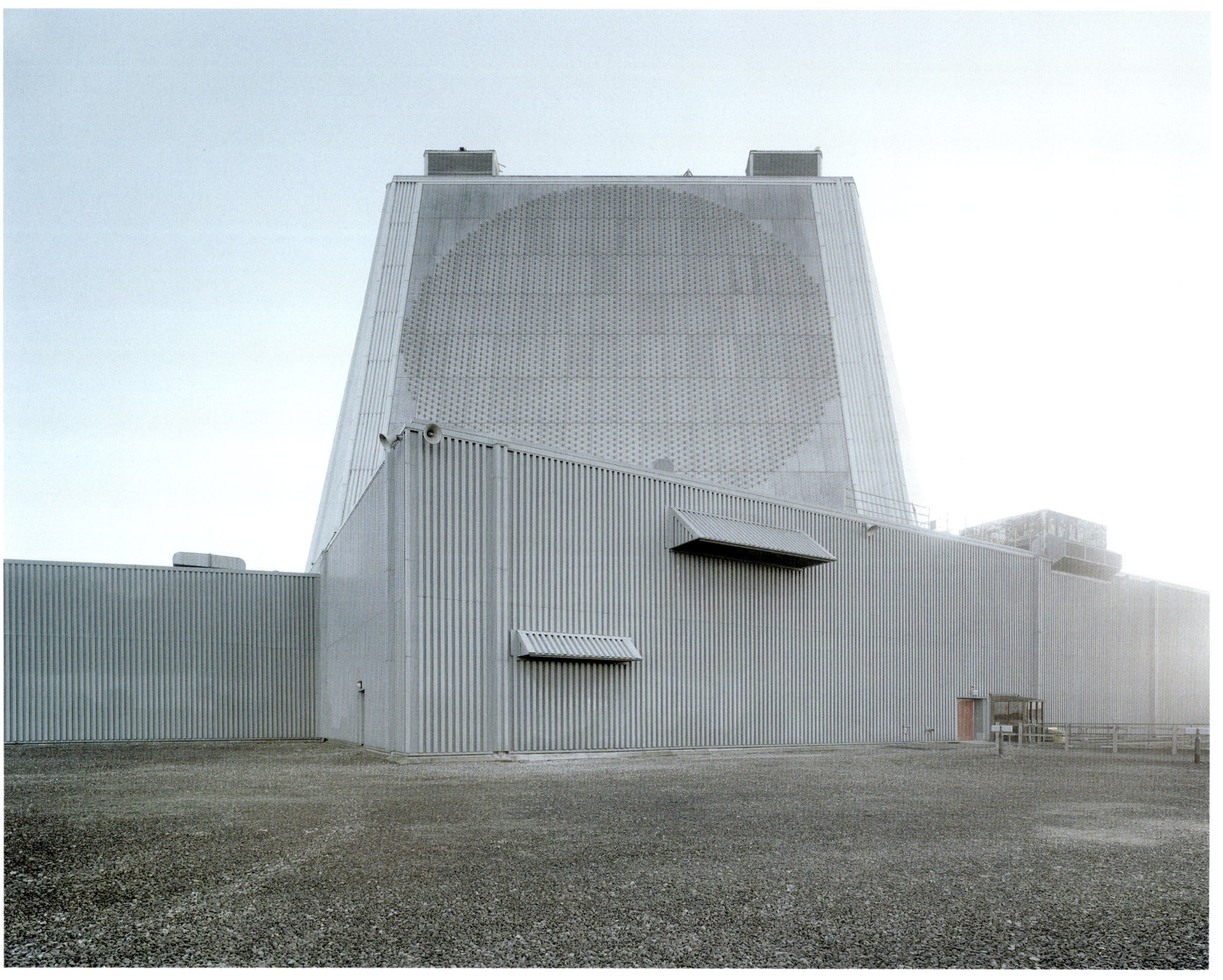

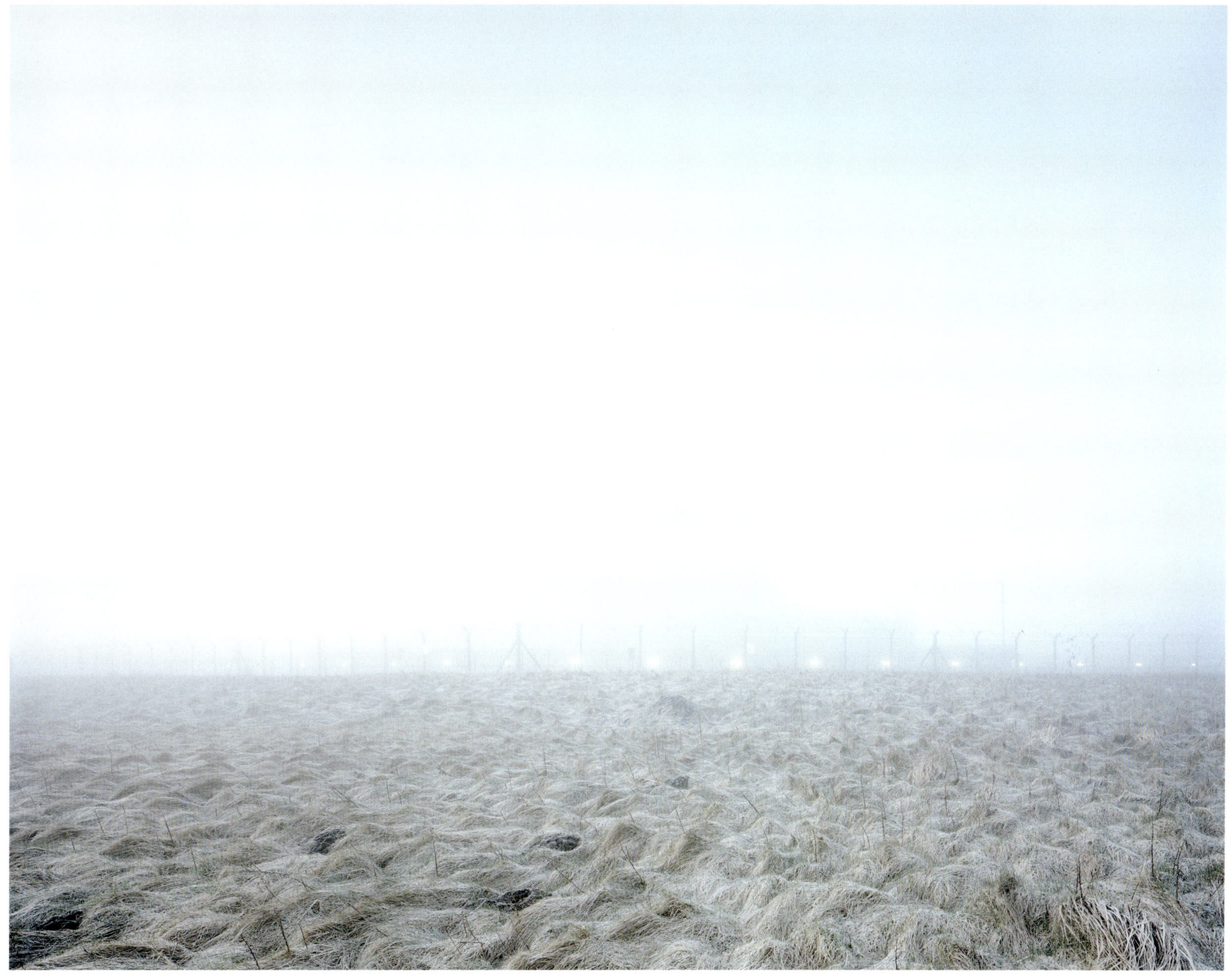

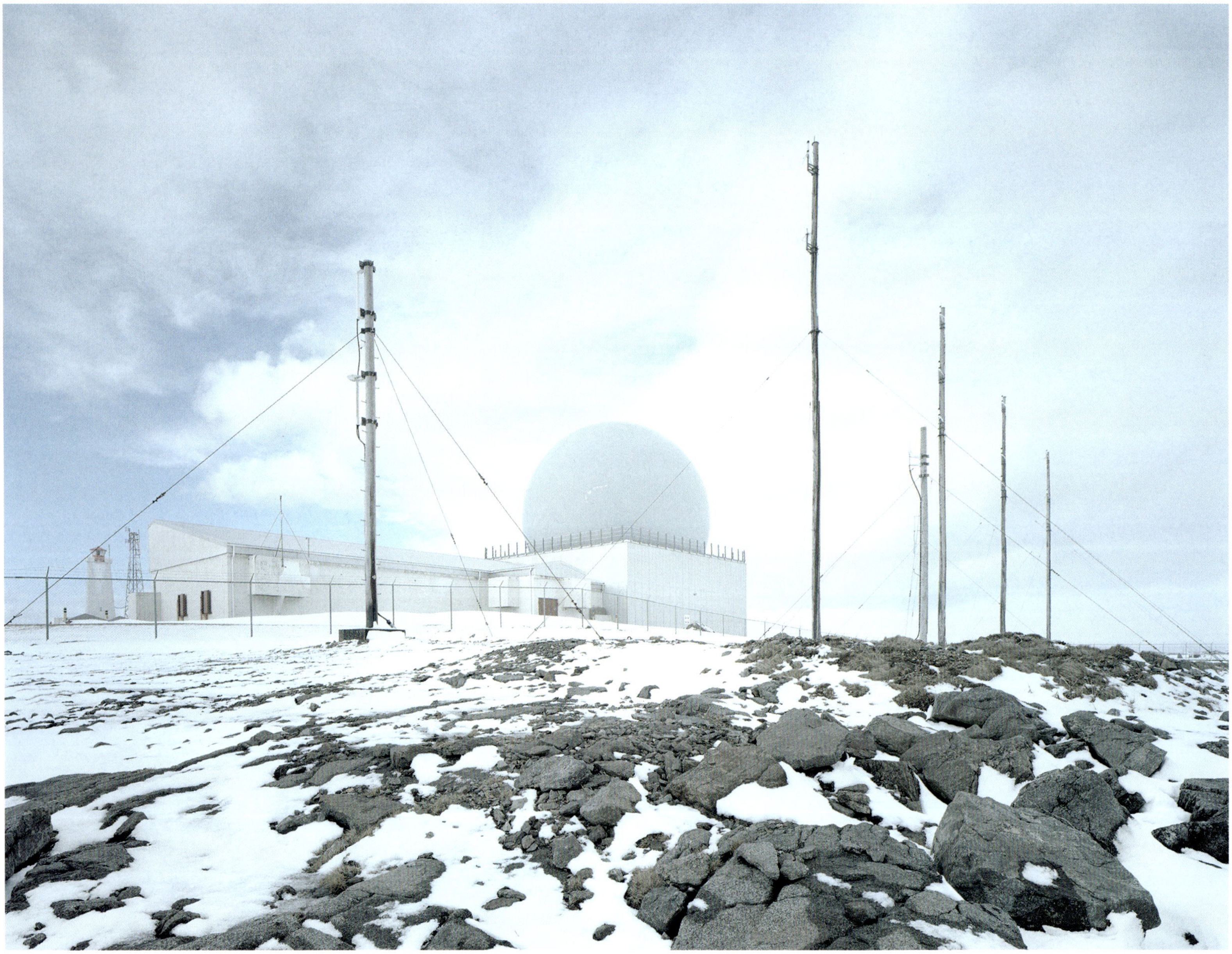

28

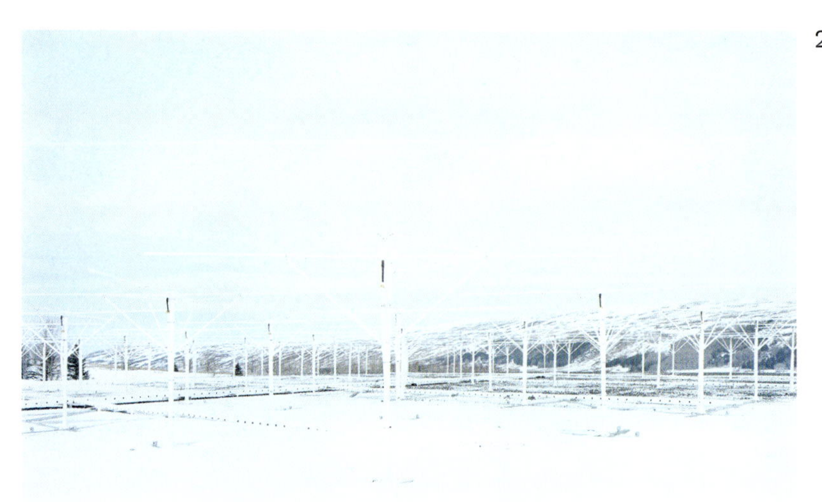

29

30
31

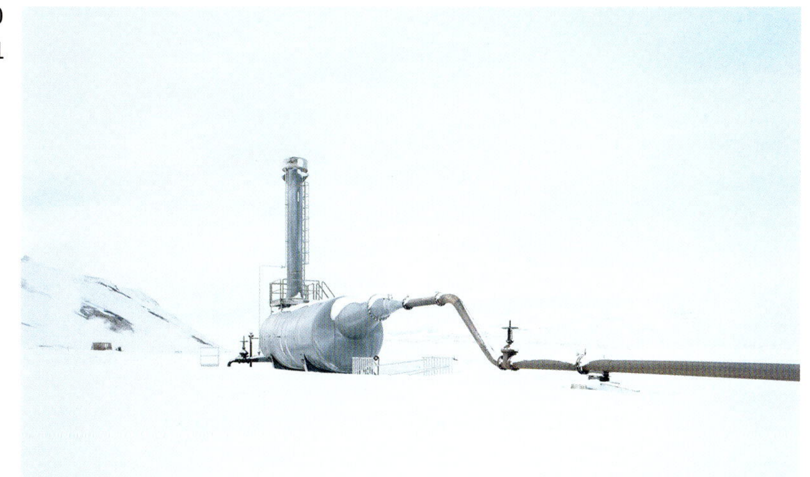

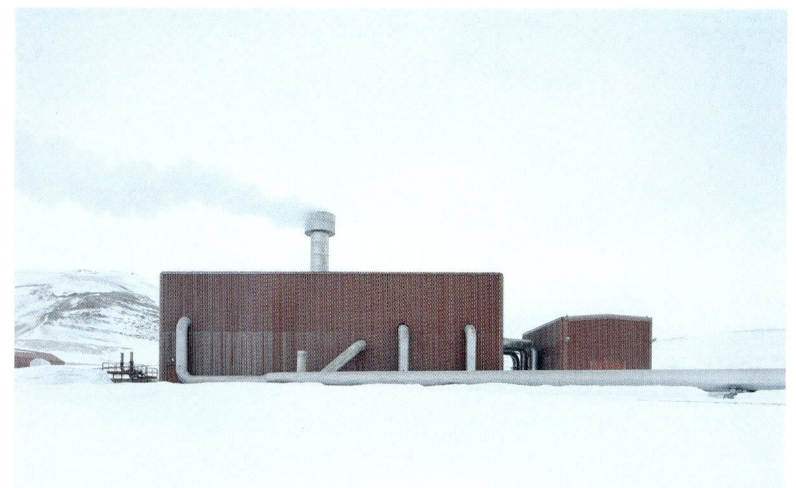

32
33

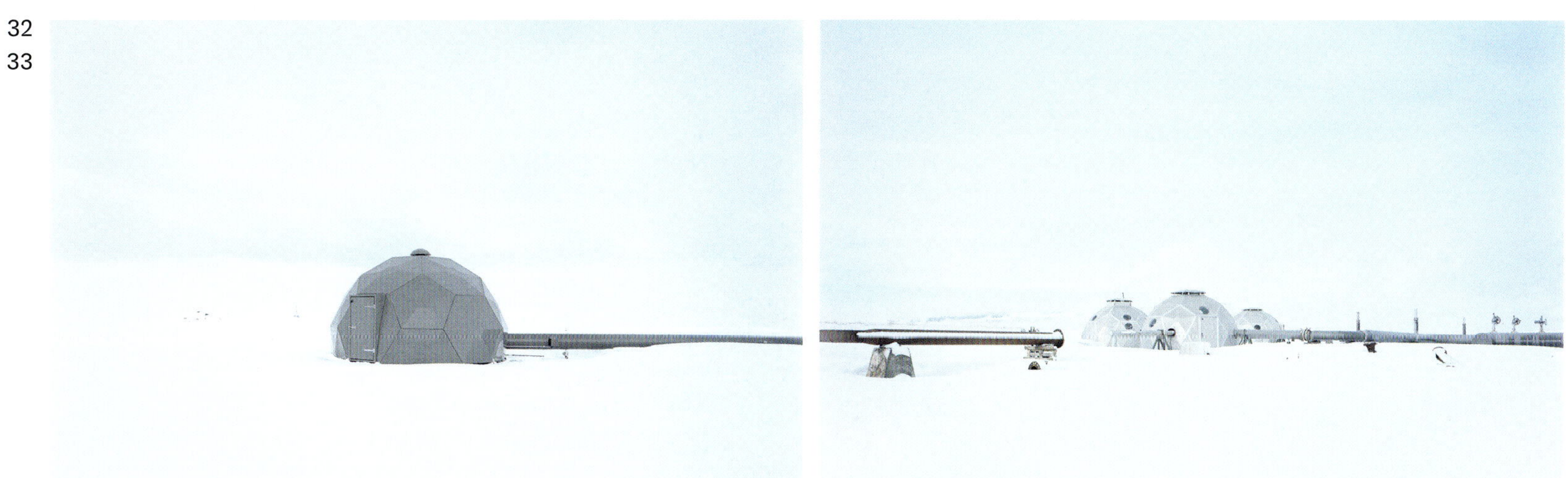

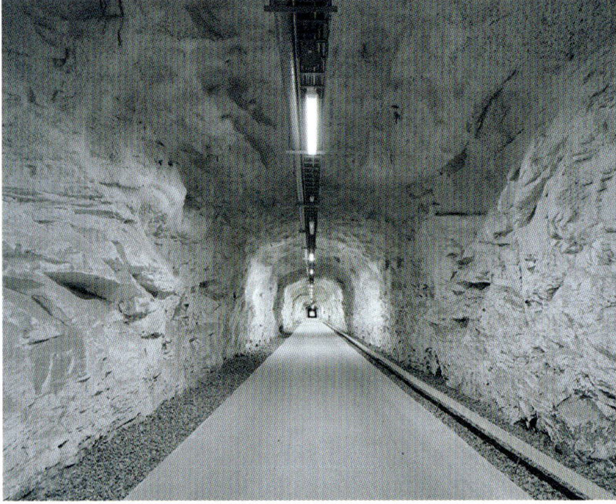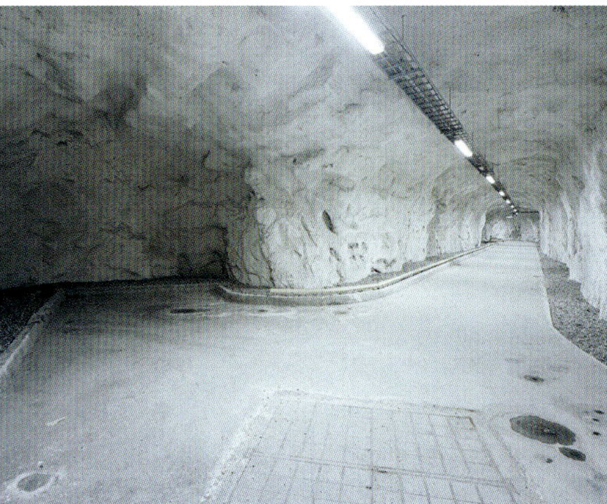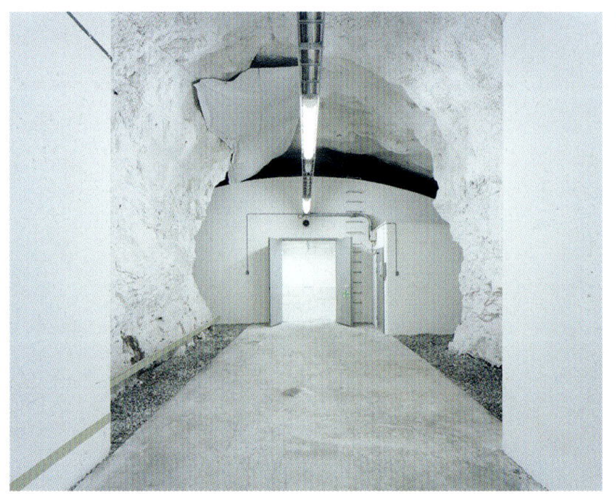

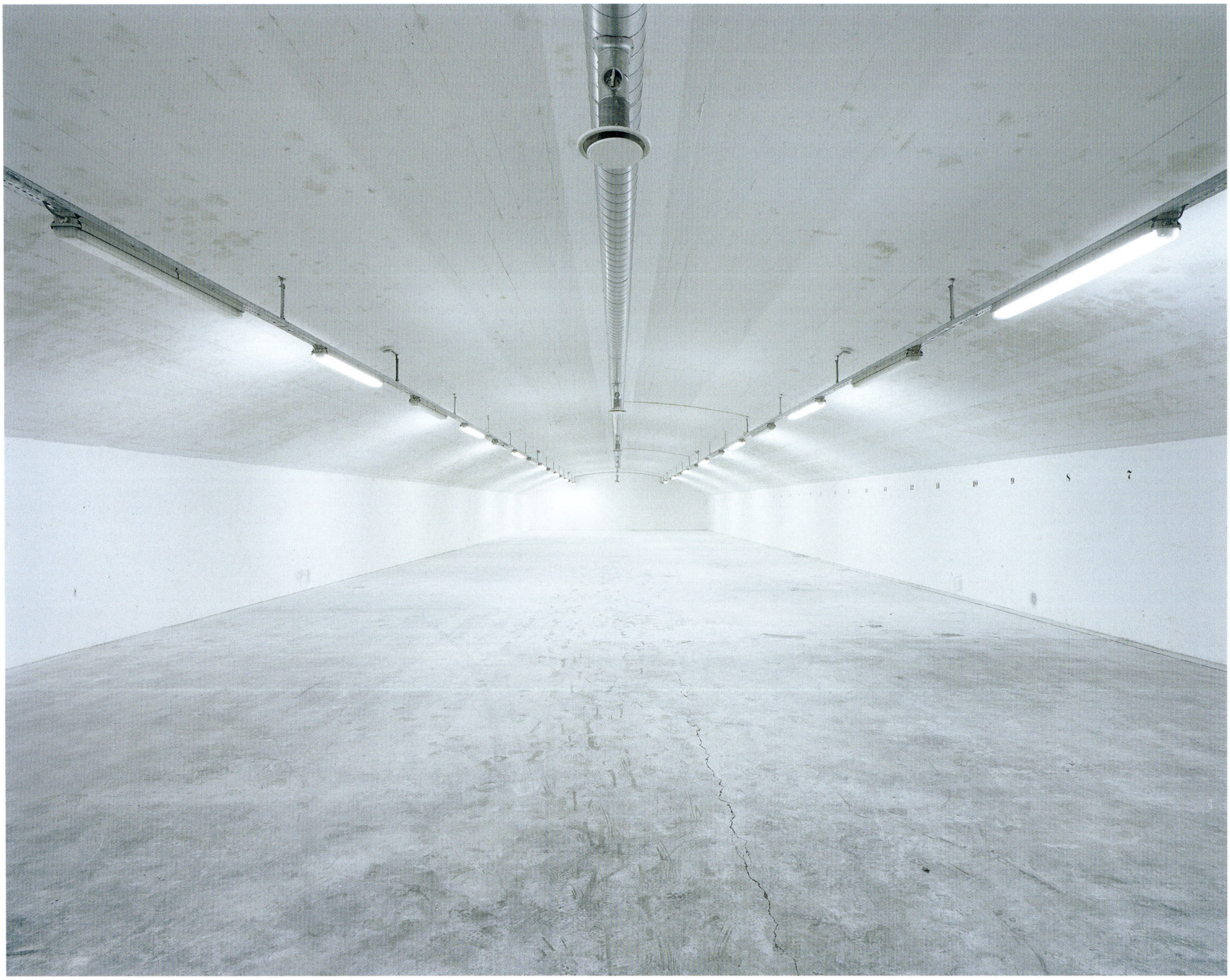

38
39

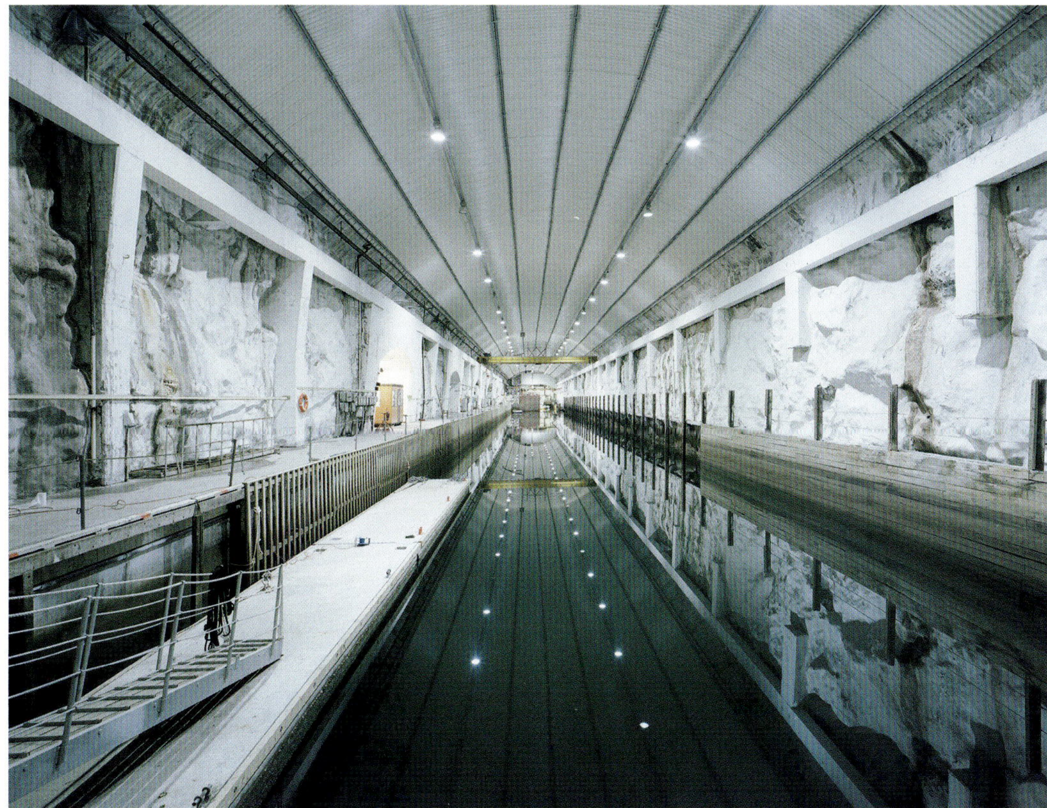

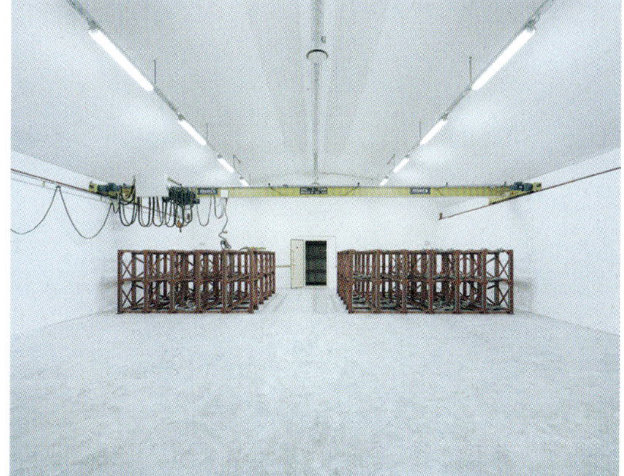

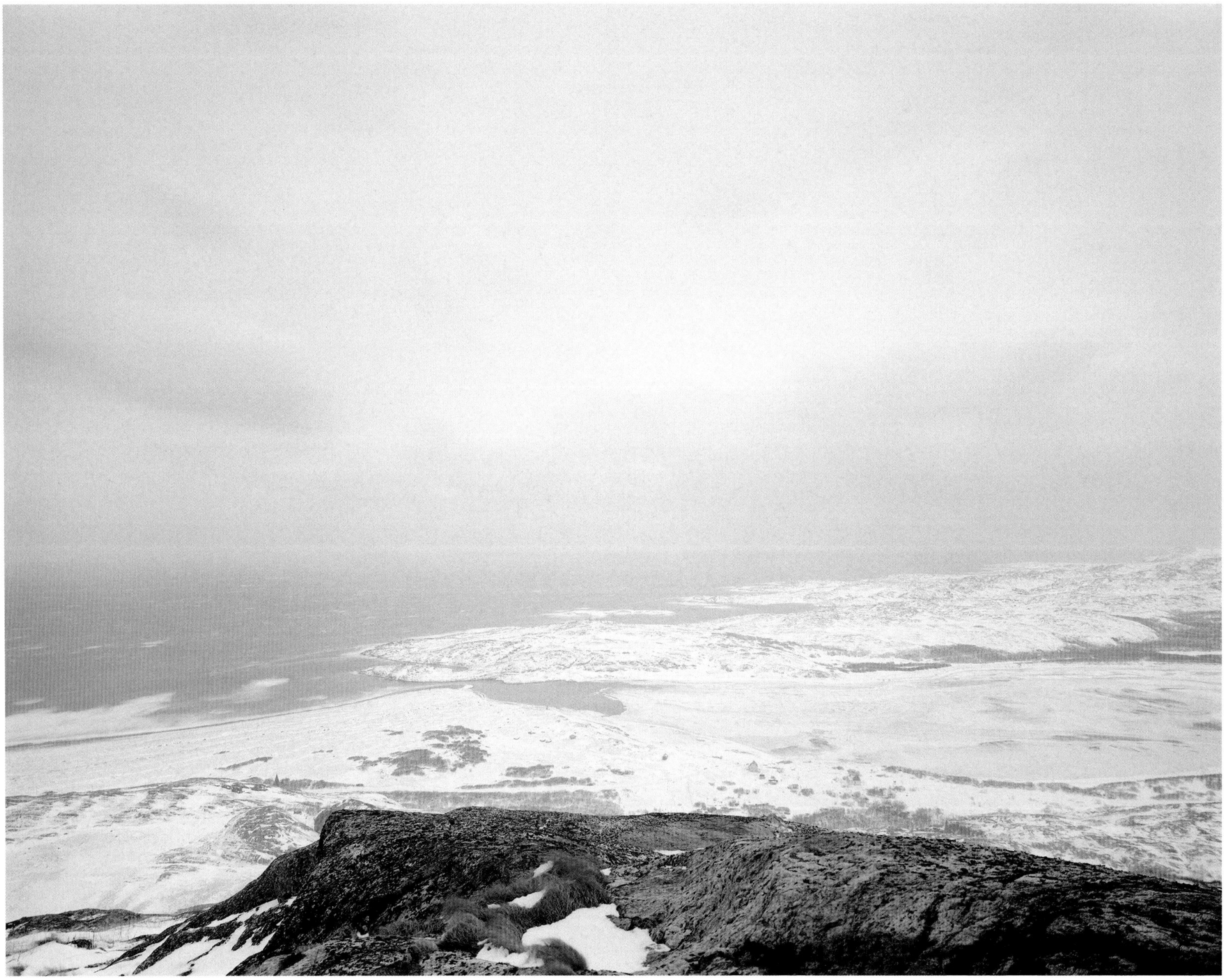

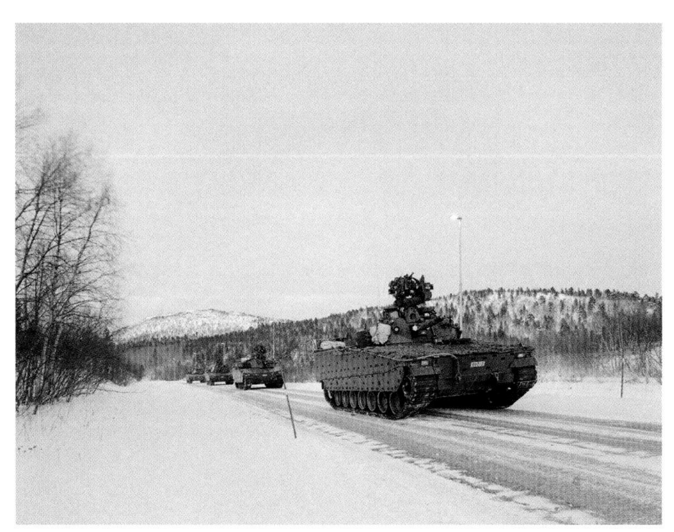
41

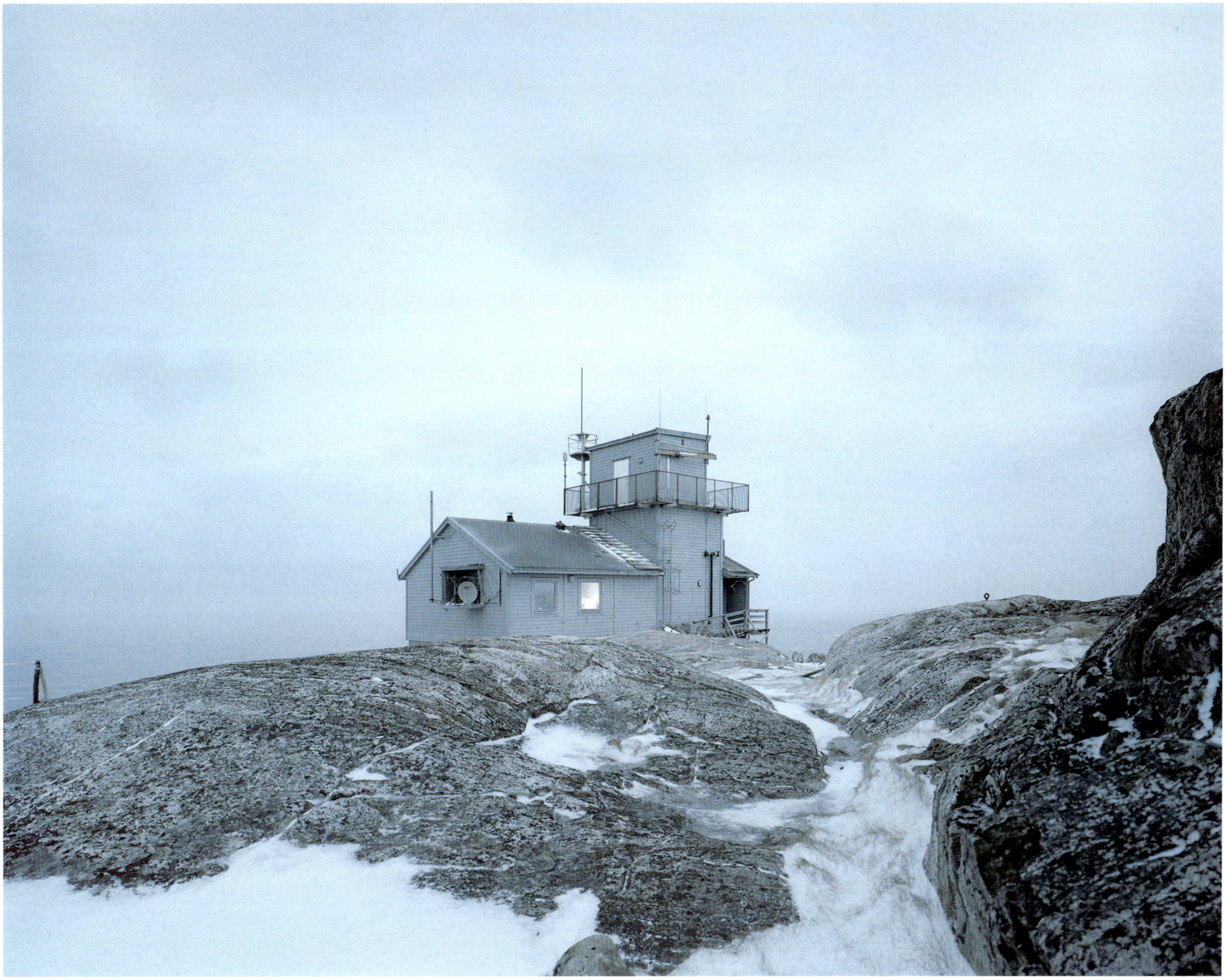

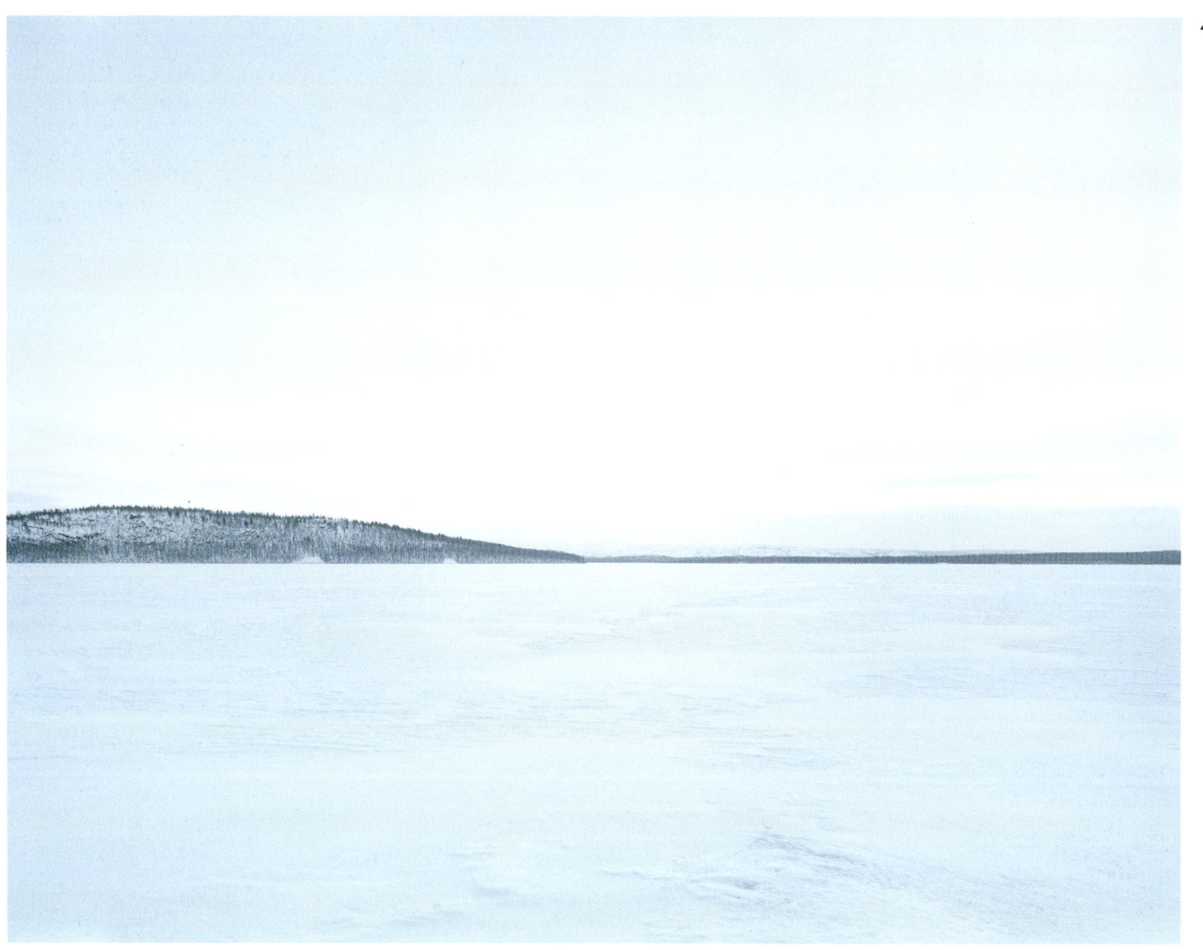

43

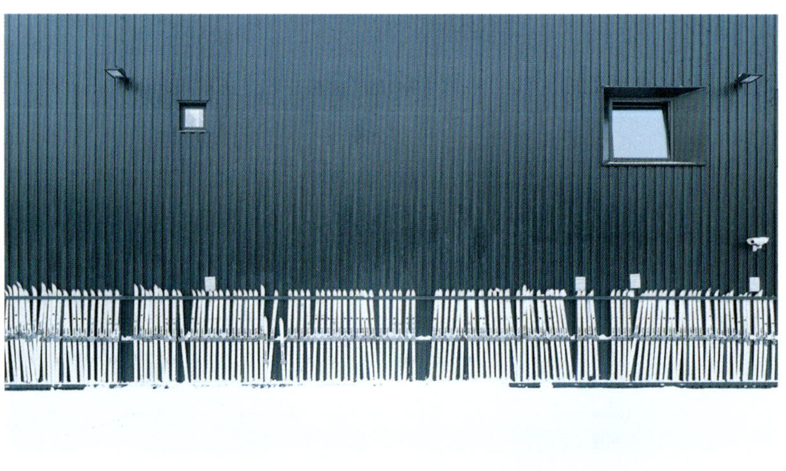

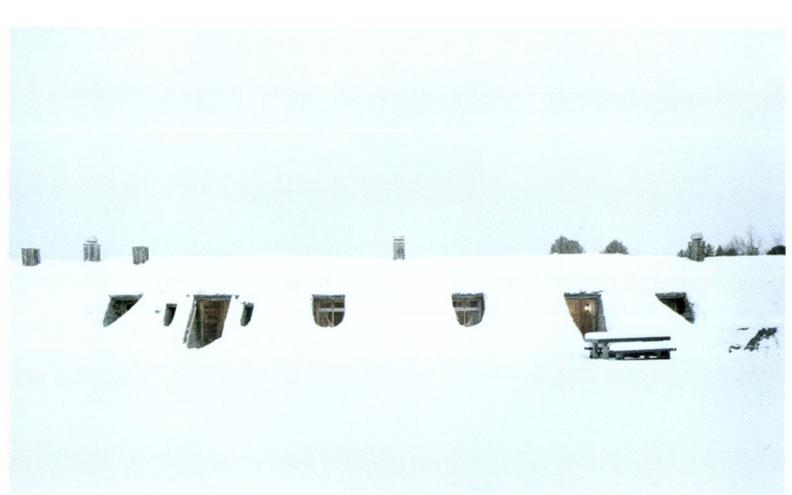

44
45

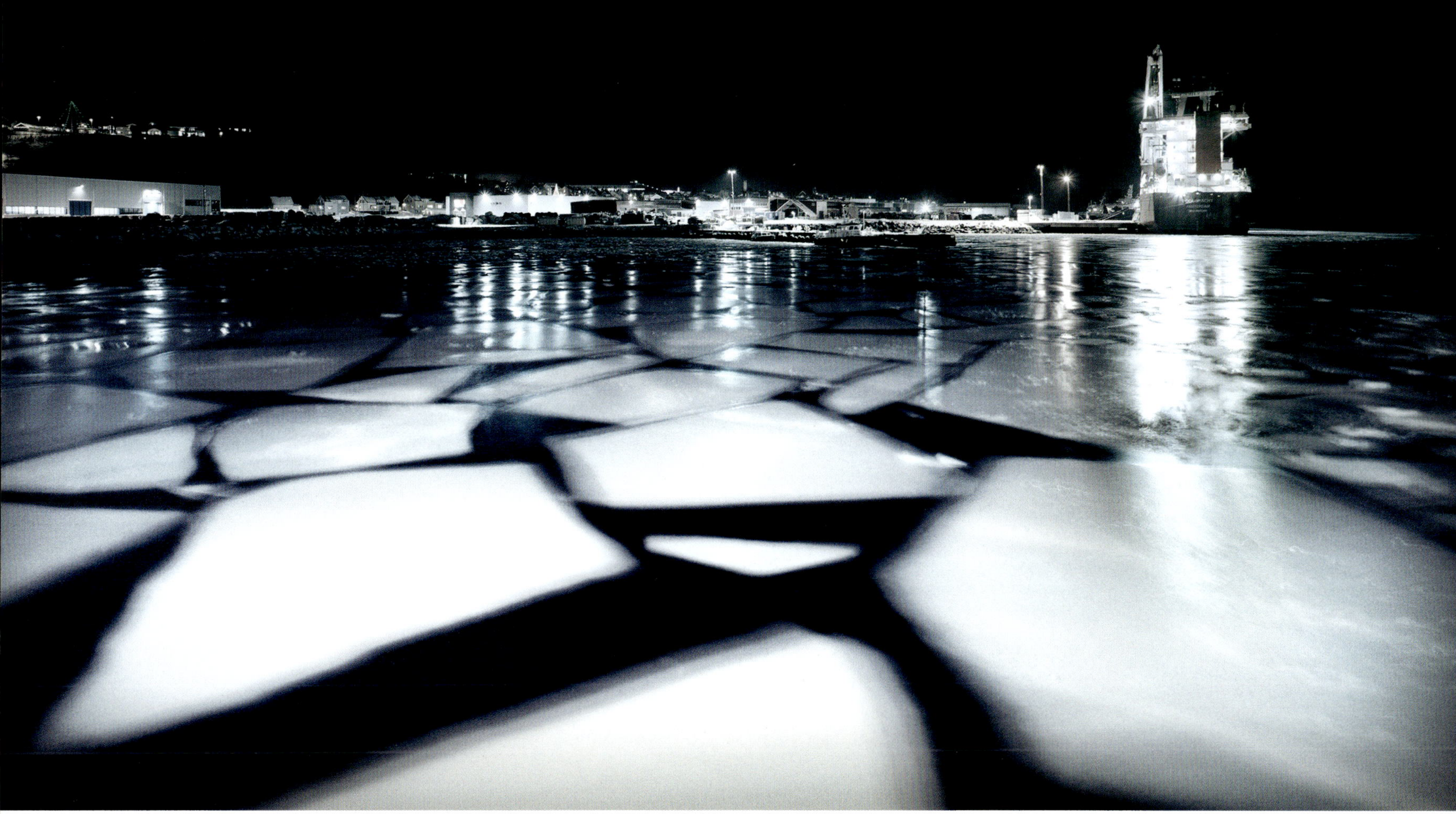

46

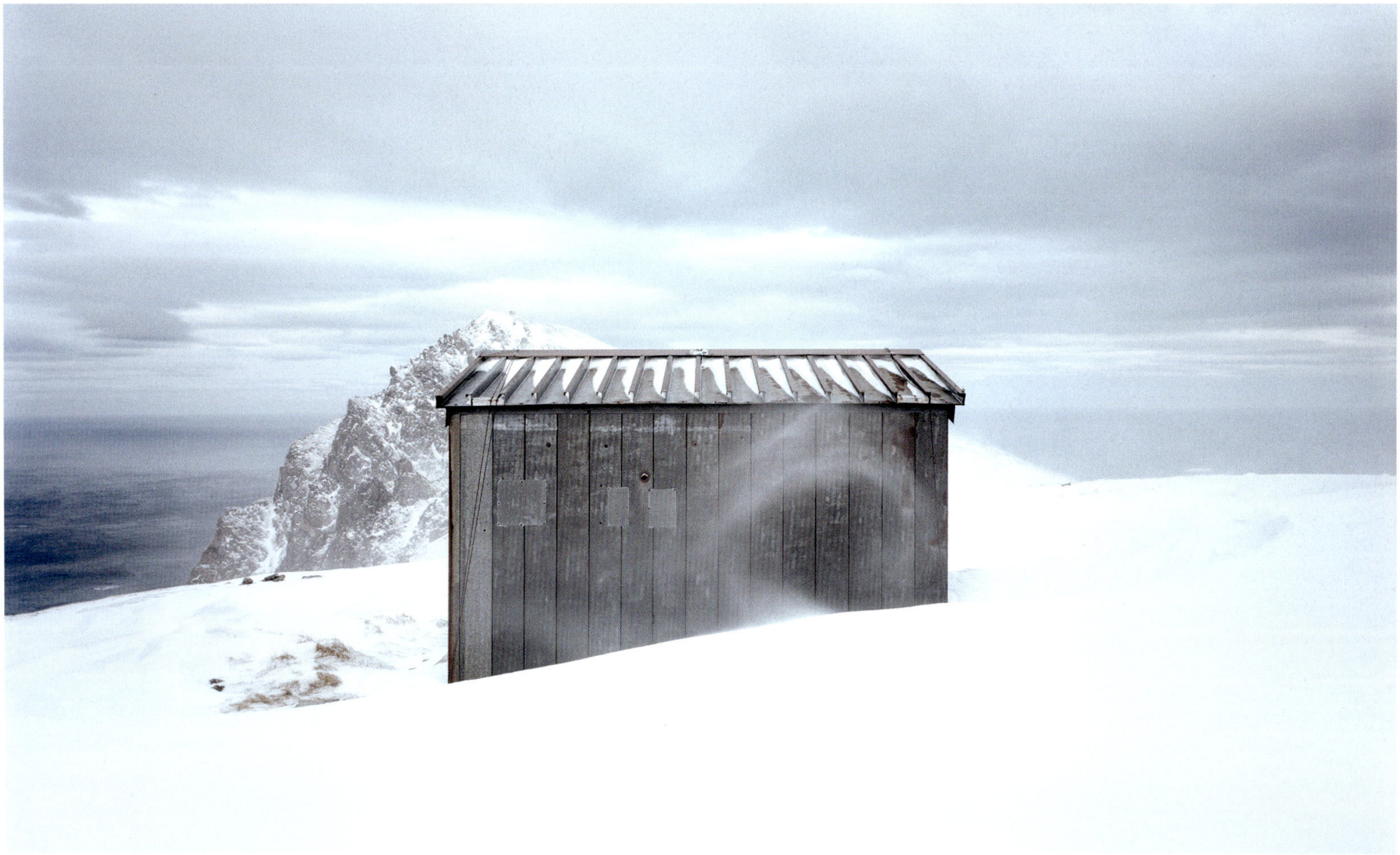

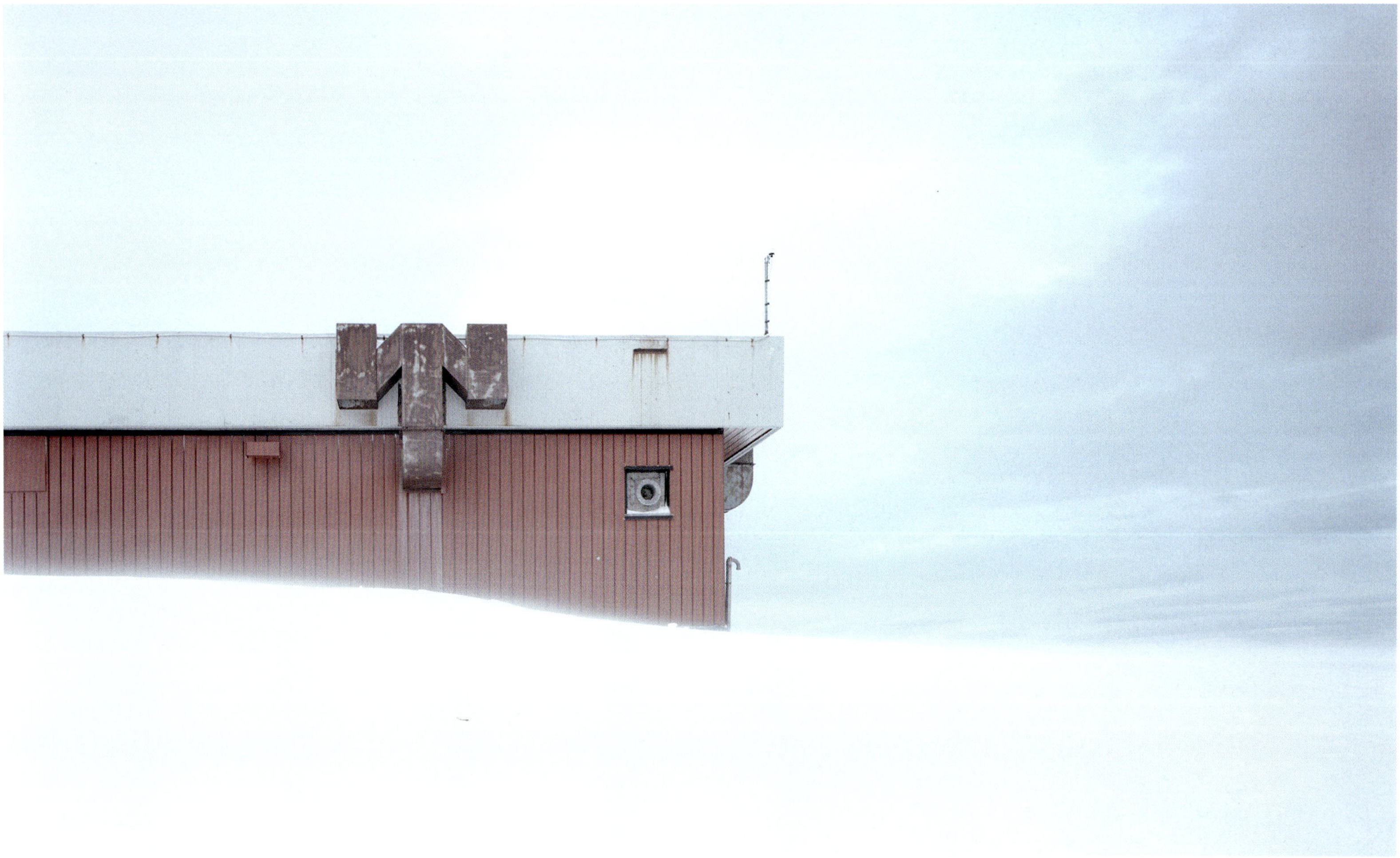

49

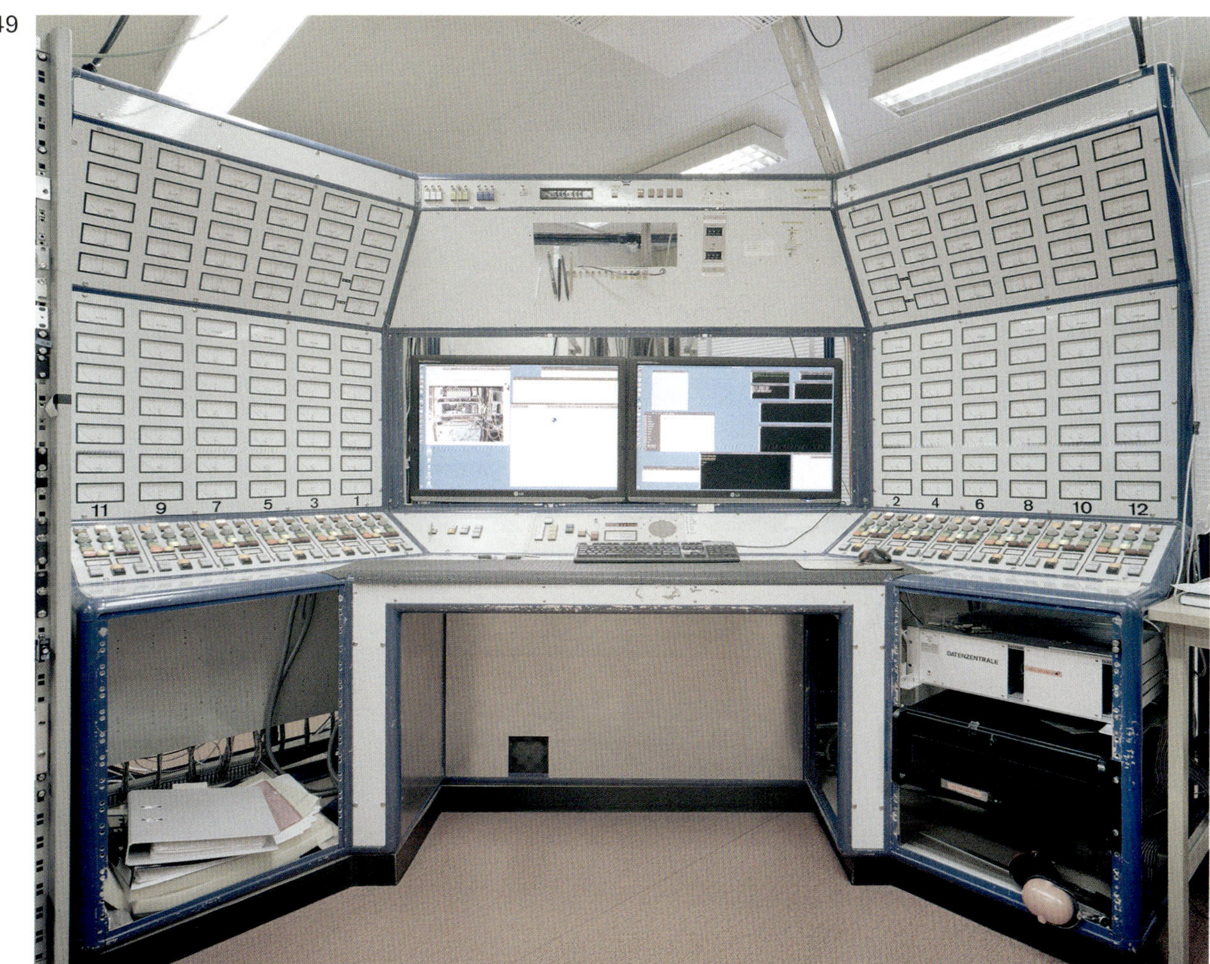

11 9 7 5 3 1
2 4 6 8 10 12
DATENZENTRALE

50

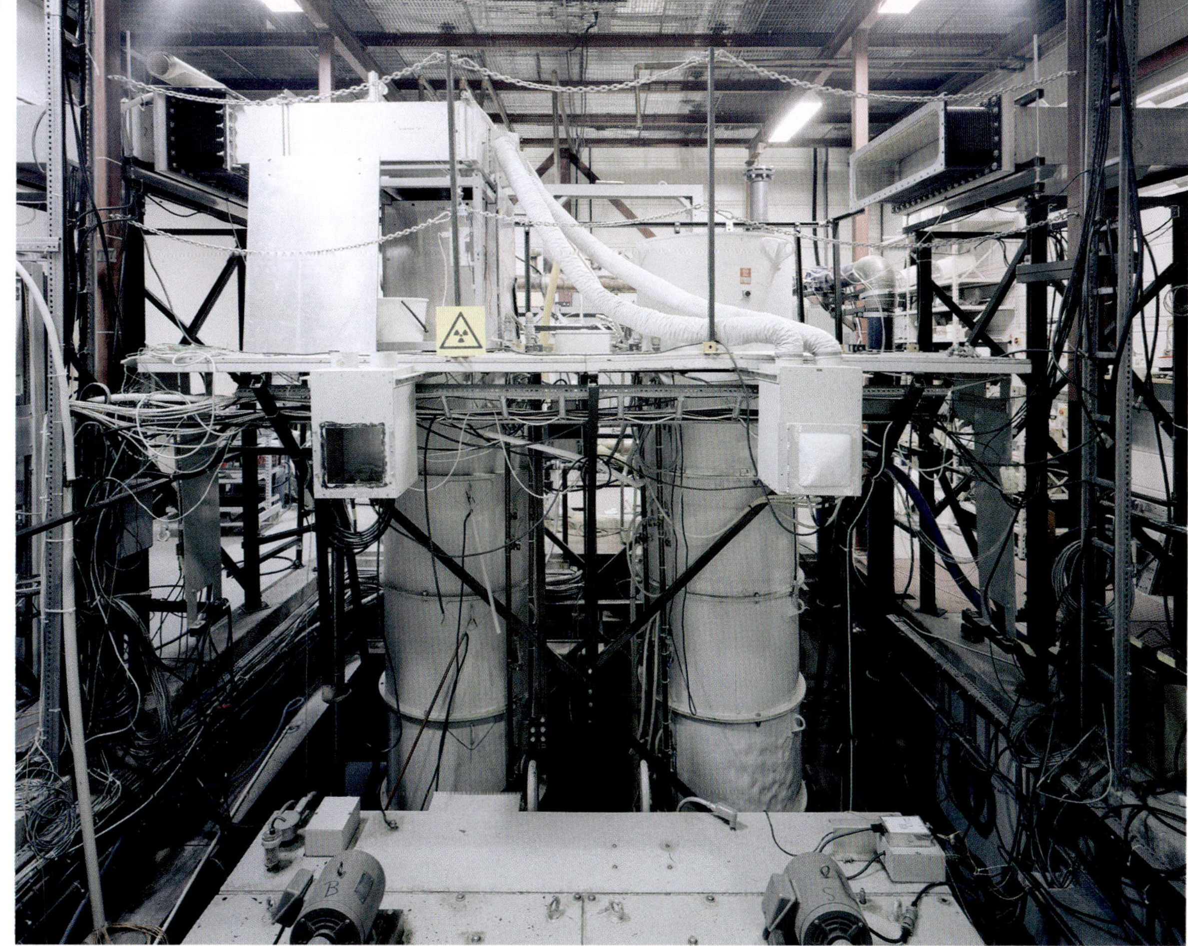

51
52

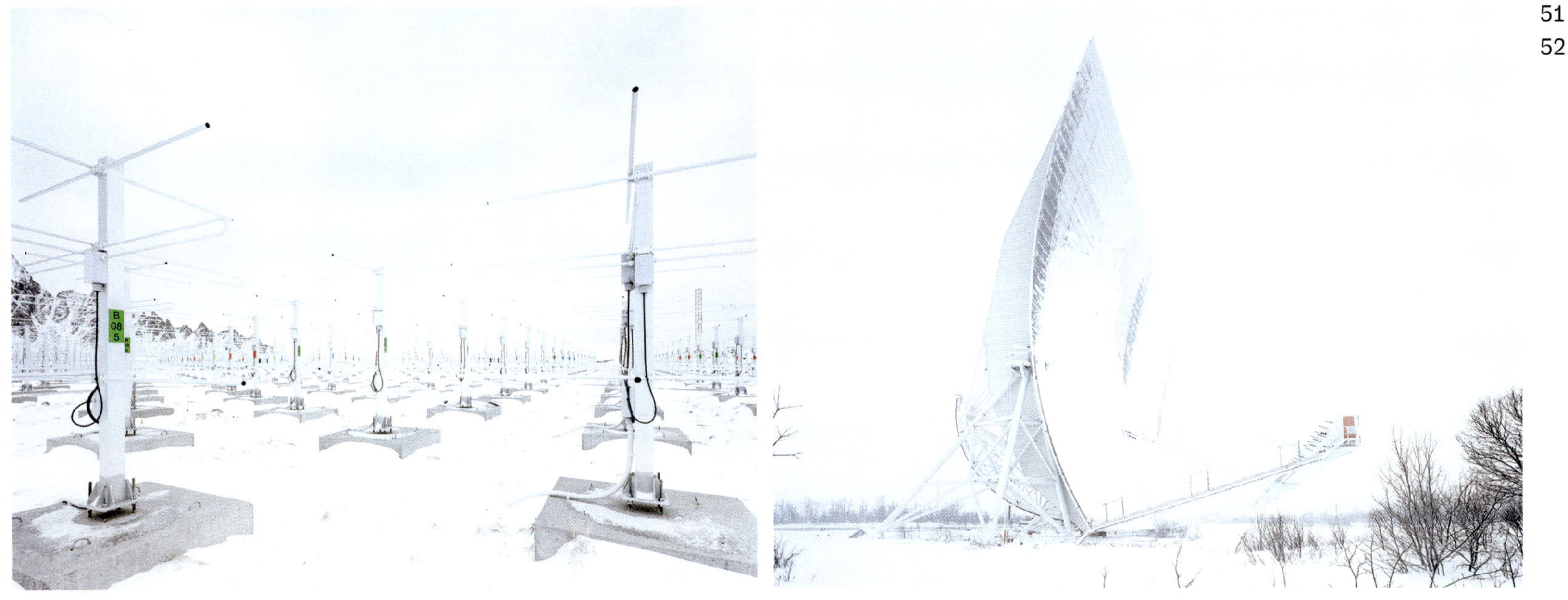

53

54

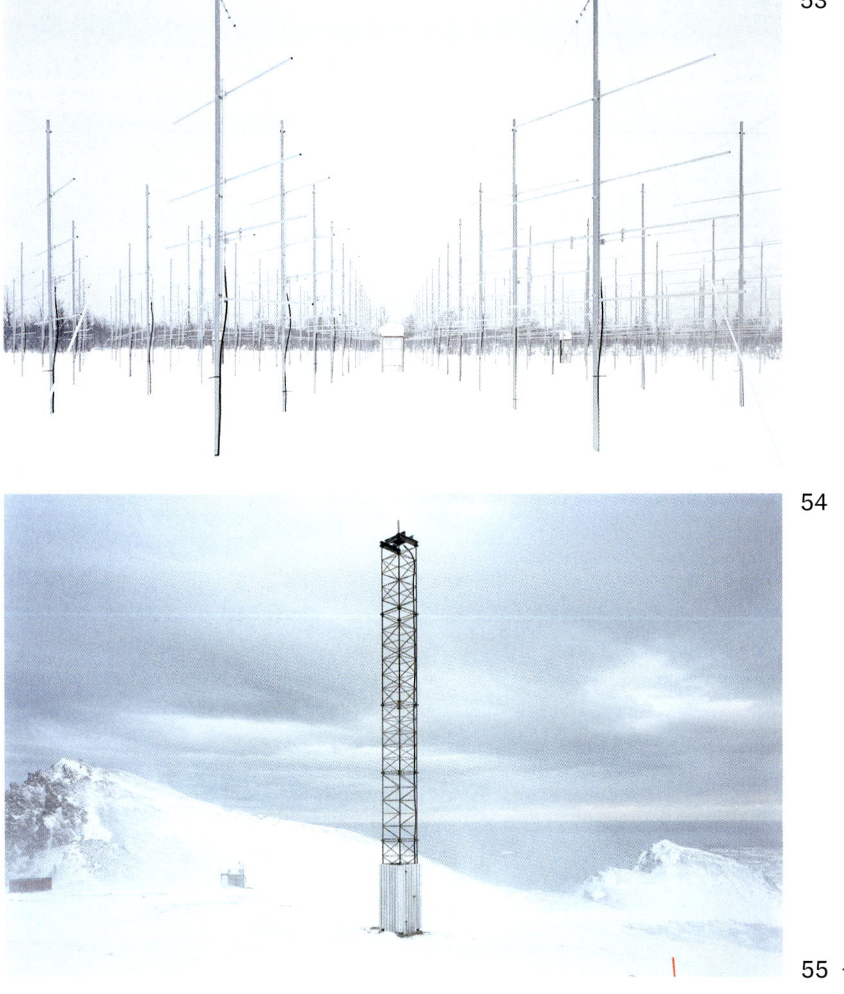

55 →

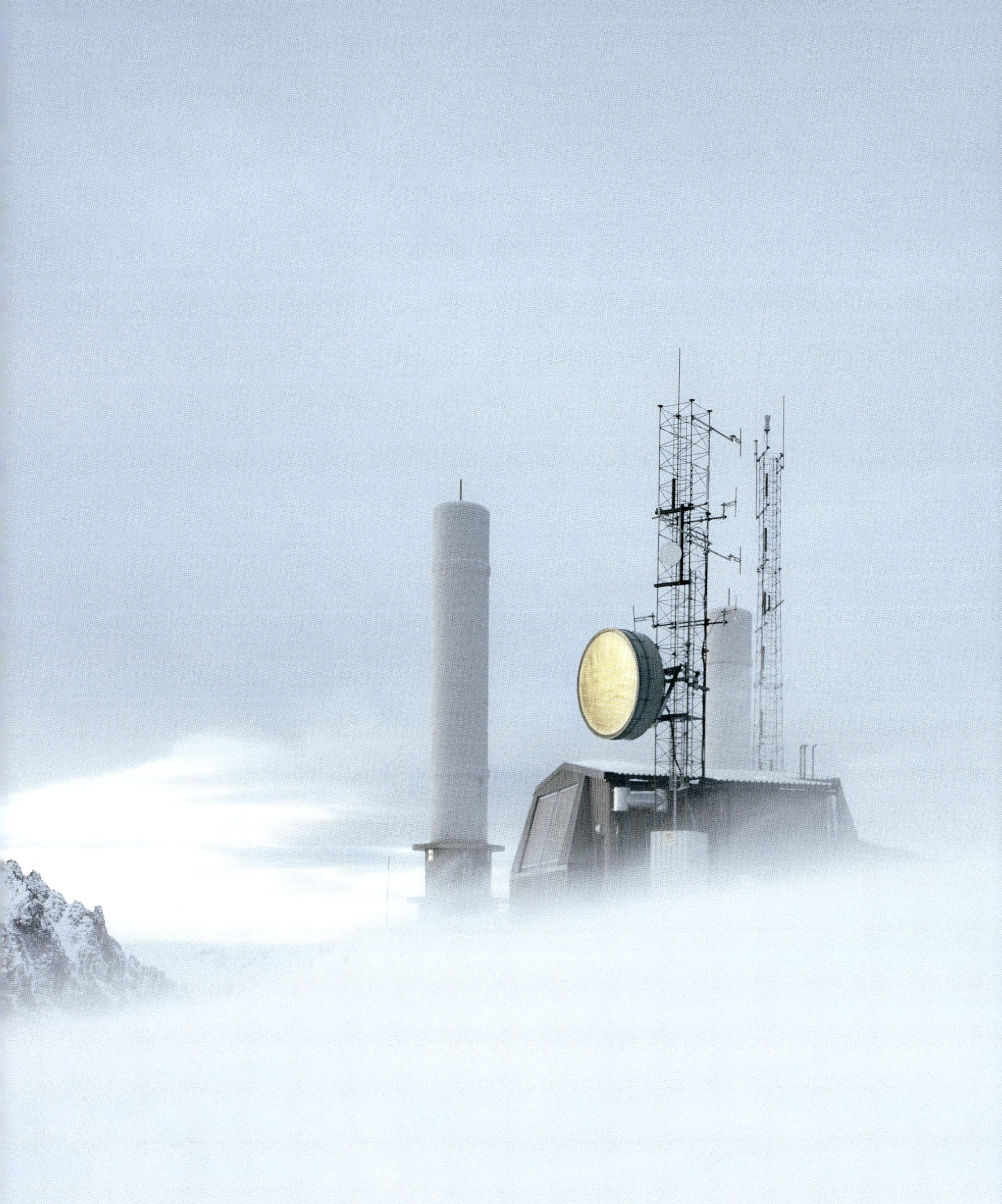

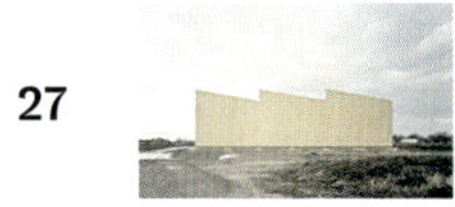

27 *Schnöggersburg V*
Deutsche Bundeswehr | German Army
Sachsen-Anhalt, Deutschland | Germany, 2017

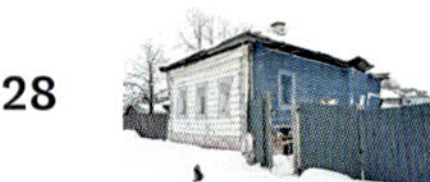

28 *Suzdal V*
Oblast Wladimir, Russland | Vladimir Oblast, Russia, 2016

29 *Suzdal IV*
Oblast Wladimir, Russland | Vladimir Oblast, Russia, 2016

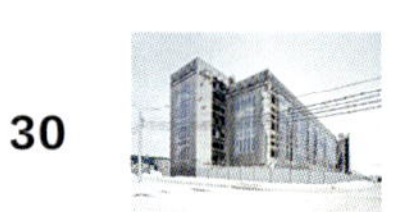

30 *Ufa I*
Baschkortostan, Russland | Bashkortostan, Russia, 2016

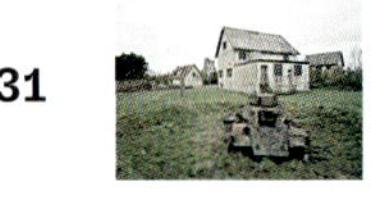

31 *Bridge Carr X*
Stanford Übungsgebiet | Stanford Training Area
Britische Armee | British Army
Norfolk, England, 2015

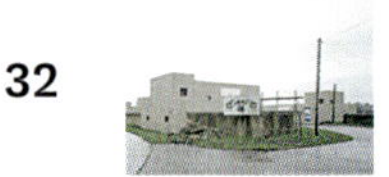

32 *Bridge Carr III*
Stanford Übungsgebiet | Stanford Training Area
Britische Armee | British Army
Norfolk, England, 2015

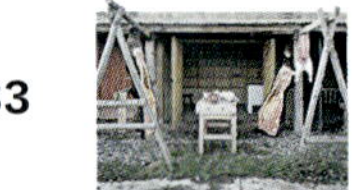

33 *Eastmere III*
Stanford Übungsgebiet | Stanford Training Area
Britische Armee | British Army
Norfolk, England, 2015

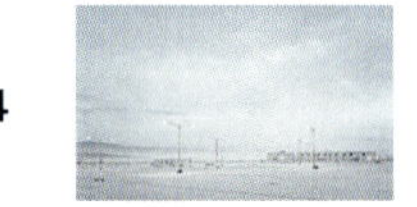

34 *Tiefort City VIII*
Fort Irwin, US-Armee | US Army
Mojave-Wüste, Kalifornien | Mojave Desert, California,
USA, 2016

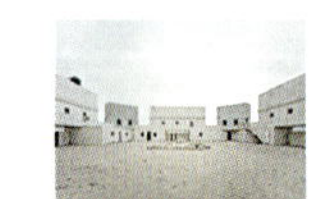

35 *Junction City IX*
Fort Irwin, US-Armee | US Army
Mojave-Wüste, Kalifornien | Mojave Desert, California,
USA, 2016

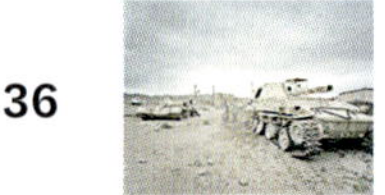

36 *Junction City X*
Fort Irwin, US-Armee | US Army
Mojave-Wüste, Kalifornien | Mojave Desert, California,
USA, 2016

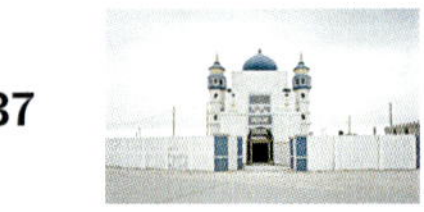

37 *Junction City XIII*
Fort Irwin, US-Armee | US Army
Mojave-Wüste, Kalifornien | Mojave Desert, California,
USA, 2016

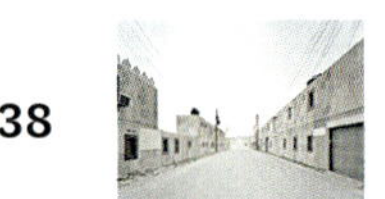

38 *Junction City VII*
Fort Irwin, US-Armee | US Army
Mojave-Wüste, Kalifornien | Mojave Desert, California,
USA, 2016

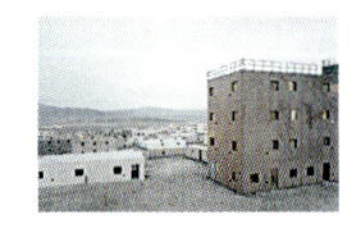

39 *Tiefort City VII*
Fort Irwin, US-Armee | US Army
Mojave-Wüste, Kalifornien | Mojave Desert, California,
USA, 2016

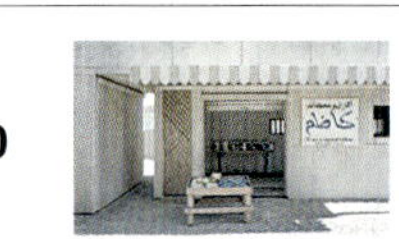

40 *Tiefort City XVI*
Fort Irwin, US-Armee | US Army
Mojave-Wüste, Kalifornien | Mojave Desert, California,
USA, 2016

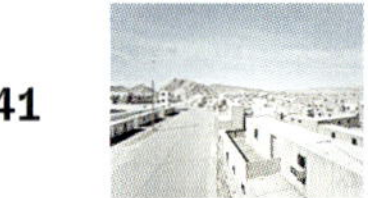

41 *Tiefort City IV*
Fort Irwin, US-Armee | US Army
Mojave-Wüste, Kalifornien | Mojave Desert, California,
USA, 2016

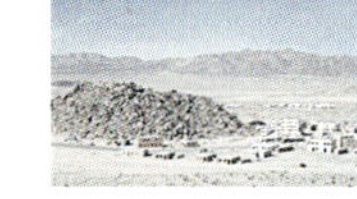

42 *Tiefort City II*
Fort Irwin, US-Armee | US Army
Mojave-Wüste, Kalifornien | Mojave Desert, California,
USA, 2016

Kokerei Hansa, 2003/2005
S. | Pp. 50–59

0 *Koksofendecke Batterie I, Füllwagen O auf Batterie O,
Fördergerüst Zeche Hansa*
Dortmund, Deutschland | Germany, 2003

1 *Kohlenbandbrücke*
Schwarze Straße | Black Street
Dortmund, Deutschland | Germany, 2003

2 *Gassaugerhaus mit NH3–Waschern (Maschinenhaus Nord)*
Weiße Straße | White Street
Dortmund, Deutschland | Germany, 2003

3 *Leitungstrasse Ammoniakfabrik mit Salzverladegleis*
Weiße Straße | White Street
Dortmund, Deutschland | Germany, 2003

4 *Ferngas-Gasometer*
Weiße Straße | White Street
Dortmund, Deutschland | Germany, 2003

5 *Kaminkühler, rechts kombinierter Kaminkühler/
Ventilatorkühlturm*
Weiße Straße | White Street
Dortmund, Deutschland | Germany, 2003

6 *Koksofendecke Batterie II,
Koksbandbrücke, Sieberei I*
Schwarze Straße | Black Street
Dortmund, Deutschland | Germany, 2003

7 *Sieberei II mit Koksbandbrücke, Batterie IV*
Schwarze Straße | Black Street
Dortmund, Deutschland | Germany, 2003

8 *Gebäudefront Hochdruckfeinreinigung*
Weiße Straße | White Street
Dortmund, Deutschland | Germany, 2003

9 *Gebäudefront Hochdruckfeinreinigung*
Weiße Straße | White Street
Dortmund, Deutschland | Germany, 2003

Ladiz, 2006/2008
S. | Pp. 60–69

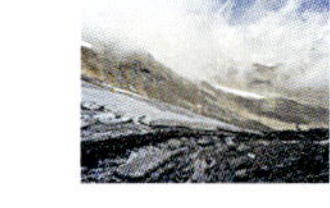

0 *Weißseeferner, Kaunertaler Gletscher, 2750–3535 m*
Ötztaler Alpen, Österreich | Ötztal Alps, Austria, 2006

1 *Eisjochferner, 2900 m*
Stubaier Alpen, Österreich | Stubai Alps, Austria, 2006

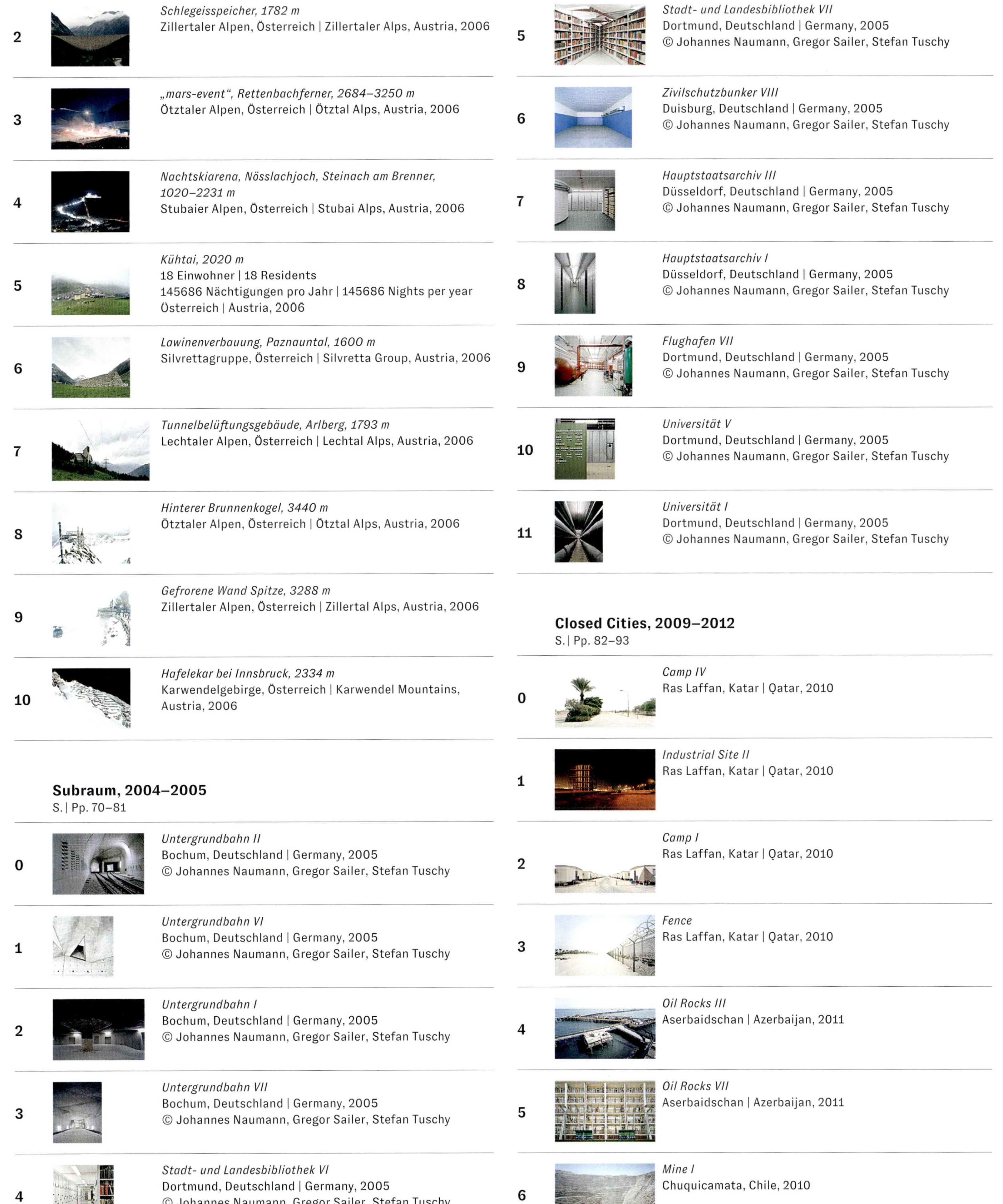

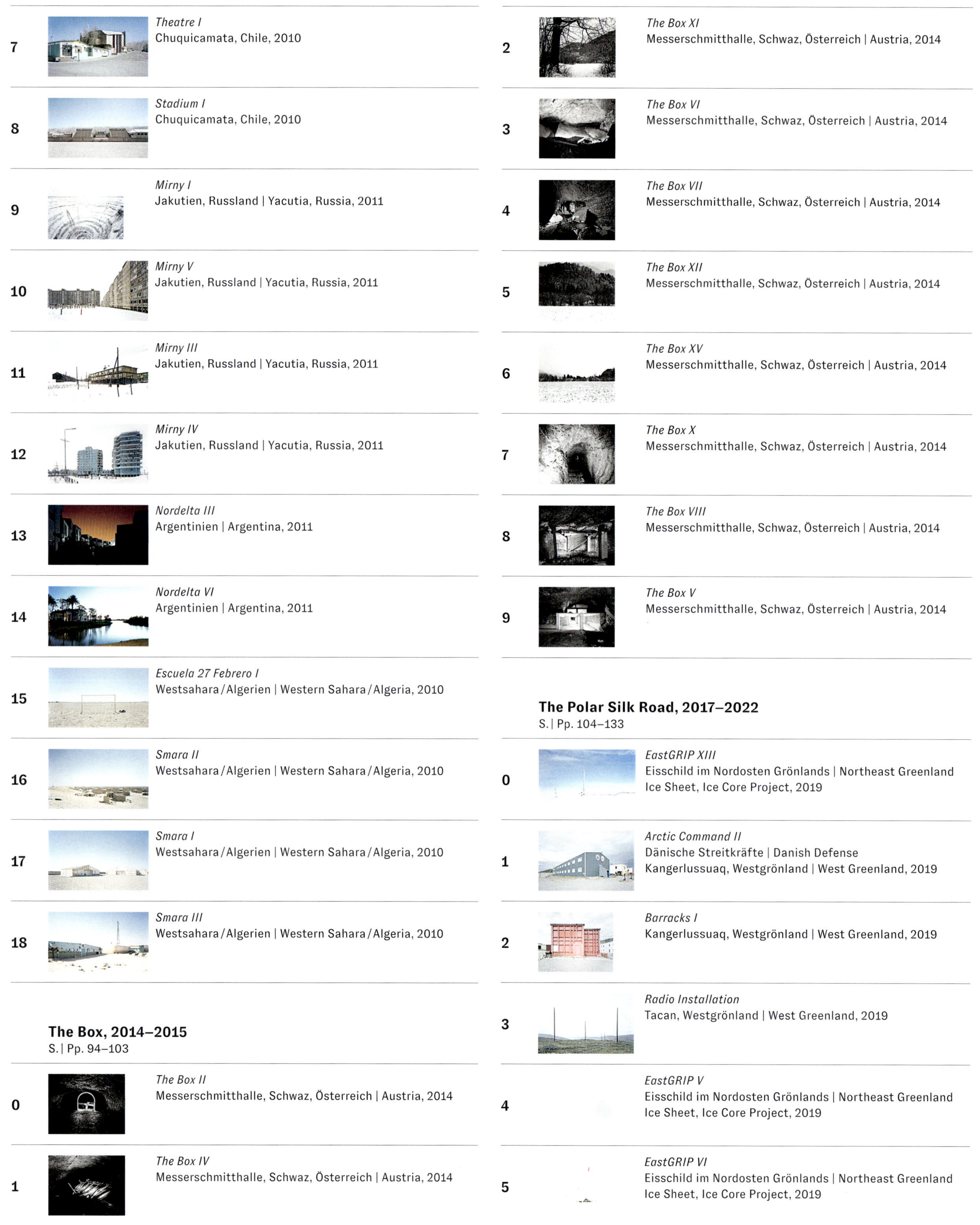

The Box, 2014–2015
S. | Pp. 94–103

The Polar Silk Road, 2017–2022
S. | Pp. 104–133

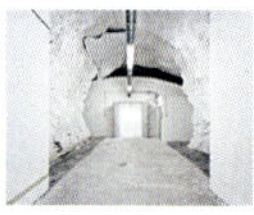

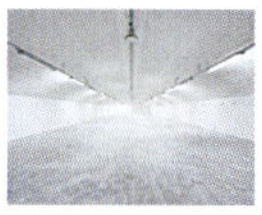

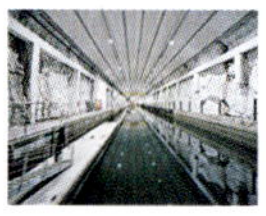

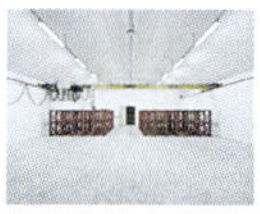

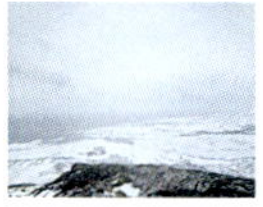

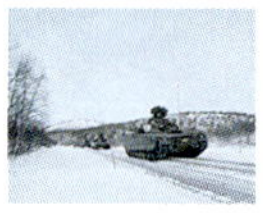

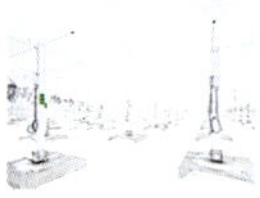

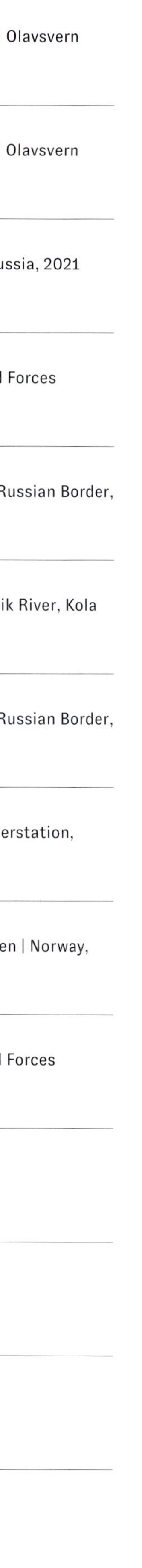
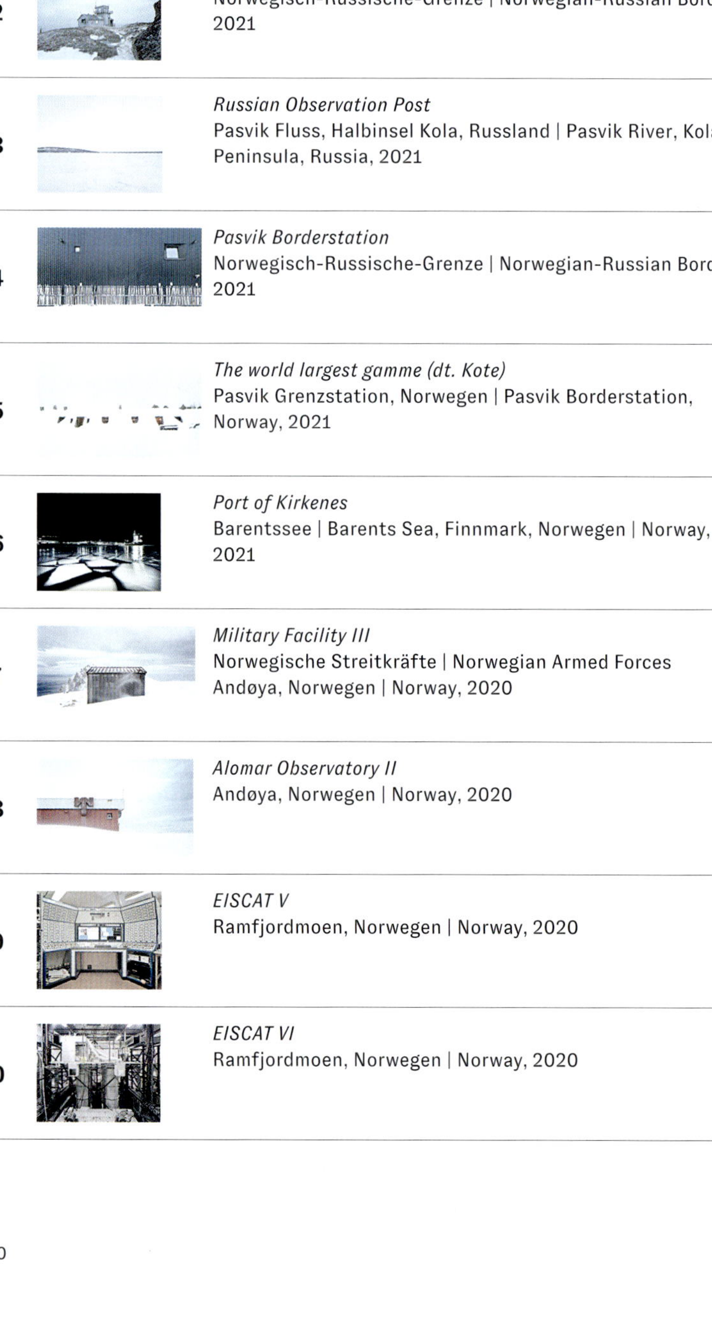

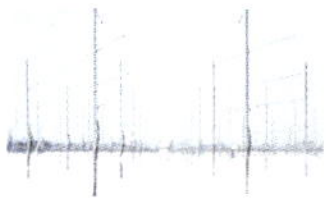

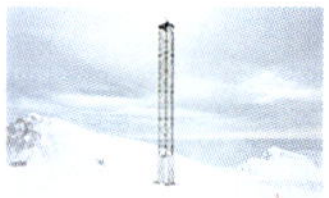

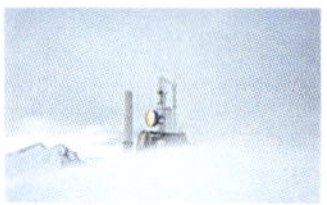

Biografie

Gregor Sailer

Geboren 1980 in Schwaz
Lebt und arbeitet in Tirol, Österreich

2002 • Diplomstudium Kommunikations-
–07 design, Schwerpunkt Fotografie und
   Experimentalfilm, Fachhochschule
   Dortmund (bei Susanne Brügger und
   Piet Wessing)
2012 • Masterstudium Photographic Studies,
–15 Fachhochschule Dortmund (bei
   Susanne Brügger, Pamela Scorzin und
   Piet Wessing)

Einzelausstellungen (Auswahl)

2023 • *The Polar Silk Road,* Alfred Ehrhardt
   Stiftung, Berlin, DE
   • *The Polar Silk Road,* Natural History
   Museum, London, UK
2022 • *Unseen Places.* Gregor Sailer,
   KUNST HAUS WIEN, AT
2021 • *The Polar Silk Road,* Museum für Berg-
   fotografie LUMEN, Bruneck/Brunico, IT
2020 • *Staged – From the Potemkin Series,*
   Atelier Sérgio Rebelo, MIP – Month of
   Photography Porto, PT
2019 • *The Potemkin Village,* Centre de la
   photographie Genève, Genf, CH
   • *The Potemkin Village,* Freelens Galerie,
   Hamburg, DE
   • *The Potemkin Village,* Atelier Jungwirth,
   Graz, AT
   • *The Potemkin Village,* Montrasio Arte,
   Mailand und Monza, IT
   • *The Potemkin Village,* Galerie Fotografic,
   Prag, CZ
2018 • *The Potemkin Village,* Les Rencontres
   d'Arles, FR
   • *The Potemkin Village,* Kehrer Galerie,
   Berlin, DE
   • *The Potemkin Village,* PhEST – Festival
   Internazionale di Fotografia e Arte,
   Monopoli, IT
2017 • *The Potemkin Village,* FO.KU.S, Foto
   Kunst Stadtforum, Innsbruck, AT
2015 • *Closed Cities,* Month of Photography,
   Klarisky, Bratislava, SK
2014 • *Grenzgänger – Closed Cities,* Gallery
   Loris, Berlin, DE
2013 • *Closed Cities,* Galerie im Taxispalais,
   Innsbruck, AT
   • *Closed Cities,* KE Gallery, Köln, DE
   • *Closed Cities,* Foto Forum, Bozen, IT
2010 • *Kokerei Hansa,* Kunsthalle Wien, AT
   • *Subraum,* Kunsthalle Wien, AT

Gruppenausstellungen (Auswahl)

2021 • *One Artist – One Minute,* Fotohof/
   Stadtgalerie Lehen, Salzburg, AT
2020 • *Subjekt und Objekt,* Foto Rhein Ruhr,
   Kunsthalle Düsseldorf, DE
   • *The Architecture of Deception,* BNKR
   München, DE
   • *Déjà Vu,* Atelier Jungwirth, Graz, AT
2019 • LiShui Photography Festival, Biennale,
   China
   • *Osmoscosmos,* Centre de la photogra-
   phie Genève, Genf, CH
   • *Alpen – Mythos Natur,* MEWO Kunst-
   halle, Memmingen, DE

• *European Architectural Photography Prize,*
   Deutsche Werkstätten Dresden, DE
2018 • Ray Triennale Frankfurt/RheinMain, DE
   • *Echt jetzt?! Klasse Kunst VI,* Landes-
   galerie Linz, AT
   • *European Architectural Photography
   Prize,* KAZimKUBA, Kassel, DE
   • *RLB Kunstpreis,* RLB Kunstbrücke,
   Innsbruck, AT
2017 • *No secrets!,* Stadtmuseum München, DE
   • *Ephemeral Urbanism,* Pinakothek der
   Moderne, München, DE
   • *Raum und Fotografie,* Mönchsberg,
   Museum der Moderne Salzburg, AT
   • *ArtTirol,* Ferdinandeum, Innsbruck, AT
   • *European Architectural Photography
   Prize,* Deutsches Architekturmuseum,
   Frankfurt am Main, DE
   • Krasnojarsk Museum Biennale, RUS
2015 • *Drap Art Festival – Closed Cities,* Centre
   de Cultura Contemporània de
   Barcelona, ES
   • *Conceptual Storytelling,* Delhi Photo
   Festival, New Delhi, IN
2014 • *Von oben gesehen. Die Vogelperspektive,*
   Germanisches Nationalmuseum,
   Nürnberg, DE
   • *Jenseits der Ansichtskarte,* Vorarlberg
   Museum, Bregenz, AT
2013 • *Under Pressure – Politik in der zeit-
   genössischen Fotografie,* Mönchsberg,
   Museum der Moderne Salzburg, AT
   • *Architecture/Landscape,* Mansion at
   Strathmore, Lockheed Martin Gallery,
   Maryland, US
   • *Fragile,* BAWAG Contemporary, Wien, AT
   • *Hohe Dosis,* Fotohof/Atterseehalle,
   Salzburg, AT
   • *Jenseits der Ansichtskarte,* Galerie
   Stihl, Waiblingen, DE
   • *5. Internationaler Marianne Brandt
   Wettbewerb,* Sächsisches Industrie-
   museum Chemnitz, DE
2012 • *Closed Cities,* Paris Photo, Grand
   Palais, Paris, FR
   • *Architecture/Landscape,* Fotoweeks DC,
   L2 Lounge Georgetown, Washington, US
   • *Schaufenster zur Sammlung II – Bilder
   von Tag und Nacht,* Rupertinum,
   Museum der Moderne Salzburg, AT
   • *Nacht,* OstLicht. Galerie für Fotografie,
   Wien, AT
   • *Bildspuren – Unruhige Gegenwarten,*
   Darmstädter Tage der Fotografie,
   Darmstadt, DE
2011 • *Alpine Desire,* ACF New York, US (in
   Kooperation mit dem Belvedere Wien)
   • *Alpen – Sehnsucht & Bühne,* Museum
   Residenzgalerie Salzburg, AT
   • *Mythos Berg,* RLB Kunstbrücke,
   Innsbruck, AT
   • *Ecopoli vs Metropoli,* Palazzo Firmian,
   Trient, IT
2010 • *Next 1,* Museum Folkwang, Essen, DE
   • *Die Welt als Kulisse,* Galerie im Taxispa-
   lais, Innsbruck, AT
   • *Iris Award,* Perth Centre of Photogra-
   phy, Perth, AU
   • *Shelf Life,* JaAliceKlarr Projects,
   Edinburgh Art Festival, GB
   • *Triennale Linz 1.0. Gegenwartskunst in
   Österreich,* Landesgalerie Linz, AT

Screenings

2019 • *Nuit de la Photo,* La-Chaux-de-Fonds, CH
2018 • *ArchFilmMatinée: Urban Fiction – Fact,
   Fiction, Fake? In-Timer 47:09:21,* Film-
   casino, Wien, AT
2017 • *Zeytinburnu International Photography
   Festival,* Istanbul, TR
2010 • *JaAliceKlarr Projects,* Edinburgh Art
   Festival, GB
2008 • *The Int'l Fest of Cinema and Technology,*
   Seattle, US
   • *Babelgum Online Film Festival,* Venedig,
   IT
   • *Broadcasting Sky Channel 195,* Propeller
   TV, England, GB
   • *Broadcasting Circuito Off Channel,*
   Venedig, IT
   • *The Int'l Fest of Cinema and Technology,*
   Melbourne, AU
2007 • *Treibhaus,* Innsbruck, AT
2006 • *Fluxus 06,* Internationales Filmfestival,
   Belo Horizonte, BR
   • *Crank Cookie Kurzfilmtage,* Passau, DE
   • *Borges en Curt,* III Festival Internacional
   de Curtmetratges de les Terres de
   Ponent, Lleida, ES
   • *Filmpremiere In-Timer 47:09:21,*
   domicil, Dortmund, DE

Monografien

2021 • *The Polar Silk Road,* Kehrer Verlag,
   Heidelberg
2020 • *Staged – From the Potemkin Series,*
   Espacio Jhannia Castro, Porto, PT
   (in Kooperation mit dem Centre de la
   photographie Genève, Genf)
2017 • *The Potemkin Village,* Kehrer Verlag,
   Heidelberg
2012 • *Closed Cities,* Kehrer Verlag,
   Heidelberg
2010 • *Subraum,* Edition Fotohof, Salzburg
   • *Dolomiti,* Actar/Birkhäuser,
   Barcelona/Basel/New York
2008 • *Ladiz,* Edition Fotohof, Salzburg
2005 • *Kokerei Hansa,* hrsg. von der Stiftung
   Industriedenkmalpflege und
   Geschichtskultur, Dortmund

Öffentliche Sammlungen

• Albertina, Wien, AT
• Artothek der Stadt und Landesbiblio-
   thek Dortmund, DE
• Belvedere, Wien, AT
• Collection Centre National des Arts
   Plastiques, Paris, FR
• Deutsches Architekturmuseum,
   Frankfurt am Main, DE
• Ferdinandeum, Sammlung des Landes
   Tirol, Innsbruck, AT
• Fotomuseum Winterthur,
   Film Collection, CH
• Galerie der Moderne, Stiftmuseum
   Klosterneuburg, AT
• Kunsthalle Wien, Ursula Blickle
   Stiftung, Videoarchive, AT
• Les Rencontres d'Arles, FR
• Museum für Bergfotografie LUMEN,
   Bruneck/Brunico, IT

• Raiffeisen Landesbank Südtirol AG,
   Bozen, IT
• Raiffeisen-Landesbank Tirol AG,
   Innsbruck, AT
• Rupertinum, Museum der Moderne
   Salzburg, AT
• Sammlung der Republik Österreich, AT
• Sammlung der Stadt Innsbruck, AT
• Tiroler Archiv für photographische
   Dokumentation und Kunst, Lienz, AT
• Wienerberger AG, Wien, AT

Zahlreiche Werke in Privatsammlungen

Preise

2020 • Förderpreis Raiffeisen-Landesbank
   Tirol AG
2018 • DAM Architectural Book Award
   • Deutsche Börse Photography Prize
   (Nominierung)
2017 • European Architectural Photography
   Prize (Commendation)
   • Prix Pictet (Nominierung)
   • Felix Schoeller Photo Award (Shortlist)
2016 • St. Leopold Friedenspreis
   • Joseph Binder Award, Digital Media
   (Bronze)
   • Staatsstipendium für Fotografie der
   Republik Österreich
2015 • The Vevey International Photography
   Award (Shortlist)
   • Staatsstipendium für Fotografie der
   Republik Österreich
2014 • Joseph Binder Award, Editorial Design
   • Deutsche Börse Photography
   Foundation Prize (Nominierung)
   • Paul Huf Award (Nominierung)
   • Kardinal-König-Kunstpreis
   (Nominierung)
   • German Photo Book-Award 2014
   (Nominierung)
2013 • PDN Photo Annual
   • Award Schönste Bücher Österreichs
   • 5. Internationaler Marianne Brandt
   Wettbewerb (Nominierung)
2012 • Förderpreis für zeitgenössische Kunst
   des Landes Tirol
   • Förderpreis Raiffeisen-Landesbank
   Tirol AG
2011 • DEW21-Kunstpreis (Nominierung)
2010 • 4. Internationaler Marianne Brandt
   Wettbewerb (Sonderpreis)
   • Alps Biennale of the Alpine and
   Mountains Landscapes
   • Iris Award, Perth Centre for
   Photography (Finalist)
2009 • Durst Photo Art Competition
   (Nominierung)
2008 • Stipendium des Landes Tirol
   • German Photo Book Award
   (Nominierung)
2007 • Red Dot Award, Communication
   Design
   • European Prize of Architectural
   Photography (Commendation)
   • Fluxus 06, Category E-CINEMA
   (Best film)

Biography

Gregor Sailer

Born in Schwaz in 1980
Lives and works in Tyrol, Austria

2002
–07 Diploma in Communications Design, focus on photography and experimental film, University of Applied Sciences and Arts, Dortmund, DE (under Susanne Brügger and Piet Wessing)

2012
–15 Master in Photographic Studies, University of Applied Sciences and Arts, Dortmund, DE (under Susanne Brügger, Pamela Scorzin, and Piet Wessing)

Solo exhibitions (selected)

2023 · *The Polar Silk Road,* Alfred Ehrhardt Stiftung, Berlin, DE
· *The Polar Silk Road,* Natural History Museum, London, UK
2022 · *Unseen Places. Gregor Sailer,* KUNST HAUS WIEN, AT
2021 · *The Polar Silk Road,* LUMEN Museum of Mountain Photography, Brunico, IT
2020 · *Staged – From the Potemkin Series,* Atelier Sérgio Rebelo, Month of Photography (MIP), Porto, PT
2019 · *The Potemkin Village,* Centre de la photographie Genève, Geneva, CH
· *The Potemkin Village,* Freelens Galerie, Hamburg, DE
· *The Potemkin Village,* Atelier Jungwirth, Graz, AT
· *The Potemkin Village,* Montrasio Arte, Milan and Monza, IT
· *The Potemkin Village,* Galerie Fotografic, Prague, CZ
2018 · *The Potemkin Village,* Les Rencontres d'Arles, FR
· *The Potemkin Village,* Kehrer Galerie, Berlin, DE
· *The Potemkin Village,* Festival Internazionale di Fotografia e Arte (PhEST), Monopoli, IT
2017 · *The Potemkin Village,* FO.KU.S, Foto Kunst Stadtforum, Innsbruck, AT
2015 · *Closed Cities,* Month of Photography, Klarisky, Bratislava, SK
2014 · *Grenzgänger — Closed Cities,* Gallery Loris, Berlin, DE
2013 · *Closed Cities,* Galerie im Taxispalais, Innsbruck, AT
· *Closed Cities,* Krings-Ernst Gallery, Cologne, DE
· *Closed Cities,* Foto Forum, Bolzano, IT
2010 · *Kokerei Hansa,* Kunsthalle Wien, AT
· *Subraum,* Kunsthalle Wien, AT

Group exhibitions (selected)

2021 · *One Artist — One Minute,* Fotohof / Stadtgalerie Lehen, Salzburg, AT
2020 · *Subjekt und Objekt,* Foto Rhein Ruhr, Kunsthalle Düsseldorf, DE
· *The Architecture of Deception,* BNKR Munich, DE
· *Déjà Vu,* Atelier Jungwirth, Graz, AT
2019 · LiShui Photography Festival, Biennale, China
· *Osmoscosmos,* Centre de la photographie Genève, Geneva, CH
· *Alpen — Mythos Natur,* MEWO Kunsthalle, Memmingen, DE
· *European Architectural Photography Prize,* Deutsche Werkstätten Dresden, DE
2018 · Ray Triennale Frankfurt/Rhine-Main, DE
· *Echt jetzt?! Klasse Kunst VI,* Landesgalerie Linz, AT
· *European Architectural Photography Prize,* KAZimKUBA, Kassel, DE
· *RLB Kunstpreis,* RLB Kunstbrücke, Innsbruck, AT
2017 · *No Secrets!,* Münchner Stadtmuseum, Munich, DE
· *Ephemeral Urbanism,* Pinakothek der Moderne, Munich, DE
· *Raum und Fotografie,* Mönchsberg, Museum der Moderne Salzburg, AT
· *ArtTirol,* Ferdinandeum, Innsbruck, AT
· *European Architectural Photography Prize,* Deutsches Architekturmuseum, Frankfurt am Main, DE
· Krasnojarsk Museum Biennale, RUS
2015 · *Drap Art Festival — Closed Cities,* Centre de Cultura Contemporània de Barcelona, ES
· *Conceptual Storytelling,* Delhi Photo Festival, New Delhi, IN
2014 · *Von oben gesehen. Die Vogelperspektive,* Germanisches Nationalmuseum, Nuremberg, DE
· *Jenseits der Ansichtskarte,* Vorarlberg Museum, Bregenz, AT
2013 · *Under Pressure — Politik in der zeitgenössischen Fotografie,* Mönchsberg, Museum der Moderne Salzburg, AT
· *Architecture / Landscape,* Mansion at Strathmore, Lockheed Martin Gallery, Maryland, US
· *Fragile,* BAWAG Contemporary, Vienna, AT
· *Hohe Dosis,* Fotohof / Atterseehalle, Salzburg, AT
· *Jenseits der Ansichtskarte,* Galerie Stihl, Waiblingen, DE
· *5th International Marianne Brandt Award,* Saxon Museum of Industry, Chemnitz, DE
2012 · *Closed Cities,* Paris Photo, Grand Palais, Paris, FR
· *Architecture / Landscape,* Fotoweeks DC, L2 Lounge Georgetown, Washington, US
· *Schaufenster zur Sammlung II — Bilder von Tag und Nacht,* Rupertinum, Museum der Moderne Salzburg, AT
· *Nacht,* OstLicht. Galerie für Fotografie, Vienna, AT
· *Bildspuren — Unruhige Gegenwarten,* Darmstädter Tage der Fotografie, Darmstadt, DE
2011 · *Alpine Desire,* ACF New York, US (in partnership with the Belvedere, Vienna)
· *Alpen — Sehnsucht & Bühne,* Museum Residenzgalerie Salzburg, AT
· *Mythos Berg,* RLB Kunstbrücke, Innsbruck, AT
· *Ecopoli vs Metropoli,* Palazzo Firmian, Trento, IT
2010 · *Next 1,* Museum Folkwang, Essen, DE
· *Die Welt als Kulisse,* Galerie im Taxispalais, Innsbruck, AT
· *Iris Award,* Perth Centre of Photography, Perth, AU
· *Shelf Life, JaAliceKlarr Projects,* Edinburgh Art Festival, GB
· *Triennale Linz 1.0. Gegenwartskunst in Österreich,* Landesgalerie Linz, AT

Screenings

2019 · *Nuit de la Photo,* La-Chaux-de-Fonds, CH
2018 · *ArchFilmMatinée: Urban Fiction – Fact, Fiction, Fake? In-Timer 47:09:21,* Filmcasino, Vienna, AT
2017 · *Zeytinburnu International Photography Festival,* Istanbul, TR
2010 · *JaAliceKlarr Projects,* Edinburgh Art Festival, GB
2008 · *The Int'l Fest of Cinema and Technology,* Seattle, US
· *Babelgum Online Film Festival,* Venice, IT
· *Broadcasting Sky Channel 195,* Propeller TV, England, GB
· *Broadcasting Circuito Off Channel,* Venice, IT
· *The Int'l Fest of Cinema and Technology,* Melbourne, AU
2007 · *Treibhaus,* Innsbruck, AT
2006 · *Fluxus 06,* Internationales Filmfestival, Belo Horizonte, BR
· *Crank Cookie Kurzfilmtage,* Passau, DE
· *Borges en Curt,* III Festival Internacional de Curtmetratges de les Terres de Ponent, Lleida, ES
· *Filmpremiere In-Timer 47:09:21,* domicil, Dortmund, DE

Monographs

2021 · *The Polar Silk Road,* Kehrer Verlag, Heidelberg, DE
2020 · *Staged — From the Potemkin Series,* Espacio Jhannia Castro, Porto, PT (in partnership with the Centre de la photographie Genève, Geneva, CH)
2017 · *The Potemkin Village,* Kehrer Verlag, Heidelberg, DE
2012 · *Closed Cities,* Kehrer Verlag, Heidelberg, DE
2010 · *Subraum,* Edition Fotohof, Salzburg, AT
· *Dolomiti,* Actar / Birkhäuser, Barcelona, ES / Basel, CH / New York, US
2008 · *Ladiz,* Edition Fotohof, Salzburg, AT
2005 · *Kokerei Hansa,* ed. Stiftung Industriedenkmalpflege und Geschichtskultur, Dortmund, DE

Public collections

· Albertina, Vienna, AT
· Artothek at the Dortmund City and State Library, DE
· Belvedere, Vienna, AT
· Collection Centre National des Arts Plastiques, Paris, FR
· Collection of the City of Innsbruck, AT
· Collection of the Republic of Austria, AT
· Deutsches Architekturmuseum, Frankfurt am Main, DE
· Ferdinandeum, Collection of the State of Tyrol, Innsbruck, AT
· Fotomuseum Winterthur, Film Collection, CH
· Galerie der Moderne, Stiftmuseum Klosterneuburg, AT
· Kunsthalle Wien, Ursula Blickle Stiftung, video archive, AT
· Les Rencontres d'Arles, FR
· LUMEN Museum of Mountain Photography, Brunico, IT
· Raiffeisen-Landesbank Südtirol AG, Bolzano, IT
· Raiffeisen-Landesbank Tirol AG, Innsbruck, AT
· Rupertinum, Museum der Moderne Salzburg, AT
· Tyrolean Archive of Photographic Documentation and Art, Linz, AT
· Wienerberger AG, Vienna, AT

Numerous works in private collections

Awards

2020 · Förderpreis Raiffeisen-Landesbank Tirol AG
2018 · DAM Architectural Book Award
· Deutsche Börse Photography Prize (Nomination)
2017 · European Architectural Photography Prize (Commendation)
· Felix Schoeller Photo Award (Shortlist)
· Prix Pictet (Nomination)
2016 · Joseph Binder Award, Digital Media (Bronze)
· St. Leopold Peace Prize
· State subsidy for photography from the Republic of Austria
2015 · State subsidy for photography from the Republic of Austria
· The Vevey International Photography Award (Shortlist)
2014 · Deutsche Börse Photography Foundation Prize (Nomination)
· German Photo Book-Award 2014 (Nomination)
· Joseph Binder Award, Editorial Design
· Kardinal-König-Kunstpreis (Nomination)
· Paul Huf Award (Nomination)
2013 · 5th International Marianne Brandt Award (Nomination)
· Award Schönste Bücher Österreichs
· PDN Photo Annual
2012 · Advancement award, Raiffeisen-Landesbank Tirol AG
· Advancement award for contemporary art from the state of Tyrol
2011 · DEW21 Art Prize (Nomination)
2010 · 4th International Marianne Brandt Award (Special Award)
· Alps Biennale of the Alpine and Mountains Landscapes
· Iris Award, Perth Centre for Photography (Finalist)
2009 · Durst Photo Art Competition (Nomination)
2008 · German Photo Book Award (Nomination)
· Subsidy from the state of Tyrol
2007 · European Prize of Architectural Photography, (Commendation)
· Fluxus 06, Category E-CINEMA (Best Film)
· Red Dot Award, Communication Design

Mein größter Dank gilt allen Beteiligten an diesem Buch- und Ausstellungsprojekt, insbesondere Verena Kaspar-Eisert und dem gesamten Team des KUNST HAUS WIEN für die kompetente und feinfühlige Zusammenarbeit, Christoph Schaden für seine präzisen Beobachtungen und den wunderbar erweiternden Text sowie Lisa Drechsel für die spannende Gestaltung des Katalogs. Nicht zuletzt bedanke ich mich bei Klaus Kehrer und seinem Team für die professionelle Kooperation.

Gregor Sailer

My biggest thanks go to all involved in this book and exhibition project, especially Verena Kaspar-Eisert and the entire team at KUNST HAUS WIEN for their competent and sensitive collaboration; to Christoph Schaden for his precise observations and the wonderfully amplificatory text, and to Lisa Drechsel for the catalogue's exciting design. Last but not least, I thank Klaus Kehrer and his team for their professional co-operation.

Gregor Sailer

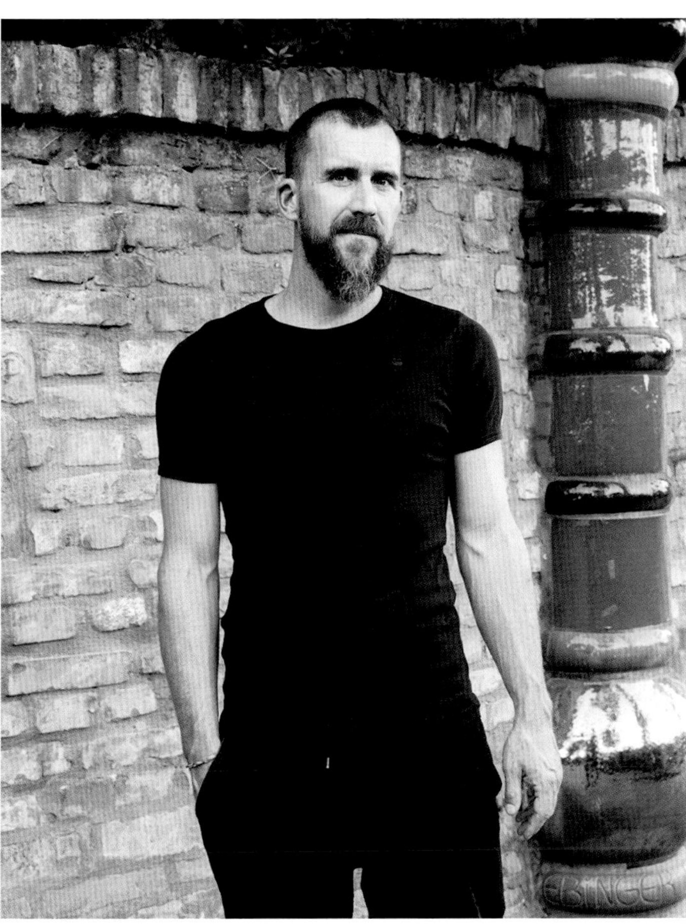

© Elsa Okazaki, 2022

Gregor Sailer fotografiert analog mit der Fachkamera Sinar p2, sowohl Großformat (4 × 5") als auch Mittelformat (6 × 9 cm). Er benutzt Objektive mit den Brennweiten 65, 90, 150 und 210 mm. Seine Fotografien werden als C-Prints oder als Silbergelatineabzüge ausgearbeitet.

Gregor Sailer takes analogue photographs in both large (4 × 5") and medium (6 × 9 cm) formats using a Sinar p2 view camera. He uses lenses with focal lengths of 65, 90, 150 and 210 mm. His photographs are processed as C-prints and gelatin silver prints.

Diese Publikation erscheint anlässlich der Ausstellung
Unseen Places. Gregor Sailer im KUNST HAUS WIEN
15. September 2022 – 19. Februar 2023

This catalogue is published to coincide with the exhibition
Unseen Places. Gregor Sailer at KUNST HAUS WIEN
September 15th, 2022 – February 19th, 2023

© 2022 Kehrer Verlag Heidelberg, KUNST HAUS WIEN GmbH,
Gregor Sailer und Autor:innen / and authors
© VG Bild-Kunst, Bonn 2022

Direktorin | Director: Gerlinde Riedl
Kuratorin | Curator: Verena Kaspar-Eisert
Team: Anna-Katharina Bischof, Ingrid Brunecová,
Sophie Haslinger, Sarah Holt, Vicky Klug, Martina Kuso,
Sabrina Linke, Jasmin Ofner, Chiara Pompermaier,
Marika Rechtacek, Malina Schartmüller, Martin Stangl,
Ádám Stecker, Maria Stephan, Brigitte Vytisk, Irene Wolfram

Herausgeberin | Editor: Verena Kaspar-Eisert,
KUNST HAUS WIEN
Texte | Texts: Verena Kaspar-Eisert, Christoph Schaden
Redaktion | Executive Editor: Anna-Katharina Bischof,
Sophie Haslinger
Übersetzungen | Translations: Stephen Grynwasser,
Alexandra Cox (Deutsch → English | German → English),
Alexandra Titze-Grabec (Englisch → Deutsch | English → German)
Lektorat | Copy Editing: Eva Luise Kühn, Kirsten Limberg
(Deutsch | German), Sandra Huber (Englisch | English)
Gestaltung | Design: Kehrer Design (Lisa Drechsel)
Bildbearbeitung | Image Processing: Gregor Sailer,
Kehrer Design (Erik Clewe)
Herstellung | Production Management: Kehrer Design
(Tom Streicher)

Bildnachweis | Credits:
S. | Pp. 16–17: © Gregor Sailer: *Kokerei Hansa,* Stiftung Indust-
riedenkmalpflege und Geschichtskultur, Dortmund 2005
S. | Pp. 17–18: © Gregor Sailer, Johannes Naumann, Stefan
Tuschy: *Subraum,* Fotohof edition, Bd. / vol. 140, Salzburg 2010
S. | Pp. 19–20: © Gregor Sailer: *Ladiz,* Fotohof edition,
Bd. / vol. 105, Salzburg 2020
S. | Pp. 22: © Gregor Sailer: *Staged – From the Potemkin Series,*
Espacio / Jhannia Castro, Porto 2020

Umschlagabbildung | Cover Illustration:
Tiefort City VIII, Fort Irwin, US-Armee | US Army
Mojave-Wüste, Kalifornien | Mojave Desert, California,
USA, 2016, aus der Serie | from the series:
The Potemkin Village, 2015 – 2017

Printed and bound in Germany
ISBN 978-3-96900-091-5

KUNST HAUS WIEN
Untere Weißgerberstraße 13
1030 Wien, Österreich | Vienna, Austria
www.kunsthauswien.com

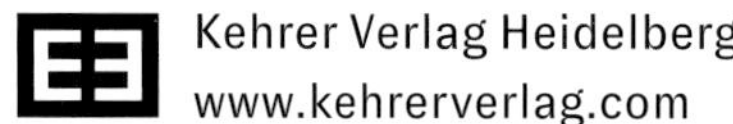

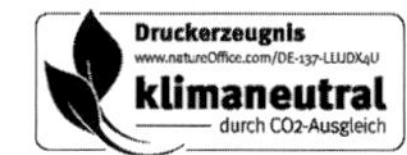
Kehrer Verlag Heidelberg
www.kehrerverlag.com

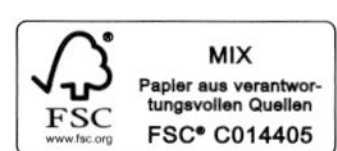